An Introduction to Islamic Philosophy

An Introduction to Islamic Philosophy

Massimo Campanini

Translated by Caroline Higgitt

Edinburgh University Press

First published in Italy by Gius. Laterza & Figli S.p.a.,
Roma-Bari, in 2004 as *Introduzione alla filosofia islamica*

English-language edition published by arrangement with
Eulama Literary Agency, Roma.

First published in English in 2008 by
Edinburgh University Press Ltd
22 George Square, Edinburgh

Typeset in Linotype Sabon by
Iolaire Typesetting, Newtonmore, and
printed and bound in Great Britain by
Cromwell Press, Trowbridge, Wilts

A CIP record for this book is available from the British Library

ISBN 978 0 7486 2607 6 (hardback)
ISBN 978 0 7486 2608 3 (paperback)

The translation of this work has been funded by SEPS
Segretariato Europeo per le Pubblicazioni Scientifiche

SEPS
SEGRETARIATO EUROPEO PER LE PUBBLICAZIONI SCIENTIFICHE

Via Val d'Aposa 7 - 40123 Bologna - Italy
seps@alma.unibo.it - www.seps.it

Contents

Foreword

This book is not a history of Islamic philosophy, nor would it claim to be. It is, rather, a reading of Islamic philosophy as it evolved in the chronological framework of what we call the Middle Ages. Necessarily not exhaustive, it seeks to give an overview in the hope that it may encourage readers to delve further into the subject. The aim, then, is to investigate how Islamic philosophers thought and what they thought about. The book is divided into two parts: in the first part I analyse the epistemological foundations of Islamic philosophy and discuss the most important and penetrating interpretative paradigms proposed by the philosophers; in the second part, I describe some of their major themes.

Methodologically, it is worth establishing from the outset how Islamic philosophy can claim to have its own identity. Islamic philosophy cannot simply be defined (as it is by Walzer) as nothing more than a philosophy inspired by ancient Greece just because it uses a language borrowed from the Greeks or deals with similar subjects. More importantly, we need to ask ourselves if it pursues the same ends and objectives. I hope that it will become clear from what follows how the ends and objectives of Islamic philosophy, albeit firmly rooted in Greek thought, were not the same, not least because any study of the world and its inhabitants was constructed in such a way as to place the one God at the head of a specifically Islamic community. It is important to emphasise that this cultural character became established without any explicit assertion of theology over philosophy. One of the presuppositions of this book, indeed, is that in medieval Islam, at least for the philosophers (the theologians taking up a rather different position), the two spheres of learning coexisted in peaceful harmony.

As far as the content of this book is concerned, while the constraints of space have meant that major themes such as logic and natural philosophy have had to be omitted, it would seem possible, nevertheless, to establish a systematic reconstruction of Islamic thought. The overall interpretative scheme that I have devised is echoed in the arrangement of the chapters of Part Two. Deriving from the basic idea of the Oneness of God, a pillar of theological, philosophic and juridical Islam, is a cosmology in which man, as a rational being, finds his precise place, entirely directed towards the attainment of perfection in the presence of higher realities. In their study of the essential idea of the Oneness of God, the Islamic philosophers went on to speculate on God's omnipotence and freedom. Stemming from the way in which they resolved these problems came new ideas about ethics and justice. Finally, it is proper that as a rational being with a place in the cosmos and responsible on Earth for the implementation of justice, the thinking man (which is to say, above all, the philosopher) takes on a political dimension, whether that involves him in social activity or retreat into the 'regime of the solitary'.

In seeking to explain, at least in part, the nature of Islamic society in the so-called Middle Ages, to assess its contribution to world history, and to establish why for no immediately obvious theoretical or philosophical reasons it fell into decline (unlike the situation in social, economic and scientific areas), it is hard to estimate the extent to which this entirely philosophical paradigm is effective. A discussion of this type would go well beyond the limits of the present work. It is clear that the cornerstone of medieval Islamic society – religious law – is one that has little to do with philosophy and one that, not infrequently, sought to put obstacles in its way. Law is Islamic science *par excellence* and, compared to it, philosophy might appear to be marginal in the context of Islamic culture. It would be impossible to understand either the evolution or the involution of the Islamic world from the Middle Ages up to modern times without a proper evaluation of the role of religious law in shaping society. Islamic law has, however, remained enclosed within the boundaries of the world that produced it, whereas currents from the Islamic philosophical paradigm flowed into Latin philosophical thought, sometimes sowing the seeds of ideas about such matters as the distinction between essence and existence, the structure of the Intelligences and the movement of the heavens, or the pursuit of happiness. One only has to think of the influence that Averroes's commentaries on Aristotle had on Scholasticism and the exercise of the profession of the intellectual in the Universities, or that of Avicenna on the writings of Albertus Magnus (Albert of Cologne), Thomas Aquinas or Duns Scotus. I do not believe that Dante's *Convivio* could ever have been written without the existence of Islamic speculation about Intelligences and the celestial spheres. The contribution made by Islamic philosophy to the universal history of philosophy can be seen as participating in what Hegel calls the Absolute Spirit. No mere finite parenthesis or momentary pause between ancient Greece and modern times, it is the mature expression of a mature civilisation; a civilisation, it goes without saying, profoundly marked by the imprint of the religion preached by Mohammad.

M. C.

Acknowledgements

The idea of writing this little book was suggested to me by Mariateresa Fumagalli Beonio Brocchieri (of Milan University) and I would like to thank her for this and much more. I discussed particular aspects of the work with friends to whom I express my gratitude: Massimo Parodi of Milan University; Augusto Illuminati of Urbino University; Oliver Leaman of Kentucky University at Lexington; Josep Puig Montada of Complutense University, Madrid; Andrés Martínez Lorca of UNED, Madrid. Any mistakes or omissions are, of course, entirely mine. Dedicated to Emanuele in the hope that, whatever he becomes and wherever he goes, he will never give up thinking.

A Note on the Translation

Where an English-language edition of a referenced volume is available, this is cited in the text under the translator's name. The full reference to a translated volume is cited in the Bibliography of English-language Versions.

The original edition of a referenced volume is cited in the Notes, so that both editions are made available to the reader. Where an English-language version of a text is not cited, the translation is my own.

Caroline Higgitt

Part One

Finding a Paradigm

Chapter 1

History

The birth of speculative thought in the Islamic world began early on, less than a century after the Arab conquest had rapidly and successfully extended over an enormous area of land, uniting it into a single cultural entity. Stretching from Morocco to the Indus and from the steppes of Central Asia to the Persian Gulf, it unified widely differing geographical regions and cultures by means of a religious message revealed to the Prophet Mohammad. The message of Islam, universal and intended for all people, was introduced as a result of the conquests but not imposed by force, the civilisations of the defeated peoples being respected by the invaders. As the Arabs conquered Egypt, Syria, Mesopotamia and Persia, they came into contact with highly developed and sophisticated cultural traditions, scientific praxis, philosophies and world views. Similarly, they were quick to integrate themselves into the preceding culture, ready to absorb new knowledge and open to every kind of spiritual and intellectual possibility. A good example of this phenomenon is the way that the late-Antique philosophical culture derived from classical Greek philosophy received new life and vigour, particularly in Syria and Mesopotamia. It is, indeed, possible to see a direct link between the birth of Arab philosophy and the concluding years of the study and teaching of pagan philosophy in the schools of the Byzantine empire.

After Emperor Justinian closed the school of Athens in 529, large numbers of Greek philosophers had emigrated (according to some sources, at least) to the East: Simplicius, for example, travelled to Gondeshapur in Persia, where there was a school that 'stands out as a major institution of Hellenic learning in Western Asia'[1] and which was famous for its medical school. Flourishing schools teaching theology, Aristotelian logic, mathematics and astronomy existed in northern Syria, not only in Harran but also in Qinnesrin, Edessa and other centres. The star-worshipping Sabaeans, including scholars like Thābit Ibn Qurra and his sons and grandsons, played an important part in the diffusion of Greek science in the Arab world. These regions and centres of learning were to experience a fruitful period of translating and cross-fertilisation between Greek, Syriac and Arab cultures. In the process of the intermingling of ideas, Arab thought, still in its infancy, had nothing to relinquish or betray and everything to gain or renew.

The fate of religions was to be rather different. At the time of the arrival of the Arabs, the greater part of the Middle East and North Africa was Christian, while in Persia the religion was Zoroastrianism. There was also a significant number of Jews. While Zoroastrianism was destined to disappear, to be replaced by Islam, Christianity and Judaism continued to be practised as before. Whereas only very few Jews converted to Islam, there were many examples of conversion by Christians, to the extent that at one point it was something of a mass phenomenon. The process was, nevertheless, a gradual one and it was probably not until the 10th or 11th century that Islam became the majority religion in the entirety of the empire. By now, this empire could no longer be called 'Arab', since it had become internationalised, absorbing many different races with their own legacies of traditions and cultures, customs and habits. They included Persians, Turks, Copts, Hindus and even Chinese. While Arabic was adopted as the language of scholarship and government, Islam became the religion not only of the elite but also of the common people. Although Islam tolerated the other religions of the Book for a few centuries, it nevertheless sought to strengthen its fundamental beliefs and refine its expressive and speculative methods, emphasising the points of difference from and opposition to religions such as Judaism and, particularly, Christianity. Both these religions already possessed a highly developed and complex theology and were aware of the need to assert their independence in the face of a new and dynamic religion that, thanks to its simplicity and clarity, was capable of attracting many proselytes. Islamic theology also came about and developed partly as a response to opposition from Judaic and Christian theologians. It shaped and constructed its own framework, discovering the characteristics of an originality that centred both on the close relationship between law and religion, and on political conviction. Like Judaism, Islam is eminently a religion of Law and, as such, laid down its juridical structure even before it had established itself theologically. On the other hand, central matters in Islamic theology, such as those relating to the legal status of sinners (when they sin, do they become misbelievers or are they still to be counted as believers?) or to human free will, had political repercussions. The Umayyad caliphs (661–750), for example, sided with those who argued that human actions are divinely predestined since this allowed them to present themselves as being predestined by God to rule the state. In contexts such as these, far from becoming contaminated by alien ideas (as it was by Greek philosophy), Islamic thought could take up a rigid attitude in defence of the Qur'an and the transmission of the *hadīth*, the 'sayings' and 'doings' of the Prophet Mohammad that acquired a prescriptive and binding force. Islamic thought could proudly counter the originality of Christian and Jewish philosophical speculation with the originality of the roots of its own jurisprudence.

The two processes at work intersect but do not overlap one another. The philosophical and scientific culture of the Near East, based on the (Neo-) Platonism and Aristotelianism of the Greek tradition, was obliged to face up to the essentially pragmatic culture of the conquerors. The three foundation stones of Islamic culture were: the Arabic language, from which were soon to arise the new sciences of grammar and lexicography; law, that, as has been said, characterises the culture of the new religion to a much greater extent than theology; and politics, insofar as the Prophet Mohammad had been not only the conveyor of God's message but also founder and ruler of the political Community, while his successors, the caliphs, inherited from him the dual responsibility of defending the faith and running the state. Thus it was that, from philosophy inspired by ancient Greece on the one side, and from Islam supported by politics and law, there emerged not so much an open conflict as a dialectic. It should be stressed at the outset that this was in no way similar to the conflict between reason and faith, as was to emerge in the West in the Middle Ages. It was, rather, an analysis and comparison of problems and different interpretative schema.

These developments can be traced in the origins and development of the first clearly developed theological movement to be established in Islam, that of the Muʿtazila. This movement flourished in Iraq in the first half of the 9th century but its influence continued to spread into later centuries, particularly in the Asian territories of the Islamic empire. The Muʿtazilites were, first and foremost, theologians, but they did not use philosophical tools merely to develop their doctrines since, alongside mainly theological and doctrinal matters, they also investigated topics of a strictly philosophical nature. They described themselves as 'those of justice and Oneness', an indication of two of the fundamental principles of their movement. By justice, they meant that God can do no evil; His actions are entirely good and He is obliged to do the best for His creatures. One consequence of this principle is that humankind is endowed with free will and so capable of choosing and performing good or evil actions. Belief in the Oneness of God meant a denial of his attributes: God is wise, powerful, living and speaking but wisdom, power, life and speech coincide with his essence. Describing Muʿtazilite belief, al-Shahrastānī says: 'According to them God is "knowing" by his essence [*dhāt*], "powerful" by his essence, "living" by his essence: not by "knowledge" or "power" or "life" considered as eternal attributes or entities, *maʿānī*, subsisting in him'[2] (Kazi and Flynn, 1984: 41–2). Separate from these attributes of the essence are the attributes of the act that represent not so much a quality belonging to God as the possibility that He does or does not do something, for example, create. One very interesting problem that greatly occupied Muʿtazilite speculative thought was that of the 'created' Qur'an. For Muslims, the Qur'an is the directly communicated word of God. But if, as the Ashʿarite 'orthodoxy' was eventually to maintain, the Qur'an were 'uncreated', it would, like God, have the attribute of eternity and so be a second God. In other words, the belief that the Qur'an was uncreated would threaten the Oneness of God and lead to polytheism. The Muʿtazilite view that attributes are inherent in God's essence was to become generally accepted by philosophers and reveals a grasp of philosophical categories such as essence, substance and accidents. In the light of this understanding, it is possible to understand how it was that the majority of Muʿtazilites were able to accept the idea that everything in the world was made up of atoms, or indivisible particles, and accidents, or how they came to speculate on the infinite divisibility of space, the void and movement. This is not to say, of course, that they were aware of the debt they owed to philosophy; indeed, some of them, including al-Sīrāfī, unambiguously attacked philosophy. Nevertheless, the evidence indicates that a process of osmosis between philosophy and theology was taking place.

Opposing the Muʿtazilites, whose ideas were regarded as too rationalist, were the Ashʿarites. This school of thought was founded by Abū'l-Hasan al-Ashʿari, a theologian who had broken with Muʿtazilism (873/4–935). It could be argued that Ashʿarism was a strictly theological movement, were it not for the fact that its method of proceeding is characterised by a rationalist element that endows it with a philosophical perspective. It would appear that a potential contradiction was emerging within Islamic theology:

> the views of philosophers were condemned on occasion as heretical and beyond the limits of Muslim belief. It is important here to distinguish between two sorts of principle. One principle shared by both Ashʿarites and Muʿtazilites is that reason is usefully employed in understanding religion. A principle that both would reject is that religion can usefully be analysed by the use of concepts derived from Greek, especially Aristotelian, philosophy. The use of such philosophical concepts were [*sic*] not regarded as helpful in an understanding of religion. But in rejecting philosophy the theologians were not rejecting reason; on the contrary, they were enthusiastic concerning the value of reason when employed in a suitably domesticated context.[3] (Leaman 1985: 12)

Reason should, in other words, be applied in a context where the reference point for any consideration of matters, whether derived directly from religion or formulated independently within the framework of philosophy, remained the essential principle of Islam. The contradiction referred to just now no longer exists if we consider how, in Islamic philosophy (and the most famous advocate of this point of view was Averroes), there was never in fact any conflict between religion and faith, the two dimensions being considered to be connected or closely integrated and working together.

The Ashʿarites put forward solutions that were frequently diametrically opposed to those of the Muʿtazilites. They maintained, for example, that God's attributes are distinct from his essence but are connected to it *bilā kayfa*, by means that we cannot understand. They asserted that the Qur'an was uncreated; that God's omnipotence does not oblige him to do what is best for his creatures; that humankind does not have freedom of action, since it is God who creates actions, humans merely 'acquiring' them (*kasb*). Most importantly, their interpretation of certain principles of philosophical origin was markedly more religious in approach. For example, as Fakhry writes:

> the interest of the Mutakallims [the Muslim theologians] (especially the Ashʿarites) in this contingent metaphysics of atoms and accidents was simply the desire to vindicate the absolute power of God and to ascribe to His direct intervention not only the coming of things into being, but also their persistence in being from one instant to another.[4]

Alessandro Bausani gives an example of a concept that is

> in some ways [. . .] more faithful to Qur'anic inspiration [. . .] cosmology as seen through an Ashʿarite perspective where the greatest emphasis is given not to the phenomena but to the aspect of greatest importance to a Muslim, God's freedom. This grandiose and occasionalistic atomism is so well known that what follows is merely the briefest of summaries. The world is made up of indivisible atoms that God creates and successively destroys in every moment and atom of time (time itself being understood as discontinuous). The seeming regularity of the flow of events in nature is an illusion, comparable to the succession of images of a film that, when projected rapidly one after another, give the impression of continuous movement. God could, if he so desired, run the film backwards, stop it, jump from one atom to another and so on. In this way any *causa secunda* is excluded.[5]

The development of Muʿtazilite thought (and, in a sense, Ashʿarite thought if, as the sources seem to confirm, the Ashʿarites emerged in reaction to Muʿtazilite rationalism) signified the consolidation of Islamic dogmatics as an autonomous and independent area of theoretical elaboration. However, although it concerned itself almost entirely with theology, it was almost certainly conditioned by the arrival and the circulation, at least, of Greek philosophical ideas, even if not necessarily in the form of texts by Greek philosophers but rather reworkings or critical rebuttals. While we are not able to trace the finer details of this process of diffusion and reworking, it is important to remember that the work of translating Greek texts received new impetus during the reign of the Abbasid caliph al-Ma'mūn (813–33), one of whose measures was to make Muʿtazilism the state theology. The texts translated from Greek and Syriac became part of the common heritage of the theological schools and the object of much debate and analysis. Although the route taken is hard to follow in detail, the influence of these works made itself felt on all those who were seeking to emancipate philosophical thought, nourished by its roots in the Greek tradition, from theological thought nourished by the Qur'an and the *hadīth*. It comes as no surprise then to find that the man who may be considered the first philosopher in the Islamic world, Abū Yusuf Yaʿqūb Ibn Ishāq al-Kindī (?–*c.* 870) and known as 'the philosopher of the Arabs', sought to integrate both Muʿtazilite problems and methods, and ideas taken directly from religious tradition with philosophical concepts borrowed from the Greek tradition. Al-Kindī maintained that there was no contradiction between reason and Qur'anic authority. On the one hand, following Aristotle, he defined philosophy as the science of causes, while, on the other hand, following the Qur'anic conception of God as the first cause and source of all reality. God creates from nothing and creation is contemporaneously *ex nihilo* and in time. 'In the place of the Aristotelian idea of an eternal world, al-Kindī put forward the theory of a world that is presently finite requiring a non-finite first cause'. The same idea of creation *ex nihilo* led 'to the consideration of all other causes and actions, and the unity of all substances, as "metaphorical", a viewpoint that, while not representing the entirety of al-Kindī's concept, is nevertheless a departure from Aristotle'[6], and probably more in tune with a more rigorously theological and Islamic mindset. He concurred with Muʿtazilite principles with regard to the 'justice' of God and human freedom of action.

The arrival of Greek texts and ideas also triggered a process of what might be termed 'secularisation' in Islamic thought. One interesting although minority tendency that emerged was that of a number of independent and heretical 'free thinkers' whose ideas pushed orthodox belief to the extreme limits or transgressed them, even to the extent of denying Islam. Notable among these marginal figures was Ibn al-Muqaffaʿ, a Persian who lived at the caliphs' court and who wrote moral and political works including some in support of the authority of the caliphate. He was, nevertheless, accused of being a Manichean dualist (or *zindīq*) and executed in 757 by the Abbasid al-Mansūr. The most eminent figure, however, was undoubtedly Abū Bakr Muhammad Ibn Zakariyyā' al-Rāzī (*c.* 865–935) or, in Latin, Rhazes. This renowned doctor, one of the most famous in the Middle Ages, launched a fierce attack on the notion of prophetism and hence on one of the pillars of monotheistic religion. He put forward the concept of five eternal principles (God, the soul, matter, space and time). We will return to Rhazes in Chapter 6, since a consideration of those figures that, to paraphrase the title of his book,[7] D. Urvoy calls the 'free thinkers of classic Islam' can help us to define the different modes of speculative thought in Islam where, on the whole, philosophy has never been ousted by religious inspiration.

While al-Kindī was something of an eclectic, Abū Nasr al-Fārābī (active in Baghdad and Syria, *c.* 870–950) made a clear distinction between philosophy and theology, establishing, for example, (as we shall see below) two well-differentiated epistemological areas and reducing reference to the Qur'an to the minimum, leaving us a reading of metaphysics that is more ontological than theological. He was able to read Plato and Aristotle unfettered by theological concerns. We will return to al-Fārābī's ideas in later chapters, confining ourselves here to noting that it was he who laid the foundations of logic, metaphysics and politics in the world of Islam, thus acquiring the honorific 'Second Master', the first master being Aristotle. We owe to him the first enunciation of the famous metaphysical distinction between essence and existence; he was the first person to describe the cosmological structure of the Intelligences in a systematic way and it was he who first sought to direct philosophy as a whole towards political philosophy, considered as a kind of enabling link between God and man, between more theoretically abstract speculation and juridical praxis. The majority of al-Fārābī's constructive works have a political aim: made explicit in the title of the *Book of Political Science*, but also in the *Virtuous City* (*Al-Madīnah al-Fādilah*) and the *Attainment of Happiness*, since, as we shall see, al-Fārābī saw a close link between knowledge, happiness and politics.

Al-Fārābī also wrote expositions and commentaries on Plato and Aristotle and was, if not the first, certainly the most important scholar to see a basic agreement of intentions and solutions in the works of these two great philosophers of Antiquity. In his introduction to his *Harmonisation of the Two Opinions of the Two Sages, the Divine Plato and Aristotle*, devoted to this subject, he states:

> Seeing the greater part of the people of our age arguing and debating about the creation of the world and its eternity and maintaining that between the two great sages, Plato and Aristotle, there is disagreement about the affirmation of the existence of the Creator and the existence of second causes from Him, and similarly about the soul and the intellect, etc., I have sought in this work to establish a harmony between their opinions and express in clear terms the meaning of authentic content of their writings, in order to make apparent the agreement between their convictions, and to dissipate doubt and hesitation from the hearts of those who study their books.[8]

This desire to reconcile the Platonic and Aristotelian systems came about from the need to defend philosophy as an authentic and certain science. If Plato and Aristotle, whose prestige was beyond question, were seen to be in contradiction, the assertion that there is a single philosophical truth would be impossible to maintain. His mission was assisted by the existence in Muslim circles of texts of a Platonic tendency that were, however, attributed to Aristotle. Although Aristotle was still regarded as the Master, Dante's '*maestro di color che sanno*' (*Inferno* 4.131), the Muslims would have been forgiven for regarding him as the most faithful interpreter of Plato's philosophy.

The two most important of these texts are: the *Theologia Aristotelis* and the *Liber de Causis*. The first of these, by an unknown author but already translated into Arabic at the time of al-Kindī, is a paraphrase of Books IV, V and VI of Plotinus's *Enneads*. The aim of the work is described in the first chapter as being

> to discuss the divine nature and exhibit it, by showing that it is the First Cause and that time and the aeon [infinite time or *dahr*] are both beneath it, and that it is the cause of causes and their author, after a fashion; and that the luminous virtue (or power) shines forth from it on it upon Reason; and through the intermediary of Reason upon the universal and heavenly Soul; and from Reason, through the intermediary of the Soul upon Nature; and from the Soul, through

> the intermediary of Nature upon the objects of generation and corruption; and that this action [of the One] issues forth from it without movement; and that the movement of all things is from it and through it; and that things gravitate toward it through a species of desire or appetite.[9]

The fundamental contribution of the pseudo-*Theologica* was to encourage the maturation in Islamic thought of

> that unitary reading of Plato that had transformed the idea of Good (*anupotheton*) of the *Republic* and the 'one' of the *Parmenides* into the First Principle – the One –; the demiurgic intellect and the world beyond the heavens of *Timaeus* and *Phaedrus* in the second principle – the *nous* –; the soul of *Timaeus* and the *Laws* in the animatory principle of the sensible world – the universal Soul.[10]

In the light of this, it was possible to cast off the presuppositions of the cosmological construction so characteristic of Islamic philosophy (see Chapter 5). As for the *Liber de Causis* or 'book of pure good' (*al-khayr al-mahd*), it is derived from Proclus's *Elementatio Theologica* and known to have been in circulation as early as the beginning of the 10th century. Like the *Theologica*, it had little connection with the original teachings of Aristotle and, like that work, it discusses

> all the germinal elements that went into Islamic Neo-Platonism: the utter transcendence of the First Principle or God; the procession or emanation of things from Him; the role of Reason as the instrument of God in his creation, and the locus of the forms of things, as well as the source of the illumination of the human mind; the position of the Soul at the periphery of the intelligible world and the link or 'horizon' between the intelligible and the sensible worlds; and finally the contempt in which matter was held, as the basest creation or emanation from the One and the lowest rung in the cosmic scale.[11]

The importance of the influence of the *Theologia Aristotelis* and the *Liber de Causis* cannot be too strongly emphasised. These texts provided Muslims with a theory – that of emanation – that many of them were to attempt to transfer to the Islamic vision of reality and the cosmos. Al-Fārābī drew on the *Theologia* in his *Harmonisation of the*

Two Opinions of the Two Sages, the Divine Plato and Aristotle, using it to support his assertion that Aristotle took up a creationist position ('He who studies his [Aristotle's] discourses on sovereignty [*rubūbiyya*, or divine metaphysics] in the book entitled *Theologia* cannot doubt that he affirms the existence of the Artist who is creator of this world. God first created matter from nothing and it received from Him and from his will corporeality and then organisation'). He also concludes that Aristotle, like Plato, demonstrated that 'the one exists in all the multiplicity and that the multiplicity in which the one does not exist is absolutely unlimited'.[12] Through the *Theologia* and the *Liber de Causis*, a version of Aristotle heavily influenced by Neo-Platonism received wide circulation in the Muslim world. As a result, even those who, like Avicenna, described themselves as 'Peripatetics' absorbed a large number of Platonic and Neo-Platonic elements. Even Averroes, that most Aristotelian of Arab-Islamic philosophers, was not entirely immune from Platonic ideas and influence.

The life and work of al-Fārābī developed at a moment that marked a crisis and a turning point in Islamic history. This was the period of the brief, almost ephemeral, triumph of Shiism: of moderate Imamite Shiism and Zaydism imposed by the dynasty of the Persian Buyid sultans on the weakened Abbasid caliphate (roughly from the mid-10th to the mid-11th century); of the extremist Ismaili Shiism represented politically by the Fatimid dynasty (rulers of North Africa and Egypt from 909 to 1171) and the Qarmati dynasty that had set up a state in Bahrain. The 10th century saw the flowering of Ismaili or Ismaili-influenced thought. An essential difference separating the Ismailis from the Imamite Shiites was that the former maintained that the line of successors descended from 'Alī (the *imām*) stopped at the seventh rather than the twelfth. The Ismailis were, nevertheless, extremist in so far as they saw the *imām* not only as a perfect man – as the Imamites also believed – but also as an incarnation of God. Some scholars have suggested that al-Fārābī himself was a Shiite, or even, more specifically, an Ismaili. One of the most interesting exponents of this particular version of Islam was Abū Yaʿqūb al-Sijistānī. Although the details of his life are obscure, it is possible that he knew al-Fārābī since there are apparent similarities between their systems. It is more likely that he was influenced by al-Fārābī than the other way round. Whatever the case, al-Sijistānī can be considered, philosophically speaking, a Neo-Platonist who attempted with great originality to integrate Islamic theological principles with Greek philosophy. Compared to al-Fārābī, he took up a position that was more markedly fideist:

> for al-Fārābī it is the philosopher, through access to demonstrative reasoning, who gains a knowledge of that truth of which religion and the law is only a similitude. For al-Sijistānī, this is not the case because at its highest level the deductive enterprise falls short and only revelation suffices.[13]

A brief description of al-Sijistānī's conception of God and the universe can be found in the first two chapters of Part Two; suffice it to note here how similar to al-Fārābī's cosmology is that of another eminent Ismaili thinker, Hamīd al-Dīn al-Kirmānī. Al-Kirmānī lived at the time of the Fatimid caliph al-Hākim (ruled 996–1021), being active in Iraq and Iran and spending some time in Cairo. Under the rule of al-Hākim, Cairo was at this time a flourishing centre of philosophical and scientific research. It had a House of Knowledge where one of the most important Muslim scientists, Ibn al-Haythem or Alhazen (died 1039), famous for his study of optics, worked. Al-Sijistānī and al-Kirmānī were both *dā'ī*, or 'missionaries' charged with disseminating Ismaili and Fatimid propaganda. This explains, on the one hand, the esoteric stamp of al-Sijistānī's work and, on the other, the active and practical character of al-Kirmānī's thinking, concerned with reform of the city and customs even when it is occupied with problems such as the soul and the calming of the mind in the service, dedicated to God, of acquiring wisdom.

One of the most representative expressions of 10th-century philosophy is the *Encyclopaedia* of the Ikhwān al-Safā', or the Brothers of Purity or 'sincere friends'. This was a mysterious confraternity about whose members nothing is known, despite a few more or less well-founded guesses. The *Encyclopaedia*, highly eclectic in nature, was produced in Iraq. It consists of a collection of fifty-two 'epistles' or *rasā'il* and provides a magnificent summa of philosophical knowledge at that time. It seems to have been intended for a narrow readership of friends and disciples, each section being introduced with the phrase 'Know, O brother'. It contains discussions of theological problems such as the question of the creation of the Qur'an as well as sections on music, language, logic, physics, metaphysics and religion. The influence of Plato and Aristotle can be detected (drawn from

Aristotle, for example, are the basic concepts relating to physics as well as a significant part of the philosophical terminology used). But of the various major figures of Antiquity, 'they seem to have understood and appreciated Pythagoras the most. His ontological approach to numbers was adapted by the Ikhwān to their own needs and a strongly Pythagorean interest in mathematics and related subjects pervades the whole of the Rasā'il'.[14] The Brothers borrowed from Neo-Platonism the concept of hierarchy that dominates all their work. This was not only the emanationist hierarchy of the One, the creator, from whom derive: firstly, the Active Universal Intellect; secondly, the Universal Soul; thirdly, Prime Matter. The brothers also divided themselves into an internal hierarchy with four levels depending on age and acquired maturity: artisans; political leaders; kings; and, lastly, prophets and philosophers. It was the duty of the best members to aspire to this fourth level. Scholars are still unable to agree whether the Brothers were Ismailis, but it is known that the Ismailis have claimed the Brothers for their own religious tendency. While a balanced historiographical view cannot fail to take account of clear indications of Shiite inclinations, it would be wise not to pronounce on any more specific affiliation to any one of the many forms of Shiism, given that the doctrine put forward by the Brothers on the *imām*, for example, cannot immediately be reconciled with the Ismaili view.

Al-Fārābī's legacy is evident in the thinkers who were central to what J. Kraemer calls, 'the humanism in the renaissance of the Buyid era'. This was a period that stands out as one of the intellectually most vibrant in the history of medieval Islam. Baghdad, in particular, became a meeting place for many of those described by Kraemer as 'humanists':

> Like Renaissance humanists, their intellectual preoccupations were not intimately bound to a specific philosophic outlook. Unlike the Renaissance humanists, however, the Islamic humanists did not shun the various branches of philosophy proper. Aristotelian thought dominated their logical investigations, their work in natural philosophy, and their reflections on ethics. But this tendency does not betoken a hardbound commitment to a specific philosophic system. Their political thought was fundamentally Platonic, and a blend of Aristotelianism and Neoplatonism pervaded their metaphysical speculation. They were selective, deferential to the entire legacy of the ancients, rather than narrowly restrictive.[15]

Some of the thinkers of the Buyid period can be considered as belonging to an ideal 'school of al-Fārābī'. Notable among them were the Christian Yahyā Ibn ʿAdī (893/4–974), a direct disciple of al-Fārābī, and the Muslim Abū Sulaymān al-Sijistānī (*c.* 913–88). Both men were celebrated particularly for their studies of logic, while Abū al-Hasan al-ʿĀmirī (?–992) formulated an amalgam of Aristotelianism and Neo-Platonism with elements borrowed from the 'epistles' written by the Brothers of Purity. These figures were interesting insofar as they provided evidence of the degree of intellectual fervour existing in the Islamic world in the 10th century, but their theoretical solutions were not particularly original. More original was the Persian Abū ʿAlī al-Miskawayh (936–1030) who, as well as a work on history, has left a treatise on ethics clearly inspired by Greek thought, the *Refinement of Character*, that seems very likely to have influenced the young al-Ghazālī. Al-Miskawayh believed that philosophy was the only true form of education and the only true way to salvation. He followed Plato and Aristotle in considering humankind to be 'social by nature'.

Abū ʿAlī al-Husayn Ibn ʿAbdallāh Ibn Sīnā (980–1037), known in Latin as Avicenna and considered by many to be the greatest Muslim philosopher, can also be described as a kind of 'disciple' of al-Fārābī. Although not a direct follower, Avicenna revisited, reworked, arranged and extended many of the fundamental concepts enunciated by his predecessor, to such an extent that it is difficult to determine how far his ideas are original and how far he was a mere cataloguer. One thing that cannot be denied, however, is that he was a genius with an encyclopaedic and protean knowledge who created an organic framework for philosophical knowledge, arranging it along the lines created by Plato and Aristotle. In his autobiography, a priceless survival from that time, Avicenna says that, by the age of 16 to 18, he had already acquired all the forms of knowledge necessary to him. In the following years, he applied or reworked these sciences without, however, adding anything of substance that was new or different. As a result, what has come down to us in practice is a series of treatises varying in length and detail that reproduce more or less the same themes. He used them to set out, in various ways, a system of thought that was relatively cohesive and homogenous. The most important of these treatises is the famous *Kitāb al-Shifā'* or *Book of Healing*, known in the West under the title *Sufficientia*, a major source for many medieval Latin philosophers. This encyclopaedia of philosophy was summarised in the *Book of Salvation*. Whereas these two books were written originally in Arabic, Avicenna also wrote a third treatise, this time in Persian. This *Book of Science* or *Dānish Nāma* (intended possibly for a non-Arabic speaking audience) was subdivided into four large sections: logic, metaphysics, natural science, and mathematics (arithmetic, geometry, astronomy and music). As might be expected, a similar arrangement can be found in the *Book of Healing*, although here the order is slightly different: logic, physics, mathematics and metaphysics. Accepting Greek-influenced thought in its entirety, Avicenna emphasises the pre-eminence of metaphysics (also known in the Muslim world as 'divine science') as the highest form of knowledge, prefiguring a kind of subalternation or *subalternatio*: 'The speculative science is of three kinds: one is named first philosophy, the science of primordials of that which is beyond nature; another is an intermediate science which is called the science of syntax and mathematics; it is also called an instructive science; the other is called a natural science or inferior science'[16] (Morewedge 1973: 12), concerned with all that which is in the material world.

The last in chronological order of Avicenna's encyclopaedic writings is the *Kitāb al-Ishārāt wa al-Tanbīhāti* or *Book of Directives and Remarks*. It is a work that has greatly intrigued scholars since it appears to show the development in the author's thought of a more esoteric and mystical viewpoint. The book is divided into two parts. The first discusses ten different kinds of problems in logic: simple predicaments; definition and description; enunciative composition; propositions and their modes; contradiction and conversion of propositions; assent; categorical syllogisms and attributative connections; hypothetical syllogisms; the demonstrative sciences; sophistical syllogisms. In apparent contradiction with this long examination of logic, the second part discusses first the substance of bodies, the celestial and terrestrial soul, being and its causes, the intellect and then goes on to speak of visible joy and of happiness, studies the stages of asceticism, piety and the Gnostic's (*ʿārif*) path to spiritual perfection, concluding with the 'secrets of the wonders'. Further evidence of this change of direction towards a more esoteric approach can be found in a number of mystical treatises written by Avicenna (including the well-known stories of *Hayy Ibn Yaqzān* and *Salāmān and Absāl*). These apparent contradictions continue to provide fuel for the most intractable aspect of Avicennan historiography, the question of 'Eastern philosophy' (*hikma mashriqiyya*). Scholars have hypothesised that Avicenna wrote yet another encyclopaedic treatise in which he reveals the secrets of a Gnostic and esoteric – eastern – wisdom. Did Avicenna believe that this 'eastern philosophy' was the true philosophy, Peripatetism and philosophy inspired by Greece being nothing more than a superficial and exoteric version of the truth? Only a few fragments remain of such a work, and they are not sufficient to resolve the scholars' questions. It is possible that 'eastern philosophy' is simply the philosophy of the inhabitants of the East, of the Persians, as opposed to that of the 'Westerners', the Greeks. Scholars have taken up one position or the other depending on how they interpret Avicenna's thought in general. Thus Henri Corbin, for example, has stressed the visionary and Gnostic character of Avicenna's authentic voice,[17] whereas Dimitri Gutas has denied the existence of any esoteric tendency, maintaining, amongst other things, that the 'eastern way/path' mentioned by Avicenna refers to his preference for intuitive knowledge rather than demonstrative knowledge.[18] Although it would not resolve the problem, it would make it easier to place in context if it were possible to decide, once and for all, whether or not Avicenna was an Ismaili and so therefore inclined to a more spiritualised reading of philosophy.

Whatever the case, Avicenna's immense intellectual activity was to provoke what could at first glance appear to be a 'traditionalist' reaction from Abū Hāmid al-Ghazālī (1058–1111) who saw his predecessor, it is worth noting, as a Peripatetic philosopher and not a mystic. Al-Ghazālī can in some ways be considered a model Muslim intellectual, not only because he was an eminent theologian and jurist but above all because he was able to unite philosophy, mysticism and law in a harmonious system that, despite a few inconsistencies and contradictions, represents the most important intellectual achievement in the Islamic world at the peak of its speculative maturity. Al-Ghazālī was a prolific writer and his most important work, the forty-volume *Revival of the Religious Sciences*, constitutes not only a summary of moral and spiritual conduct, but also of theological knowledge. Al-Ghazālī's intended this work to lay the foundations for a revived Islamic religion that he saw as being in crisis. He maintained that the aim of knowledge is action, with the result that his thought is shot through with ethical tension. His reforming zeal persuaded him of the fact that philosophy – and by this he meant, and dealt with almost exclusively, Avicennian philosophy in so far as it interpreted the legacy of the great Greek philosophers – represented, if not a threat, then a dangerous temptation, for any truly religious mind. In his work *Aims of the Philosophers*, he takes the theories of his opponents and analyses each one with dispassionate objectivity. In his famous *Incoherence of the Philosophers* (*Tahāfut al-Falāsifa*), he demolishes them. He extrapolates twenty propositions, describing seventeen of them as 'blameworthy innovations' (*bidʿa*) and three as clear examples of misbelief (*kufr*). These three are: the eternity of the world, a theory taken directly from Aristotle that obviously excludes the creative action of God; the denial of God's awareness of the individual since He knows only the universal and hence, for example, could not know that Mohammad was a Prophet; and the denial of the resurrection of the body, explicitly affirmed in the Qur'an (Avicenna favoured the idea of the survival of souls as pure spirit).

Despite his intention to refute the ideas of the philosophers, al-Ghazālī was anything but an 'irrationalist'. In the first place, he sought to oppose philosophy not with anathemas and theological dogma but with philosophical, dialectic and demonstrative tools – in other words, opposing philosophy with philosophy. Secondly, in expressing his own original ideas, he often makes use of terms, categories and concepts that are clearly derived from philosophy. In a work with a more mystical intent, the *Niche of Lights*, a kind of commentary on a fundamental Qur'anic verse in the *sūrah* called 'Light' (24,35), the debt to Avicenna is clear. Recent historiography (see R. Frank, for example)[19] is increasingly inclined to see al-Ghazālī as a crypto-philosopher – something that would no doubt have enraged him. Whatever the case, a close study of the *Incoherence of the Philosophers* (to which we shall return in more depth in Chapter 7) is of great utility in determining the characteristics of a rationality or way of thinking that might be defined as 'Islamic'.

Around the mid-11th century, philosophy in the true sense of the word made its appearance in the western Islamic world, in North Africa and in al-Andalus (Spain). The Iberian peninsula had been conquered by the Arabs in 711 and the following centuries saw a transfer of culture and knowledge from East to West. This process, according to M. Cruz Hernández, came about by means of four routes: Muʿtazilism;

bātinism, a tendency where the Qur'an is given an allegorical interpretation that is, in fact, characteristic of Shiism and, obviously, of Ishmaelism; scientific thought; and mysticism.[20] The ascetic Ibn Masarra (died 931) seems to have been one of the first to introduce philosophical ideas into al-Andalus, if it is indeed possible to attribute to him pseudo-Empedoclian influences (something that has recently been questioned by some scholars). Traces of Muʿtazilite and Neo-Platonism can be identified in Ibn Masarra's work, but the history of when and how philosophy reached this area is complicated and, even now, not definitive. It is difficult, for example, to establish the exact date when the classic Greek works began to circulate, or what form – commentaries or translations – they took. It would be no easy task, and very possibly meaningless, to identify the 'first' Andalusian philosopher. What is highly probable is that philosophy emerged late in al-Andalus and not before the 11th century.[21]

Bearing these comments in mind, it could justifiably be argued that the first major exponent of philosophy in al-Andalus was Abū Bakr Ibn al-Sā'igh Ibn Bājja, known in Latin as Avempace (?–1139). If 'rationalism' means anything, Avempace was certainly a rationalist, firstly in that, unlike Avicenna and even, at a later date, Averroes, he did not make use of the texts of the Qur'an and the religious traditions of Islam as points of reference. Secondly, and more importantly, he saw the development of spiritual forms and the realisation of intellectual excellence as the main aims of human perfection, in fact all of human life worthy of being lived. His mysticism is a mysticism not of the emotions but of the intellect, rigorously applied: 'With corporeality, man is an existing being; with spirituality he is nobler; with intellect he is divine and virtuous'.[22] These views emerge clearly from works such as his *Treatise on the Union of the Intellect with Man* and, particularly, one of several unfinished works, the *Regimen of the Solitary* (*Tadbīr al-mutawahhid*, also known as *The Hermit's Guide*). He had a thorough knowledge of Greek philosophy: there are clear traces of the influence of Plato's *Republic* on his work and he produced direct commentaries of works by Aristotle including the *Physics* and *De generatione et corruptione*. Avempace's influence was long lasting, affecting succeeding thinkers including Averroes who, in his youth, was greatly impressed by Avempace. The famous rabbi Maimonides makes it clear that he knew Avempace's work in detail: he judges him to be an 'excellent philosopher' and provides us with evidence of, amongst other things, his important work as a scientist and astronomer and of how, for example, he had the courage to question the prevailing Ptolemaic viewpoint, denying the existence of epicycles.[23]

Another contemporary and successor who similarly admired Avempace was Abū Bakr Ibn Tufayl (1110–*c.* 1185), although he reproaches him for being too taken up with worldly affairs. In fact, Ibn Tufayl, too, held public position, being doctor at the court of the Almohad caliphs. Of his philosophic works, the only one to survive is his famous novel *Epistle of Hayy Ibn Yaqzān*, in which the author professes himself a follower of Avicenna and says that he has written this work because he had been invited to 'unfold for you, as well as I am able, the secrets of the oriental philosophy mentioned by the prince of philosophers, Avicenna [Abū ʿAlī Ibn Sīnā]'[24] (Goodman 1972: 95). The tone of the epistle is undoubtedly Gnostic (the name of the protagonist means 'the Living son of the Awakened One'), but appears to be linked to a view of the cosmos that is still strongly influenced by Neo-Platonism and Aristotle, seeming to draw little from esoteric cosmologies. Growing up alone on a deserted island, Hayy, who is endowed with a high level of intuitive and speculative abilities, is able to identify the fundamental laws of the functioning of the universe through his observation of nature. His discoveries range from the ontological difference between the mortal body and the immortal soul to the concept of the planetary system of homocentric spheres, from Aristotelian physics (with the division of heavy and light bodies that determines the relative movements, and the distinction between matter and form) to the Neo-Platonic metaphysical intuition that imperfection is nothing other than pure non-being. On the other hand, Hayy is undoubtedly a mystic: he realises that corporeality is evil; he intuits the existence of an incorporeal body, single and necessary, which leads him to lose himself in ecstatic adoration, freeing himself of the bonds of the material world. Hayy's vision fuses the philosophical idea of God as First Being and Prime Mover, cause of causes, with the Qur'anic image of He who holds the most beautiful of Names and who endures outside the transience of generation and corruption:

> How could He not transcend privation when the very concept means no more than absolute or relative non-being – and how could no-being be associated or confused with Him who is pure being, Whose

> essence is necessary existence, Who gives being to all that is? There is no existence but Him. He is being, perfection and wholeness. He is goodness, beauty, power and knowledge. He is He. 'All things perish except His face' (Qur'an, 28.88).[25] (Goodman 1972: 134)

Hayy is a solitary, a mystic, but his point of view, though different and alternative, is not in contradiction with that of those who, living in the city and acquainted with prophetic revelation, conceive the social aspect, the regulator of communal life, as a potential bastion against the temptations of the devil. It is clear that Ibn Tufayl preferred meditation, spiritual study and profound enquiry into the meaning of things to the literalism and exotericism of those who went no further than the Law, which is not to say that he rejected the validity of the Law which he considered to be appropriate for ordinary people even if insufficient to meet the spiritual demands of the true philosopher.

By presenting him at the court of the Almohad caliph, Ibn Tufayl was to play a decisive role in the fortunes of Averroes whose primacy as the greatest philosopher in the Islamic world rivals that of Avicenna. Since we shall return at length to Averroes in later chapters, we will confine ourselves here to an historical and political evaluation of his importance. For it is possible, I would argue, to read the greater part of the work of Abū al-Walīd Muhammad Ibn Rushd (1126–98) in a political light. It should be borne in mind that he lived at the court and was closely connected to the Almohad regime: not only was he the caliph's personal doctor, but he also held the prestigious posts of supreme judge in Seville and Cordova. While it is true that, in later years, his fortunes changed and he was sent into exile, it is likely that this came about not so much because of the opposition of conservative circles to his philosophical activities as through court rivalries or one of the many political intrigues with which the caliph's entourage was rife. Above all, the entirety of Averroes's work can be understood in the light of the Almohad reforms. The Almohads, a Berber dynasty that had united North Africa and al-Andalus in the mid-12th century, had a triple aim: to oppose the rigid traditionalism of the dominant caste of Mālikite jurists in the name of a return to the scriptural sources (the Qur'an and the *hadīth*) and of an uncompromising proclamation of the Oneness of God; to preach the religious faith to the masses by means of education and able, at the same time, to pursue philosophical and speculative research (it is no accident that Ibn

Tufayl and Averroes were close to the sovereigns and that sovereigns like Abū Yaʿqūb Yūsuf were well versed in the sciences and philosophy); to consolidate the political unity of the Muslim West in the face of the *reconquista* of Spain initiated by the Christian states that had been making offensive forays for several decades. As Marc Geoffroy writes, the Almohad regime

> can be credited with – at one and the same time – *opening* in relation to the élite made up of the class of those who dedicate themselves to rational enquiry, the philosophers; of *closing* in relation to both the adepts of imitative conformism, the Mālikite traditionalists, and the dialectic theologians, both rejected in favour of a 'middle way' between the defects of the first and the excesses of the second that would ensure the proper teaching of the masses.[26]

In the context of these intentions, Averroes's contribution would be decisive. Reflecting Almohad policy, his manual on jurisprudence, *The Distinguished Jurist's Primer*, sought to establish the pre-eminence of the principles of law (the *usūl*, or the Qur'an and the *hadīth*) over its ramifications (*furūʿ*), and to assert the superiority of reference to the basic texts over any religious school tradition (*taqlīd*), including the Mālikite school to which Averroes officially belonged. The composition of the theological works such as the famous *Decisive Treatise* (*Kitāb Fasl al-Maqāl*) or the *Unveiling of the Methods of Proof concerning the Principles of Religion* made it possible to define the limits of theology, and to encourage the philosophers to practise their calling freely and the masses to be content with the teachings of religion and to live their lives with the practical support of faith. In the *Decisive Treatise*, in particular, Averroes advanced a juridical opinion according to which he judged that philosophy was permitted with regard to the religious Law and, in fact, obligatory, so that the characteristics of one imply the practice of the other:

> Since it has been determined that the Law makes it obligatory to reflect upon existing things by means of the intellect, and to consider them; and consideration is nothing more than inferring and drawing out the unknown from the known, therefore, it is obligatory that we go about reflecting upon the existing things by means of intellectual syllogistic reasoning.[27] (Butterworth 2001: 2)

The composition of the commentaries on Aristotle to which Averroes owed his fame ('*colui che'l gran Comento feo*', as Dante puts it [in the *Divine Comedy*, *Inferno* 4.144]), and which was to have a profound and lasting influence on Western philosophy for which his name will always be remembered, was begun at the suggestion of the Almohad caliph Abū Yaʿqūb Yūsuf. Although marginal in relation to his public activities as doctor and jurist, the work was consistent with the rationalist outlook of the sovereigns. Averroes's philosophical work can, therefore, be described as having a rationalist approach, even if it should be added that it was a rationalism that was able to combine the Greek philosophical tradition with the Muslim mentality, a combination that was to prove fruitful. Averroes believed that true philosophical knowledge should be based on Aristotle, who was in his opinion the master of rationality. In this, he opposed the too-Platonic Avicenna and rejected any tendency towards esotericism. He challenged al-Ghazālī, seeking to demonstrate, in his *Tahāfut al-tahāfut*, the 'incoherence of the incoherence' of the enemies of philosophy. Nevertheless, his rationalism led him to admit that 'religious laws are necessary political arts'[28] (Van Den Bergh 1954: 359) and that Islam is the best of religions since it has been able to integrate speculative enquiry with prophetic inspiration.[29] Averroes's aim was to bring about a reform in the political society of his time and in the *Commentary on Plato's Republic* in which he analyses Plato's *Republic* in the absence of Aristotle's *Politics*, a text that did not reach al-Andalus, he criticises the Muslim regimes, describing them variously as timocratic, democratic or even tyrannical. He did not, however, abandon his dream of founding an ideal city where the coexistence of philosophical teaching alongside the practice of the true religion would be guaranteed by the enlightened government of the Almohad caliphs. Elsewhere, complaining that sectarian quarrels were posing a threat to religion and civil peace, Averroes praises Almohad government, saying:

> God has removed many of these evils, ignorant occurrences, and misguided paths by means of this triumphant rule [or 'victorious power' as Geoffroy translates *amr ghālib*[30]]. By means of it, He has brought many good things closer, especially for that sort who follow the path of reflection and yearn for cognizance of the truth. That is, this rule calls the multitude to a middle method for being cognizant of

> God (glorious is He), raised above the low level of the traditionalists yet below the turbulence of the dialectical theologians, and alerts the select to the obligation for complete reflection on the root of the Law. (Butterworth 2001: 33)

The Almohads did not just defend philosophy, they also sought to ensure that the people acquired a correct version of religion.

Although his dream of philosophical reform was never realised, not least because of the decline of Almohadism, Averroes marks a watershed in the history of Islamic philosophy. Historiographical convention has long asserted – and to some extent continues to do so – that al-Ghazālī inflicted a mortal blow on philosophy from which it never fully recovered and that Averroes was the last Islamic philosopher. Both statements are groundless, and more especially the first. Quite apart from the fact that he was much more of a philosopher than he himself was prepared to admit, not only did al-Ghazālī not in any way hold back the development of philosophy in the Islamic West, but neither did he impede the emergence of an Avicennan tradition in the East. Indeed, it is certainly true that Avicenna was the archetype and point of reference for a long tradition of philosophy that, detaching itself clearly from the rigorous Peripatetism influenced by Averroes, continued in various parts of the Islamic world. While no longer representing the high point of Islamic philosophy, its influence continued to be felt well into the Ottoman period. Abū'l-Barakāt al-Baghdādī and Sayf al-Dīn al-Āmidī were just two of those who variously criticised or defended Avicennan doctrines in the 12th and 13th centuries. But the most important Avicennan tendency was that which flourished in Persia right up to the 17th century.

What is clear is that with Averroes a particular type of Islamic philosophy came to an end, never to be revived. While continuing to operate against an ideal Muslim background, it sought, both in its areas of study and its methodology, to uphold the ideas of the Greek philosophers. Some scholars have suggested that perhaps 'Islamic philosophy' is a misnomer and that it might be more accurate to say that a number of Muslim thinkers, from al-Kindī to Averroes, studied philosophy and that, after them, when the Muslim world's interest in philosophy declined, attention turned to other areas of knowledge.

This provocative point of view[32] implies that, on the one hand, 'philosophy' is a specifically 'western' area of learning and, on the other, that the continuity of Islamic thought developed along lines other than philosophical ones. It cannot be denied that Averroes was the last in the Islamic world to support his ideas by the application of rigorously demonstrative, Aristotelian and syllogistic methods. The end of this type of philosophising coincided with the progressive decline in originality of Islamic thought. A special case must be made for al-Ghazālī who addressed and interpreted the many faces – rational, juridical and mystical – of Islam. An intellectual of his calibre is rare in any age.

The Avicennan tradition took many different forms, some of which can be seen as somewhat ambiguous. Indeed, if we apply the parameters set out above it is not always easy to categorise it as 'philosophic'. Two figures who well illustrate some of its characteristics are al-Suhrawardī and Mullā Sadrā al-Shirāzī, both Persians.

Shihāb al-Dīn al-Suhrawardī (1155–91), known as the 'executed one' (*maqtūl*) because he was executed by Saladin at the citadel in Aleppo, started from Avicenna, not to follow him but to oppose and defeat him. He proclaimed himself the true theoretician of that 'eastern philosophy' that Avicenna had been unable factually to enunciate because 'he was in ignorance of the principle, the "Oriental source" (*al-asl al-mashriqī*) itself, which authenticates the qualification "Oriental". Avicenna was unaware of this source, disclosed by the Sages of ancient Persia (the Khusrowanids) and identified with theosophia, divine wisdom par excellence'[33] (Sherrard 1993: 207). Al-Suhrawardī was, then, more of a theosophist than a philosopher and the profoundly esoteric Gnostic bent of his ideas led him to construct a fantastic cosmology centred round the idea of a cascade of 'longitudinal' lights emanating from a First Light, the Light of Lights only very distantly connected with the transcendent One God of Islam. His cosmos is constructed in such a way that the hierarchy of lights is interconnected by relationships of 'dominance' (*qahr*) and 'attraction' (*ʿishq*, or 'love'). The universe of Primordial Lights is an archangelic universe and it forms the longitudinal order, descending from the supreme sovereign lights at the top to the 'world of the Mothers' at the bottom and which is placed over the world of elements. The latitudinal order is formed by the archetypal archangels identified with Platonic ideas in that they are hypostases of Light.

The philosophy put forward by al-Suhrawardī is known as 'Illuminationism' (*ishrāqī*). Although the Illuminationist hierarchy draws on many ideas found in Neo-Platonism and is comparable with the cosmic structure of intelligences formulated by Avicenna, it differs significantly from the Islamic conceptual context in that it is also influenced by Zoroastrian and Hermetic sources prefiguring an ambiguous perennial philosophy (*philosophia perennis*) that is entirely alien to the historical and revolutionary message of the Qur'an. As G. C. Anawati writes:

> The Platonists of ancient Persia loomed large in the ideas of the Illuminationists (*Ishrāqiyyūn*): Hermes who was to be identified with the prophet Idrīs and considered to be not only the ancestor of all wisdom but also the archetypical hero of mystical ecstasy, Zoroaster and Plato. Other figures from the Iranian past were added, making a whole known as the 'holy line of gnosis' (*silsilat al-ʿārifīn*). The Platonists of Islamic Persia were to interpret Platonic ideas in terms of Zoroastrian angelology.[34]

It should be said, however, that other scholars such as Hossein Ziai have denied al-Suhrawardī's esoteric leanings, maintaining that '[his] critique of certain problems of logic, epistemology, physics, mathematics and metaphysics in his Philosophy of Illumination draws upon established Peripatetic texts. No other textual source can be presumed to have been available to him'.[35] Whatever the case, illuminative cosmology and cosmogony were to have a radical effect on the Avicennan cosmological system. While the latter, as we shall see in Chapter 5, is an attempt to explain Islamic monotheism in the light of a Neo-Platonised Aristotle, the illuminative cosmology is the presupposition of a path to sapiential liberation and the study of salvation that al-Suhrawardī described in esoteric and allegorical treatises such as *The Western Exile*. In this work, he describes the process of liberation from matter and of acquisition of the science of Lights as a journey taken by an initiate from Qayrawān (Kairouan) in North Africa to Mount Sinai and beyond.

The Gnostic and dualistic elements in the work of thinkers like al-Suhrawardī, may appear to marginalise, if not actually betray, Islamic ideas. There are a number of other post-Avicennan Persian philosophers whose ideas place them on the very edge of Islam, or even outside it. They include Sayyid Ahmad ʿAlawī (died 1640), also known as Mir-Fendereskī, in whose work dualist Zoroastrian or even Hinduistic elements are much in evidence. Mullā Sadrā al-Shirāzī (1572–1641), on the other hand, remained closer to Shiism, by then the state religion of Safavid Persia. Nevertheless, his ideas appear to be tinged with a Gnosticism that transgresses the positive determinism of the Qur'anic message (which is, as Bausani might put it, active, practical and juridically anti-Gnostic), where God has given origin to the world through an act of creation that brought into being, in a single moment, the heaven and the earth, the soul and humankind. In his commentaries on Avicenna and al-Suhrawardī, Mullā Sadrā substituted 'the metaphysical tradition of essences with a metaphysics of existence, emphasising existence over quiddity'. Above all, he

> is the philosopher of metamorphoses, of transubstantiations. His anthropology is in full agreement with that postulated by Shi'ite eschatology, expressed in the expectation of the coming of the Twelfth Imām as the coming of the Perfect Man. This anthropology is itself bound up with a grandiose cosmogony and psychogony: the fall of the Soul into the abyss of abysses; its slow ascent from level to level up to the human form, which is the point where it emerges onto the threshold of the *malakūt* (the trans-physical spiritual world), the extension of anthropology into a physics and metaphysics of the resurrection.[36] (Sherrard 1993: 343)

Here again, in the case of Mullā Sadrā, it is possible to talk of a theosophy that envisages the sapiential as having a continuity through many epochs. According to him, the Greeks, originally star-worshippers, were told of and instructed in monotheistic theology by Abraham. This *philosophia perennis* is, in my opinion, a distortion of the Qur'anic message which is firmly rooted in the history of prophecy.

If, given these reservations and queries, it is possible to say that an Islamic philosophical tradition survived in the East and particularly in Persia, it might be safe to say that, in the West (including Egypt and the Fertile Crescent), philosophy suffered a decline. This was not because there were no longer any philosophers, but because, on the one hand, there was a traditionalist reaction and, on the other, because, objectively, Averroes had no heirs. To speak of a traditionalist reaction is, however, to risk giving a false impression. Two highly influential and important thinkers of those to speak out against philosophy – Ibn Hazm and Ibn Taymiyya – were anything but irrationalist and certainly did not uphold backward-looking and retrograde positions with regard to cultural matters. However, they both make use of epistemological structures of a particularly Islamic type that are likely to conflict with certain presuppositions of philosophy.

Ibn Hazm of Córdoba (994–1064) was a theologian of the Zāhirite juridical school. This school (no longer in existence today) taught a literal adherence to the sacred texts, ignoring any of the allegorical interpretations so dear to the hearts of the philosophers and similarly rejecting all forms of reasoning by analogy or deduction. Thus it was unsurprising that Ibn Hazm regarded not only philosophy but also Muʿtazilite and Ashʿarite theology with suspicion. Nevertheless, he subjected the legacy of philosophical, theological and religious doctrines to critical examination in his major doxographical work, *The Book of Sects and of Religious Confessions*. In addition, he formulated a remarkable theory of language based on the realistic presupposition according to which the name is a direct indication of the meaning (*al-ism dalla ʿalā al-maʿnà*).[37] Consequently, language is not conventional, but has a sacral value being, in the last analysis, divinely instituted.

> The words of language were dictated by God to Adam, and later the words of the revelation were dictated to Mohammad. We find here the root of a fundamental attitude in Islam: reason and faith are not antinomic; they have the same source and the same object, that can be called 'truth-word'.[38]

As happened in the case of the Ashʿarites, Ibn Hazm's supposed 'traditionalism' does not lead him to see religion and reason as antithetical – rather the reverse since, as we shall see in a later section, he is seen by modern Muslim scholars as a champion of rationalism.

Taqī al-Dīn Ahmad Ibn Taymiyya (1263–1328) lived in Syria and Mameluk Egypt. He was a Hanbalite jurist and, like Ibn Hazm, advocated a strict adherence to the sacred texts. He was, though, a firm believer in the need to attempt an elaboration of the principles of law (*ijtihād*) along rational lines. He was also a moralist, advocating a return to the purity of intention and the usages of the first generation of Muslims, the *salaf*. He wrote a *Confutation of the Logicians* and a work on the conformity of rational and revealed knowledge. His attack on logicians, and on Aristotelian logic in particular, reveals his sceptical distrust of the ability of reason to produce an effective knowledge of the defined thing through definition. While this might not have had any significant implications (scepticism is a widespread tendency in the history of philosophy and yet does not for this reason cease to be philosophy), the Islamic rationalism championed by Ibn Taymiyya gives pre-eminent importance to juridical culture and maintains that the sources of the Law, as interpreted by the *salaf*, are sufficient in themselves to lay the basis of any type of knowledge. Ibn Hazm's Zāhirism, too, relying on the literal meaning of the text, could be seen to imply a significant degree of scepticism in relation to rational methods of knowledge. If applied too rigorously, however, it will lead inevitably to anthropomorphism which is in contradiction with the philosophers' view of God.

The reasons that brought about the decline of philosophy are at one and the same time historical and sociological, political and economic. To investigate them in depth would be to venture into the realms of one of the major problems of Islamic civilisation and culture: its stasis in the face of modernity, its inability to keep step with scientific and technological progress, the exhaustion of the fruitful modes of thinking that reached astonishing heights with the speculative work of al-Fārābī, Avicenna and Averroes. We are forced to conclude that, if Averroes had no emulators, it was because his rationalism no longer answered the needs of 13th-century Islamic society in the way that the rationalism of al-Fārābī and his 'school' had met the requirements of Islamic society in the 10th century. While this assertion should properly be supported by a full comparative study of the economic, political and social life of the two periods, broadly speaking we can say that, while Islamic society was enjoying a period of expansion in the 10th century as a result of flourishing trading and commercial activities,[39] by the 13th century, it had retreated into a 'feudal' regime, the first indications of which had already begun to appear under the Buyid dynasty.[40] In the field of purely intellectual matters, it is hard to say whether the militant rigour, deeply impregnated with juridical culture, of a man like Ibn Taymiyya was more or less responsible for the decline of philosophy than the theosophical deviations of the Avicennian school. After a consideration of the meaning of Islamic philosophy and, particularly, on 'ways of philosophising', it should be possible, to some extent, to resolve these questions at the end. This is also an appropriate moment to consider critically the most important figure in the declining years of medieval Islamic thought, Ibn Khaldūn.

As a young man, ʿAbd al-Rahmān Ibn Khaldūn (1332–1406) was an open-minded politician, living a restless and wandering life in the various courts of North Africa, in Tunis, Bougie and Fez. Moving to Cairo, flourishing under the rule of the Mameluk dynasty of soldier slaves, he devoted himself to teaching and practising law. He composed a monumental work on the history of the Islamic dynasties and, in particular, the Berber and African dynasties (the *Book of Examples*), which he prefaced with an important *Introduction* (or *Muqaddima*). Here, he sets down the guidelines of his interpretation of the political and social realities of Islam, starting out from a clearly Aristotelian philosophical definition of the role and function of the science of history as the science of the 'causes' of events:

> The inner meaning of history [. . .] involves speculation and an attempt to get at the truth, subtle explanation of the causes and origins of existing things, and deep knowledge of the how and why of events. History, therefore, is firmly rooted in philosophy (*hikma*). It deserves to be accounted a branch of it'.[41] (Rosenthal 2005: 5)

The essential innovation in Ibn Khaldūn's work lies in the enunciation of an analytical method in his approach to history that is not idealistic but is instead coldly realistic. Society lies at the centre of history while politics lies at the centre of society. Politics is the heart of sociology and sociology is the heart of history. History, sociology and politics are the three tools of an investigation of reality that is both objective and philosophically based.

Ibn Khaldūn identifies a precise law of historical evolution. In the beginning, it is possible to see a natural passage from primitive life to complex life, determined by the increasingly complex and developing needs and demands and the related satisfying of these needs and responses to demands. There then exist two basic phases of 'civilisation', the rural life of the Bedouins and the sedentary life of the city dwellers. He emphasises not so much the contrast between nomadic and sedentary life as that between rural and city life. The primitive culture is that of the countryside and may be, but is not necessarily, nomadic. Evolved culture is that of the cities. This is obviously sedentary, but is characterised above all by the bonds of cooperation and conditioning that subsist in the city. The move from a Bedouin civilisation to a sedentary one is the natural transition from a society of simple needs to one whose needs are complicated and sophisticated. In this sense, Bedouin culture is earlier than the sedentary culture. The evolution from the basic society to the more elaborate society of the city obviously implies a transition from anarchy to the state, which is to say, from a situation where rival clans predominated to one where a sovereign power becomes established. The element that makes it possible for one tribal group to assert itself over others and form a state is *ʿasabiyya* or 'group feeling'. When young and vigorous, this sense of the group is aggressive and warlike, resulting in the crushing of its adversaries and the setting-up of a centralised government. When the sense of solidarity declines and becomes weak, the state becomes similarly weakened. Ibn Khaldūn emphasises how the sedentary phase of monarchy follows on from the Bedouin phase and how this process is necessary; it is, in fact, the laws of historical development that mean that group feeling comes to an end and is replaced by monarchical power based on force. Once the cities have been built, however, luxury triumphs and with luxury the bonds of kinship weaken and individualism predominates. Civilisation, that had been laboriously constructed through the move away from the wild life of the desert and the countryside, is in crisis; civilisation ends up by devouring itself as excess, luxury and decadence corrupt the original and pure customs of the Bedouin. These factors, in combination with others, such as the spread of injustice and the crisis of the sovereign power, bring about an inversion of the progress of history: from the constructive phase of the founding of the state, there is a return to the anarchy of the Bedouin period, from urban civilisation there is a return to a rural civilisation.

This cyclical process of historic evolution does not, however, preclude the possibility of society moving onwards and upwards to ever more complex and sophisticated levels of organisation. It is on the basis of this paradigm that Ibn Khaldūn develops his theory of state and power, to which we shall return in Chapter 8. Suffice it here to say that Ibn Khaldūn's theory delves deeply into the crisis of the Islamic societies that was unfolding at that time. While he was speaking first and foremost of those of North Africa, he clearly intended his remarks to be understood in a more general way. He intuited

> that it is among the urban populations, whose structures were very different from those of the *bled* [countryside], that we should seek the chief cause of the crises that bring about the failure of attempts at centralisation and monarchical consolidation. Indeed, [Ibn Khaldūn] goes beyond intuition. He grasps the historically negative characteristics of the city populations: he is describing, in fact, the absence of a bourgeoisie.[42]

Ibn Khaldūn does not, however, confine himself to a pessimistic description of a social phenomenon the repercussions of which long made themselves felt in the history of the Islamic states. He reflects, instead, on philosophy from an epistemologically 'traditionalist' viewpoint.

> Ibn Khaldūn takes up an innovative and original position in relation to philosophy. Although it proceeds from a logical and clearly positivistic point of view, it casts doubt on the epistemological foundations on which the philosophers base their metaphysical systems. He does not refute philosophy in the manner of a rigorous jurist [such as Ibn Taymiyya], nor does he even attack aspects of philosophy from a philosophical or theological angle [like al-Ghazālī]. His aim is nothing less than to demolish its epistemological basis by revealing the falsity of its fundamental metaphysical thesis.[43]

In his epistemological criticism of philosophy, Ibn Khaldūn denies that it is possible to arrive at an understanding of either the reality of the sensible world or of the supersensible world through apodictic and deductive reasoning (he was, of course, referring to an 'Aristotelian' model of reason to which one might perhaps oppose a model of specifically 'Islamic' reason). As a consequence, not only does he discount entirely the importance of scientific and physical understanding of the world, but he also rejects one of the most characteristic and particular results of Islamic philosophy: the possibility for the philosopher to aspire to perfect knowledge and, though it, union with God and thus to attain that happiness that represents, among other things, one of the essential goals of political philosophy. While Ibn Khaldūn may not have had such radically destructive intentions towards philosophy (as we have said, he recognises, for example, the philosophical value of history), he nevertheless casts a significant shadow of doubt over this intellectual discipline.

Thus, with Ibn Khaldūn, philosophy appeared, in the 15th century, to be writing its own epitaph. With him, we conclude this brief sketch. It justifies, amongst other things, why I called this book an 'introduction to Islamic *philosophy*' and not an 'introduction to Islamic *thought*'. If the whole of Islamic 'thought' were to be tackled, it would have been necessary to discuss in detail at least three other subjects: theology in the strict sense of the word, particularly in its juridical implications (Ibn Hazm and Ibn Taymiyya being notable examples); science, that enjoyed a notable flowering in the Islamic area; and, last but not least, mysticism or *tasawwuf*, that at times has taken on philosophical elements. A theologian and commentator on the Qur'an like the famous Fakhr al-Dīn al-Rāzī (1149–1209), one of the most advanced thinkers of Ashʿarism and author of a critical commentary on Avicenna, was profoundly influenced by philosophy and was not immune from the contamination of Muʿtazilite 'rationalism'. Thinkers of this type are not, however, strictly speaking 'philosophers', and for this reason are not discussed in this work. On the other hand, if we return to some of the mystics like Ibn ʿArabī (1165–1240) when discussing the Oneness of God in Islamic thought (see Chapter 4), it should be remembered that some encyclopaedic Islamic philosophers, such as al-Kindī and Avicenna or even to a lesser extent Averroes, studied widely in the field of the sciences, from mathematics to astronomy and from chemistry to medicine. Obviously their philosophical concepts influenced the direction of their scientific research. The reverse is also true, however, with a large number of Islamic scientists, including the physicist Ibn al-Haytham and the mathematician al-Khwārazmī, taking little or no interest in philosophy. They are therefore not considered here. A fact that is worth bearing in mind is that Islamic science, yielding such a wealth of results in the fields of medicine, optics and trigonometry, was unable to elaborate a conscious 'discourse on method' which is why it did not experience the 'revolution' that, with Galileo, Descartes and Newton, allowed Western Europe to produce and dominate the modern world.

Chapter 2

What is Medieval Islamic Philosophy?

There are two matters that need to be clarified from the outset. The first relates to the notion of the Middle Ages, a concept that even in the historiography of the western Latin Middle Ages has become increasingly problematic. In European history, the Middle Ages was an 'invention' of, in the first place, the Humanists and then more particularly of the historians of the Enlightenment who, by stigmatising the period between the classical world and the modern age as backward and obscurantist, sought to exalt the progressiveness and the enlightened ideas of their age and their culture. The notion of the 'medieval', with all its negative implications, is even less meaningful for Islam, since it was precisely in the period between the 9th and the 14th centuries that it had its most creative and fruitful phase. The new ideas about science and philosophy emerging from the Islamic world were hugely influential, spreading through the whole of the known world and particularly into the countries around the Mediterranean. If there is such a thing as the Islamic Middle Ages, it is situated between the 16th and 18th centuries, the period when, by contrast, science and philosophy were to come to maturity in the West.

To resolve the second matter, it needs to be recognised that Islamic philosophy and Arab philosophy are not interchangeable. Not all Arab philosophy is Islamic and not all Islamic philosophy is Arab. The term Islamic philosophy means, specifically, the philosophy developed by men (or women) whose professed religion is Islam or who, at least, live according to Islamic customs. The term Arab philosophy refers, by contrast, to philosophy written in the Arabic language. Both a 'Jewish' philosophy and a 'Christian' philosophy existed in the Islamic world and they often used Arabic as their mode of expression, not least because, for example, the Christian philosophers in Islamic areas were, ethnically speaking, Arabs. As such, they can rightly be considered to be part of Arab philosophy. On the other hand, not only were some Islamic philosophers not ethnic Arabs, but they also wrote in other languages, particularly Persian, but, in more recent times, also in Turkish and Urdu. These distinctions having been made, it should not be supposed that the different philosophers studied lacked their own specific characteristics or cannot be identified – which is to say, precisely defined – as Muslims or Arabs. It is, on the other hand, possible to speak of Muslim philosophy insofar as this philosophy relates to the Qur'an and Islamic principles.

It is worth pausing to take a closer look at one or two aspects of what has been said above. Christian Arabs made an important contribution to the development of Islamic philosophy, both Arabic and non-Arabic. This contribution was both direct and indirect. It should be recalled, above all, that the majority of the most important translators of the philosophical and scientific works of Ancient Greece from Greek into Syriac and from Syriac and Greek into Arabic were Christians. The Nestorians Hunayn Ibn Ishāq (809–73), his son Ishāq Ibn Hunayn and his grandson Hubaysh translated almost the entire Aristotelian corpus, as well as other works including some by Plato, the Peripatetics and Galen's medical treatises. Abū Bishr Mattā Ibn Yūnus (died 940), who continued this work of translation, was also a close friend of al-Fārābī and an important exponent of Aristotle's logic. Also interested in the study of logic was another translator of Greek texts, the Jacobite Yahyā Ibn ʿAdī. Qustā Ibn Lūqā (died *c.* 910) was a doctor, philosopher and mathematician. He translated Diophantos and Heron into Arabic and even much later in Islamic history was regarded as a kind of personification of the wisdom of the ancients. The Jews too, who lived in Islamic territories freely carrying on their activities without fear of persecution, made a direct contribution to Islamic philosophy. From Saadia Gaon (882–942) in Egypt to Salomon Ibn Gebirol (1021–50) in al-Andalus, Jewish philosophers wrote as often in Arabic as in Hebrew.

The great Maimonides (1138–1204) composed his most important work, *Dalāla al-Ḥā'irīn* (*Guide for the Perplexed*), in Arabic. Although not a Muslim, he tackled the same problems as the Islamic philosophers, discussing the doctrines of the *mutakallimūn* theologians and using the works of al-Fārābī and Avempace, whom he greatly admired, as a starting point for the development of his own theories. The declining years of the Middle Ages, finally, saw the flowering of a fully fledged Jewish Averroism starting with the work of Isaac Albalag and culminating with, particularly, Moses Narboni (1300–62), an enthusiastic exponent of thoroughly Averroist ideas.[1] Narboni also wrote commentaries on works by Avicenna, al-Ghazālī and Avempace.

Thus, Abū Bishr Mattā and Maimonides and Narboni can in a sense be considered to be 'Arab' but not, of course, 'Islamic' philosophers. Conversely, there were many Muslim philosophers who wrote in their mother tongue, particularly Persian. As is the position of English today, Arabic remained the international language of cultural communication. Nevertheless, Avicenna wrote the *Book of Science* in Persian, the language used by al-Ghazālī for his *Advice to Kings*, which follows in the footsteps of the Iranian tradition of 'mirrors for princes', and the *Alchemy of Happiness*, a shortened version of his most important work (written in Arabic), *The Revival of the Religious Sciences*. These are just a few of many examples. Later, in the Ottoman period, it is not surprising to find Turkish intellectuals turning away from Arabic in favour of Turkish. The fact that Arab and Islamic philosophy cannot necessarily be identified with one another has a precise conceptual value that explains why, in this book, I discuss only those philosophers whose ideas were formed within the context of Islam, which is to say of a religion that provided them with a clear ideological reference point.

Islamic philosophy is, of course, profoundly rooted in Arabic in that the Qur'an, the direct word of God, was revealed in 'plain Arabic speech' (as is stated in many verses of the Qur'an, including 26.195) because it was an 'admonition' to all people (according to many verses, including 6.90). The Qur'an is obviously not a work of philosophy, nor one of science. Nevertheless, Muslim philosophers made considerable use of it to lend weight, with the light of revelation, to the theoretical conclusions at which they had arrived. This was evidently considered possible because the Qur'an was considered to be rational and to contain a message inviting humankind to reason and speculate. Seeking, in his *Decisive Treatise*, to demonstrate that 'the Law calls for consideration of existing things by means of the intellect and for pursuing cognizance of them'[2] (Butterworth 2001: 2), Averroes goes to the lengths of quoting five different verses from the Qur'an to support his argument. Indeed, the Qur'an devotes as much space to explicit references to the dignity of rational speculation as it does to unequivocal affirmations about the rational character of divine creation. Again and again, verses tell us to 'study' nature, or to understand it with the intellect and to reflect speculatively about it. One example runs:

> It was He who spread out the earth and placed upon it mountains and rivers. He gave all plants their male and female parts and drew the veil of night over the day. Surely in these there are signs for thinking men.
>
> And in the land there are adjoining plots: vineyards and cornfields and groves of palms, the single and the clustered. Their fruits are nourished by the same water: yet We make the taste of some more favoured than the taste of others. Surely in this there are signs for men of understanding (*yaʿqilūna*). (13.3–4)

Those who are endowed with reason speculate about nature and things and discern in them a plan perfect in its construction: 'He created seven heavens, one above the other. You will not see a flaw in the Merciful's creation. Turn up your eyes; can you detect a single crack?' (67.3).

The two terms most frequently used to refer to philosophic 'science' and 'knowledge', *ʿilm* and *hikma*, are similarly drawn from the Qur'an. The word *ʿilm* is used in the Qur'an in the sense both of 'to know' and 'to learn without effort'. In verse 3.7 there is a reference to 'those who are well grounded in knowledge' (*al-rāsikhūn fī 'l-ʿilm*). Although interpretations vary, these are thought to be either those who, with God, understand the philosophical and allegorical interpretation of particularly ambiguous and uncertain sacred texts, or those who profess to believe unwaveringly in the Book and its teachings, reserving to God the ultimate knowledge of the secret. The Prophet, anxious to recite the Qur'an and to learn the truth, utters the words: 'Lord, increase my knowledge (*ʿilman*)!' (20.114). In this way, scholars have been able to assert that *ʿilm* mean religious knowledge as opposed to *maʿrifa* or profane knowledge. The distinction is, however, an artificial one and, in many cases, the meanings are reversed: the word *ʿilm* and its plural *ʿulūm* can be used to mean the sciences of nature which would never be called '*maʿārif*' (the plural of *maʿrifa*). In fact, *maʿrifa* is a term of particular importance in the language of the mystics (*ʿārif*, that can be translated as 'wise', is, however, the technical term used to define a 'Gnostic').

More usually, the term 'philosophy' is translated into Arabic as *falsafa*, a word clearly derived from the Greek *philosophia*. But *falsafa* is used above all of that current of thought that includes figures such as al-Fārābī, Avicenna and Averroes and acknowledges Plato and Aristotle as its masters. In other words, *falsafa* refers to Islamic (or more generally Arab) philosophy influenced by Greek philosophy. The characteristically Arabic word used to express the concept of philosophy is *hikma*. This term embraces a group of intellectual operations covering a broad spectrum of philosophical work and could be said to be the most general and all-embracing term used to refer both to conscious reflection about humankind and the world, and to wisdom. Used like this, it is perhaps more appropriately equivalent to the Greek *sophia*. To understand philosophy as only *falsafa* could give rise to misunderstandings. The many aspects of this problem can clearly be seen in the doctrines of the Brothers of Purity. In a single passage of their epistles they use three different words for knowledge: *falsafa*, *ʿilm* and *maʿrifa*: 'The principle of philosophy (*falsafa*) is the love of the sciences (*ʿulūm*); its means the knowledge (*maʿrifa*) of the reality of things as far as is possible for human capacities, and its aim is to profess them and to act (*ʿamal*) in accordance with this science (*ʿilm*)'. The Brothers of Purity assert their superiority over other scholars because they have succeeded in harmonising the philosophical sciences (*ʿulūm hikmiyya*) with the prophetic sciences (*ʿulūm nabawiyya*).[3] The first are based on typically rationalistic Aristotelian (and also Platonic) foundations: 'science is the form of the known impressed in the soul of the knower'; the second are based on authority: 'faith is the acceptance given to he who knows more than you'[4]. Without entirely falling into Gnostic error, it is possible to say that, in Islamic thought, there is no effective contradiction between the two terms of the question, between the concept grasped through the use of reason and the precept received through revelation. Instead, the two are integrated with one another, representing at most two differentiated aspects of a single truth. This implies a 'rationalistic' reading of the Qur'an. And this is also what Averroes wanted to convey when he affirms, in the *Decisive Treatise*, that one Truth (*haqq*) cannot oppose another Truth and that religion, far from being the enemy of philosophy, encourages its study.

The search for a suitable vocabulary that could convey concepts and make them as precise as possible is an indication that Muslim philosophers were at the same time seeking to define their own meaning of philosophy. In 1953, Richard Walzer wrote that 'Islamic philosophy is [. . .] a "productive assimilation" of Greek thought by open-minded and far-sighted representatives of a very different tradition and thus a serious attempt to make this foreign element an integral part of the Islamic tradition'.[5] This thesis, that has led Walzer to posit the necessary existence of Greek sources, some entirely unknown and hypothetical, for each and every idea developed by the Islamic philosophers, is certainly overstated and may even need to be rejected entirely. Not so much, or at least not only, because it might have the effect of devaluing the overall value of Islamic thought by reducing it to a mere re-elaboration – albeit often original and informed – of Greek ideas, but mainly because it appears to resolve – but incorrectly, I believe – a basic problem. This can be formulated as follows: did Muslim philosophers try to explain the essence of Islam in the terms of Greek philosophy as Philo of Alexandria tried to do for the essence of Judaism and as Clement and Origen tried to do for the essence of Christianity? Or is the contrary true: that Muslim philosophers tried to explain Greek philosophy in Islamic terms? To answer this it is necessary to start from the proposal that there was no serious attempt to Islamicise Plato and Aristotle in the same way as occurred in the Latin West where medieval and, to some extent, Humanist philosophers attempted to Christianise them. No Islamic philosopher has ever suggested that the great Greek philosophers anticipated – let alone were standard-bearers of – the revelation of Islam. Even Averroes, who passionately admired Aristotle, limited himself to describing him as the most perfect man ever created by nature, and did not attribute to him any prophetic qualities. Rather the reverse, since it is the philosophers who are grouped together under the name 'heirs of the prophet'. Revelation, in any case, has a dignity that is entirely autonomous and impervious to philosophical speculation. At most, it might be possible to presume or suspect that a 'free thinker' like Rhazes discounted the very notion of revelation. Al-Fārābī, Avempace and Averroes saw religion and philosophy as having different spheres of expression and application, maintaining that philosophical and religious conclusions were not contradictory, even if they had been arrived at by different routes. This lack of any contradiction is not in any way to imply that philosophy has a religious dimension. On the other hand, it certainly means that religion has a rational dimension. That said however, it is highly probable that al-Kindī and Avicenna saw philosophy as having a religious dimension. Post-Avicennan philosophers like al-Suhrawardī and Mullā Sadrā certainly operated within a theosophical context. Philosophers despite themselves and conditioned by philosophy, al-Ghazālī and Ibn Khaldūn nevertheless were hostile to it in the name of religious truth. We can conclude that Islamic philosophers did not attempt to explain Islam in the terms of Greek philosophy and, indeed, for some of them the opposite was true. Let us examine the most important characteristics of the relationship between Islam and Greek philosophy.

The first impact of Greek philosophy on Islamic thought came about through translations of Greek texts into Arabic. Dimitri Gutas, writing in 1991, puts forwards a persuasive analysis of this process that is worth reconsidering despite some debate and objections to details. Put briefly, his thesis is that the translations were carried out because they were useful to the policies of the first Abbasid caliphs. Thus, after coming to power and finding himself faced with a series of rebellions and breakaway groups, al-Mansūr (754–5)

> not only dealt decisively with all of them but also adopted a policy of ideological cooptation, that is, he appropriated as ʿAbbāsid the Zoroastrian ideology. [. . .] Al-Mansūr's decision to coopt Zoroastrian ideology and transfer it to Baghdad appears not even particularly wise, just pragmatic and sensible.
>
> Once Zoroastrian Sasanian cultural attitudes became acceptable in Baghdad, right after its foundation, the translation of secular learning into Arabic became part of the process.[6] (Gutas 1998: 49–50)

Thus Greek texts, particularly astrological texts, began to appear in Arabic by way of the Pehlevi language. Al-Mahdī (775–85) found himself caught up in bitter debates between intellectuals on matters relating to cosmology. Questions about the atomistic structure of matter, space and the void would appear to have had dualistic origins. There was an 'orthodox' reaction seeking to outline a philosophy of nature that was acceptable to Islam and which could interact dialectically with opponents. The result was the promotion of translations of books of Aristotelian logic and, in Gutas's view,[7] the entry of Aristotelian physics into Arab thought. Al-Ma'mūn (813–33), the sovereign who made Muʿtazilism the state theology, pursued a policy of political and doctrinal centralisation around the figure of the caliph, an objective that

> involved taking control of the religious discussion in the capital and by extension in the Islamic world, and fostering an intellectual elite that would conduct this discussion in acceptable ways. This was necessary both to maintain the image of the caliph as champion of Islam, strengthen his religious and hence political authority, and, as a most important corollary to the preceding, weaken the religious authority of leaders among the masses.[8] (Gutas 1998: 95)

Policies of this kind would, according to Gutas's analysis, have required a process of translation that could provide Muslim thinkers and the intellectual elite with new ideas and new tools. The first Greek texts to be translated were, therefore, those that dealt with astrology, physics and dialectical logic, subjects that were most useful to the caliph's political ends. Prompted by an ever increasing and specialised interest, these were followed by books and treatises that were more strictly philosophical. This reconstruction of events suggests that the approach to Greek philosophy was, first and foremost, political and intended to bolster up Islam. 'The Byzantines turned their backs on ancient science because of Christianity, while the Muslims had welcomed it because of Islam'[9] (Gutas 1998: 85). It is said that Caliph al-Ma'mūn embarked on his reforming initiative after Aristotle appeared to him in a dream. The Moroccan philosopher al-Jābrī, presenting a somewhat different view from that of Gutas, asserts that

> whether or not it really occurred, al-Ma'mūn's famous 'dream' was not as innocent as it might appear. It was not inspired by pure interest in Aristotle but by a desire to oppose Zoroaster and Mani. The task of Arab-Islamic philosophy in future was therefore clearly defined even in the earliest years of its development, the period of the first translations. Philosophy was to be a weapon against the ideological attack of Gnosticism that threatened the very foundations of the state.[10]

This leads to the question of whether Muslims looked to Greek thought for a new model of rationality.

It is generally accepted that much of the credit for initiating the diffusion of philosophy among Muslims is due to al-Kindī. Gutas writes,

> The introduction of philosophy into the Islamic world is indelibly linked with the name of al-Kindī, the first philosopher in Arabic, and the circle of scientists and collaborators that he gathered around him. To understand this development it is important, first of all, to keep in mind that al-Kindī was not a philosopher in the sense that he was only or primarily a philosopher. He was a polymath in the translated sciences and as such very much a product of his age.[11] (Gutas 1998: 119–20)

Al-Kindī's encyclopaedic knowledge explains how, amongst other things, he was able to attempt to harmonise Greek philosophy with Islam and with Muʿtazilite theology. It was he who first used philosophical terms to characterise the Islamic idea of the one and transcendent God who is at the same time lord and ruler of all that is created:

> The first principle [*primo principio*] of philosophic Islamic theology will remain characterised as the 'pure' and transcendent One and, at the same time, as a supreme intellectual substance; will exercise its causality according to Neo-Platonic laws, but will always be regarded also as the first fixed principle of the movement of the spheres; will be conceived of as transcendent in relation to every one of our predications, without, however, losing the characteristics of a monarch who rules the course of both the heavens and human events.[12]

From al-Kindī onwards, Islamic philosophy was to express itself through a synthesis of Plato (and perhaps particularly of Neo-Platonism) and Aristotle:

> a student of Greek philosophy in Islam in the classical period will normally follow Aristotle in all the basic epistemological and metaphysical options, but will crown his own doctrine of the first principle with a number of elements, including that of perfect unity, absolute simplicity and radical transcendence, drawn from the Neo-Platonist analysis of the conditions of intelligibility of reality.[13]

While we can certainly see Plato and the Neo-Platonists and Aristotle coupled together and integrated into Islamic philosophy, the approach to the themes of the Greek philosophers is very free, partly because

> while it is certainly true that the Arabs took the first foundations of their philosophy, and their sciences, from foreign cultures, they were to go on to develop these foundations in original ways, finding new solutions to old problems. In the case of philosophy, this can in great part be explained by the influence of their profoundly monotheistic religion that found itself interacting with theories of Greek origin. A particularly important role was played by the ideas of oneness, divine attributes, the creation of the world, rewards and punishment in the afterlife, all elements that Islamic philosophy returned to again and again. The result is a philosophy that assumed a profoundly religious form.[14]

So it would appear that Muslim philosophers were not so much seeking a 'new' model of rationalism as a particularly effective and organised prop for their own religious ideas. What Gutas calls Muslim 'philhellenism' never implied the renunciation of an Islamic basis for knowledge. This fact can be deduced from an analysis of how Islamic philosophers dealt with the works of their great Greek predecessors. Al-Fārābī, for example, would seem to have used Plato's *Republic* as the reference text for works such as the *Virtuous City* and the *Book of Political Science*. According to Walzer,[15] al-Fārābī wanted to set out a radical reform of the caliphate in Platonic terms, suggesting that the caliph should model himself on the principles of Plato's *Republic*. Many similarities can, not surprisingly, be detected, starting with the qualities that al-Fārābī maintains are essential for the ruler of the virtuous city and which he draws from Books VIII and IX of the *Republic*. I would argue, however, that examples of divergence are as consistent and striking as examples of convergence and that it would be wrong to seek very close parallels between al-Fārābī's treatise and Plato's work.

In the first place, there is the actual structure of the treatise. It is not a dialogue, being systematic in form. There are no hints of those elements of myth and poetry that are so characteristic of Plato's philosophy. Secondly, the ordering of the arguments follows a precise scheme more reminiscent of Neo-platonic emanationism than Platonic dialectic. Al-Fārābī first discusses God (Chapters I–IV and IX) (the division of the chapters is that established by A. Nader[16]); then the cosmic hierarchy and how all beings come from God (Chapters VII–VIII and X); he goes on to discuss the nature of the relationship between matter and form in relation to the causes and structure of the heavenly bodies (Chapters XI–XIX); this is followed by the parts of the soul in relation to corporeality (Chapters XX–XXI) and to the intellectual and psychic faculties (Chapters XXII–XXIV), including a section of dreams that, in particular conditions, may imply inspiration and prophecy (Chapters XXV–XXVI). The last part of the treatise (Chapters XXVII–XXXVII) is the most strictly political, with chapters dedicated to the ruler of the perfect society, to the difference between the virtuous city and those which are ignorant or imperfect, to justice and to religious piety. Al-Fārābī's arrangement is thus entirely different from that used by Plato. His basic aim was to give political doctrine a metaphysical basis. While it is true that this idea can also be found in Plato, the metaphysics and the physics in the *Virtuous City* are more Aristotelian than Platonic, while the metaphysical basis that al-Fārābī attempts to establish is clearly Islamic in inspiration: the idea of God (the First Being and not Good) set out in the *Virtuous City* is clearly monotheistic and draws its inspiration from the Islamic principle of *tawhīd*. It is true that a unitary doctrine could have been conceived in a Neo-Platonic environment, but the negative theology, characteristic of Neo-Platonism, was also typical of the Muʿtazilite tradition and was used, not much later, by mature Ismaili traditions (see Chapter 4) of which al-Fārābī may have been a precursor.

Thirdly, even if in al-Fārābī the philosopher is the guide to the virtuous city as in Plato, when he is identified with the figure of the *imām*, a figure with Shiite religious connotations, he does not seem to follow Plato's philosopher at all closely. There are many reasons to justify this observation. Firstly, as Miriam Galston has noted, it does not appear to be true, unlike the situation in the Republic, that philosophy is a discipline necessary to the government of states and, particularly, of virtuous cities. It is, according to Galston, the concrete government of a city that can do without philosophy, regarding it as an essentially practical art[17] – or at least one that is linked to the formulation of legislation derived from Islam. I would take the opposite view and say that, for al-Fārābī, the inhabitants of the virtuous city share 'ideas' and principles based on philosophy and that the virtuous ruler cannot do without philosophy. I would agree, however, that such a ruler need not be tied to one particular type of philosophy, or at least that his philosophical ideas should not conflict with Islamic principles, thus distancing the philosopher-king of the virtuous city from the philosopher-king of Plato's *Republic*.

Secondly, al-Fārābī attributes prophetic qualities to the philosopher-*imām* that are clearly not Platonic even if a number of the qualificative attributes of the philosopher-*imām* correspond to those of the philosophers of Plato's *Republic*. The ruler of the virtuous city is, at one and the same time, philosopher, prophet and king: as a philosopher, he possesses the intellectual tools that allow him to lay the ideological foundations of the perfect society; as a prophet he possesses the rhetorical tools that allow him to speak to, and convince, the common people; as a king he is a legislator and rules the city according to explicit political ends. While the distinctive attributes of the philosopher-*imām* recall some of the qualities that Plato also gives his philosopher, they also correspond to the qualities that will later be recognised in the Sunni caliph (and the main theoretician of the Sunni caliphate, al-Māwardī, was certainly not influenced by Platonism): physical and mental health; moderation in habits; a love of science and justice; eloquence to lead his subjects; the ability to protect the Law; and the ability and the courage to go to war. To conclude, while al-Fārābī takes the *Republic* as his starting point, he quickly moves away from it, revealing himself to be, on the one hand, indebted to the Islamic tradition and, on the other, anxious to define an authentically functioning model of the virtuous city.

Averroes's writings can be grouped into two, apparently antithetical, types. One is directly inspired by Islam and includes the *Decisive Treatise* and the *Incoherence of the Incoherence*. The other is of those that, to varying extents, comment on and analyse the writings of Aristotle and, as such, can be described as particularly 'Greek'. The many years that Averroes devoted to the study of Aristotle, from the age of about 30 until his death, resulted in three types of commentaries: the summaries or epitomes (*jawāmiʿ*), also known as 'minor' commentaries; the so-called 'medium' (*talkhīs*, plural *talākhis*); and the 'great' commentaries or literal commentaries (*tafsīr*, plural *tafāsīr*). The *tafāsīr* were, for the most part, written in the later and last years of Averroes's life, at the time when he was turning away from a use of the *talākhis* (with the exception of the *talkhīs* on Galen's *Treatise on Fevers* composed in 1193 and the *talkhīs* on Plato's *Republic*, probably written around 1195), and had also abandoned the simple expositional style of the *jawāmiʿ*. These mature works represent a determined and highly original attempt to rediscover and rework Aristotle's ideas. Puig Montada has written that

> *talkhīs* and *tafsīr* (sometimes *sharh*) are two genres used by Averroes to arrive at a fundamental understanding of Aristotle; the other forms are secondary. In the case of both genres, Averroes takes his basic inspiration from Hellenistic commentators, Alexander of Aphrodisias and Themistius. I have found no examples of Qur'anic commentaries as models. The type of commentary produced by Avempace may have influenced the so-called 'minor commentaries', but not here [in the 'medium' and 'great' commentaries]. On the other hand, al-Fārābī is the author of commentaries that are parallel in form to the *tafāsīr* of Averroes.[18]

In fact, both al-Fārābī and Avempace had produced commentaries on Aristotle. The former, for example, wrote commentaries of the *Physica*, *De Coelo* and the *Meteorologia* as well as a lost *Commentary on the Nichomachean Ethics*. In this last work, it would appear that he entirely revised his previous ideas about happiness and the possibility of conjunction between human intellect and the Agent Intellect. Avempace too is thought to have written a commentary on the *Physica* as well as works on *De generatione et corruptione* and the *Historia animalium*.

The three types of commentaries produced by Averroes, from the *jawāmiʿ* to the *tafāsīr*, can be seen as forming an ascending and systematic series that becomes progressively ever more elaborate in structural conception, being much more than mere compilations with each type bearing the hallmark of the author's personal involvement. The *jawāmiʿ* take many liberties in relation to the summarised texts and give the impression of being more original. The *talākhis*, while commentaries in the proper sense of the work, seem to convey a desire to examine and analyse specific aspects of the texts. The *tafāsīr* adhere closely to the Arisototelian text, but enunciate definitive formulations of Averroes's opinions on a number of crucial questions (such as the cosmic structure of the Intelligences and the motors in the commentaries to the *Physica* and the *Metaphisica*, or the oneness of the possible intellect in the commentary on *De Anima*). This evolving process clearly indicates how Averroes's thought became more rigorous and increasingly subtle. As he gradually came to grips with Aristotle's ideas, he became increasingly aware of the need to express them with coherence and accuracy, delving ever more deeply into the secrets of nature of which

Aristotle was – in his opinion – the undisputed master. It can be argued, therefore, that Averroes's work, progressing from the *jawāmiʿ* to the *tafāsīr*, corresponds to an intention (not always respected, however) to study and adhere ever more diligently to Aristotle's text. This adherence of Peripatetism to reality implies that the commentaries prefigure a sort of 'encyclopaedia' that organises knowledge in a single homogeneous entity. An 'encyclopaedia' of knowledge of this kind needs no external supports: Aristotelian logic provides it with a model and conceptual structures; physics, metaphysics or psychology its thematic development. It is arranged as a kind of tree of sciences through which, starting out from the originality of the *jawāmiʿ*, the faithfulness of the *tafāsīr* can eventually be reached through a process that seeks to 'set out strictly human knowledge and to address those who have a desire to possess such knowledge'. Thus, for Cruz Hernández, the compendia have a propaedeutic function, with the *talākhis* constituting a 're-creation of the fundamental problems of the *falsafa*', the *tafāsīr* seeking to cleanse philosophy 'of the theological connections of the *kalām ashʿarī* [that is, of Ashʿarite theology], of the syncretic simplifications of the Muʿtazilites or of the Neo-Platonic formalisation of Ibn Sīnā'.[19]

This assertion of the autonomy of philosophy by Averroes in no way contradicts either the principles of faith and religion or the views put forward in 'Islamic' works such as the *Decisive Treatise* or the *Incoherence of Incoherence*. Thus there is little point in asking whether Averroes is more original in the commentaries or in his 'Islamic' works, or whether there is a contradiction of aims between the two types of work, or whether, as a disbeliever, he was seeking to put forward his own heterodox philosophical opinions in writings reserved for a small elite. Works of this kind belong, of course, to different areas and deal with the same truths from two different angles. Greek philosophy is not an alternative to Islam, nor does it incorporate it. Islam does not oppose philosophy, nor does it condemn it. Greek philosophy deals with philosophical, and political problems; Islam deals with philosophical, theological and religious matters. Greek philosophy and Islam do not, however, arrive at diverging conclusions on the most important and basic questions. There is a reciprocal compossibility between religion and philosophy.

Philosophy in the Islamic world was never a profession in the sense that it was for the *magistri artium* of the University of Paris in the 13th century. The reason was that there was no institution comparable to the medieval universities of the West. Teachers often gathered disciples around them outside publicly organised schools and knowledge was imparted directly. Such teaching would take place in mosques or in areas and institutions attached to the mosques. When the Fatimids conquered Egypt in 969, they built the Azhar mosque in Cairo with the intention of making it a centre of Ismaili education and propaganda. But here, only theology and those disciplines linked to theology (for example, grammar which in Islam is a discipline linked to religion in that it is used to interpret or decipher the Sacred Text) were studied. The same thing was to happen later. When the Seljuk grand vizier Nizām al-Mulk (died 1092) set up the famous *madrase nizāmiyye* all over the Islamic East, in Baghdad and in Persia, his intention was to promote, through them, the study of law (particularly the Shafite version) and the religious disciplines, with an emphasis on anti-Shiite and anti-Ismaili teaching. The *madrase* (or 'schools') are the institutions that most closely resemble the western universities, but no profane knowledge such as medicine or philosophy was taught in them. It should not be forgotten that, in Islam, law is a religious science.

If the philosophers did not have their own 'place' in which to practise their calling, it is also true to say that philosophy was not, strictly speaking, their profession. In almost every case, the Islamic philosophers were professional jurists, doctors or statesmen with patrons in high places. Al-Kindī enjoyed the protection of some of the 'Hellenising' Abbasid caliphs including al-Ma'mūn and al-Muʿtasim, but he was also very rich and appears to have lived on a private income. Not enough is known about the life of al-Fārābī to make any assumptions but we know that in his last years he lived under the protection of the Hamdanid Shiite sultans of Aleppo. Al-Ghazālī studied philosophy in any free time remaining from his hours of teaching Shafite law at the Baghdad *nizāmiyya*. He was an intimate of the Seljuk sultans and the caliphs, at least until he decided to dedicate himself to mysticism. Avicenna studied in the sultan's library in his native city, Kharmaithen (near Bukhara) in Central Asia (now Uzbekistan). He became famous as a doctor and for many years held the office of vizier. Avempace too was a vizier, in this case to the sovereigns of Saragossa, and a doctor. Ibn Tufayl and Averroes were doctors. Averroes held the prestigious post of supreme judge of Seville and Cordova and was a friend of the Almohad caliphs. Maimonides was a doctor and a rabbi. Ibn Khaldūn spent his turbulent years in Tunis, Fez and the Maghreb as a courtier, ambassador and politician. When he moved to Cairo, he taught Malikite law under the protection of the Mameluks.

Although philosophy may not have been a profession, the Islamic philosophers nevertheless cultivated the myth of the philosophical life. One such was Abū Bakr al-Rāzī, or Rhazes. In one of his surviving works, with the apposite title of *The Philosophical Life*, Rhazes affirms that, naturally, the model would be Socrates although given the temperate life he led, avoiding all excess and disinclined to flatter the powerful, he would be an almost unattainable ideal. Rhazes seems to offer, instead, more modest practical advice. The nub of his argument is that the way that human beings behave in this earthly life will inevitably have repercussions for the state in which they will find themselves in eternity. In the most significant passage in the work, Rhazes explains that:

> we shall find ourselves in a situation (*hāla*) after death that will be praiseworthy or blameworthy depending on how our conduct (*sīra*) has been during that period when our soul was attached to the body. The most noble aim for which we were created, and which represents our ultimate goal, is not to enjoy bodily pleasures, but to acquire knowledge and behave justly, so as to save ourselves from this world and attain to that world where there is no death nor pain. Nature (*tabīʿa*) and passion incline us to present pleasures, while the intellect (*ʿaql*) invites us to set them aside in favour of better things. There is a Lord (*mālik*) whose reward we desire and whose punishment we fear who looks down on us with mercy and who does not want us to suffer, making us hate injustice and ignorance and love science and justice. The Lord makes those people suffer who deserve it, making the suffering proportionate to the extent that they have deserved it, while it is not appropriate that we suffer pain together with pleasure in such a way that the pain is greater than the pleasure in quantity and quality. In truth, the Sublime and Powerful Creator has made us responsible for all those small things that make up our needs, like weaving and farming, and we must rejoice in this in order to ensure the life of the world and society (*maʿīsha*). Now we say: since material pleasures and pains are transitory and end with the ending of

life, while the pleasures of that world where death is unknown have no end and are infinite, anyone who chose to forego permanent, continuous and infinite pleasures for transient and finite pleasures would be regarded as mad.[20]

Although Rhazes is often described as an 'atheist' or 'free thinker', in this passage he shows not only that he believes in God, but also that God rewards and punishes. In a way that is consistent with Islam, the world of the Beyond seems to be the objective of an upright and temperate life during our earthly existence. The intellect is the teacher that must guide us to prefer the permanent over the ephemeral, since it is science and justice that prepare the way, during our ethically motivated existence in this life, for eternal joy. In a possible echo of Epicurean ideas,[21] however, Rhazes shows that he fears, first and foremost, pain and considers that it is a moral duty to struggle against suffering. In his *Philosophical Life*, not only does he assert that, just as the Creator does not torment us, so we should not torment or cause any animal to suffer without reason unless it is to avoid a greater pain or to satisfy an indispensable need (to eat). But he enunciates as a general principle that 'seeing that man, according to justice and reason, must not cause suffering to his neighbour, so it follows that he must not inflict [unnecessary] suffering upon himself'.[22] A wise detachment from everyday life can indeed enable a man to attain greater serenity.

The other great upholder of the philosophical life was Avempace. He was convinced that human perfection consisted in the full development and application of the intellectual faculties. The intellectual faculties make it possible to act freely according to reason, and only a rational act determined by free will is a truly human act. By choosing according to reason, man makes himself like God: 'It is right that the actions of the individual who acts under the prompting of rational ideas and from [the concept of] uprightness, without giving in to the bestial soul and that which it produces, be called divine rather than human'.[23] Man in the full sense of the word is the philosopher. The philosopher can best express his own gifts and abilities in an ideal society where the state is ruled by philosophers. From this point of view, Avempace was a Platonist. He was, however, convinced that in his time society had become irredeemably corrupted and perverted. The philosopher living in such a society should not participate in political life. He is a 'plant', a fruit-bearing bush surrounded by dried-up and barren scrubland. In the introductory chapter to the *Regime of the Solitary*, Avempace states that in the perfect city doctors and judges are not necessary because the inhabitants do not commit crimes or overindulge in the pleasures of the senses. Furthermore, they share the same opinions:

> as far as the perfect city is concerned, we will not consider those who hold different opinions from those of the city's inhabitants or carry out actions different from those that are carried out there. In relation to the four [imperfect] cities, by contrast, this is possible, since there are people who transgress in their actions and are guided to this whether by nature or because they have learned such behaviour from others – and they know this. They hold false opinions and anyone will become aware of such falsities; [in these cities] sciences exist that lead to error and in which one can place no trust, or sciences in the greater part of which one falls into contradiction, even if a man, through natural talent or education received from elsewhere, is able to discover what is the truth among the contradictory ideas. There is no appropriate name for this type of person who performs [good] actions and possesses an upright science that cannot be found in the [imperfect] city. And yet, those who profess good opinions who do not dwell in that [imperfect] city and who, indeed, profess the opposite of what is believed there, these people are called 'plants' (*nawābit*). And the more numerous and important their doctrines, the more this name is appropriate to them.[24]

In the imperfect cities, the philosopher is a 'solitary' (*mutawahhid*) who pursues three goals: the perfecting of corporeal forms, of individual spiritual forms and of universal spiritual forms. 'Reflection (*ru'ya*), [rational] enquiry (*bahth*) and reasoning (*istidlāl*), or thought (*fikra*) assist [the solitary] to pursue each of these goals, since if he did not take pleasure in his meditations, his actions would be purely those of an animal and would in no way share in [the qualities] of humanity'.[25] By refining his own spiritual and intellectual perfection, the solitary prefigures the teleological possibility of the ideal society and represents he who embodies the hope of the transformation of the erring city into the virtuous city. 'It is evident that one of the characteristics of the perfect city is that, seeing how in it there are no false opinions, nor are there any 'plants'. [. . .] 'Plants' are found, on the other hand, in the [other] four ways of living [of the imperfect cities], and their existence is the cause that brings about the perfect city'.[26] The philosophical life is the condition of such a potential transformation and thus has a political goal.

If Avempace predicated, in some way, the withdrawal of the sage from the imperfect societies, in order to live to the full the philosophical life, Averroes was convinced of the need for the philosopher to live and work among the common people: 'the existence of the learned class is only perfected and its full happiness attained by participation with the multitude'[27] (Van Den Bergh 1954: 360). This leads on to a consideration of the relations between the philosophical elite and the common people. The philosophers master the secrets of nature; they know how to interpret the divine dictates and discourse on the essence of the divinity. They are believers, but their knowledge places them on a higher level in relation to that of the ordinary believer, although the latter too has the right to know and to save himself and to be happy. But, the question follows, how is it possible to speak to someone who does not possess the speculative (and linguistic) tools needed to attain to highest and most sublime truths? How will the non-philosopher be able to practise his religion correctly, using it for the happiness and good of humankind without having control of theoretical knowledge? Religion is the depository of a universal message, while philosophy is directed towards a narrow circle of privileged individuals. Averroes says that 'the religions are, according to the philosophers, obligatory, since they lead towards wisdom [*hikma*] in a way universal to all human beings, for philosophy [*falsafa*] only leads a certain number of intelligent people to the knowledge of happiness'.[28] Religion concentrates on the prophecy that set down the fundamental truths not only of faith, but also of reason, available to all in a simple and accessible language. Philosophy is a kind of prophecy intended for those who possess superior and more refined tools and abilities. It is – as we have already said – no accident that according to a well-known adage in Islam sages are the heirs of the prophets.

The discussion of the relationship between the philosophical elite and the common people leads inevitably to a consideration of the themes of prophetism and the relations between religion and philosophy. The doctrine of prophetism is a subject tackled by almost all of the Islamic philosophers. Avicenna was convinced that prophetism coincides with the highest level of philosophical wisdom. The gifts of prophecy are, therefore, natural and not, as the ordinary people think, the result of a special intervention by God. For Avicenna, a prophet is not only endowed with superior imaginative abilities but also, and most importantly, with an extraordinary intellectual acumen that becomes increasingly refined with practice. He possesses what is called in Islamic terms 'holy intellect' (*ʿaql qudsī* – and it should be remembered that the Qur'an speaks of a 'Spirit of sanctity' or *rūh al-quds*, perhaps identifiable with the Archangel Gabriel, God's messenger to Mohammed). The active intellect is subordinate to the holy intellect, as are the material and practical intellects. Below these there come in descending order the various qualities of soul, the estimative faculty and the imagination, right down to the nutritive and sensible faculties. The prophets are exceptional men endowed with the ability to intervene in natural phenomena and to produce those that are conventionally called 'miracles'. In other words, a miracle does not involve an *extra legem* intervention from God which would modify the regular course of nature.

While with Avicenna prophetism amounts to a rational quality, Rhazes considered it to be completely unnecessary since reason is perfectly capable of attaining an understanding of truth unaided. Furthermore, prophetism gives rise to religious fanaticism because a person who believes he has received the gift of prophecy also believes that he has been singled out by God over other people, which has led to conflict and the shedding of blood. Two treatises against prophetism have been attributed to Rhazes, but the most direct evidence of his doctrinal position comes from the account of a contemporary who bitterly opposed his views, the Ismaili Abū Hātim al-Rāzī. While it should, of course, be borne in mind that Abū Hātim's fierce objections to Rhazes's ideas may result in a somewhat partisan presentation, we read as follows in his polemic in dialogue form (as paraphrased by A. Bausani):

> He said (Rhazes): What prompts you to assert that God elected one people from among others to receive the Prophecy, making it noble among humankind? How can you think that a wise God would thus have created hate and enmity between the peoples?
>
> I said (Abū Hātim): And how do you think that a wise God should act?

> He said: By inspiring his servants with the knowledge of that which is useful to them and that which is harmful, but without preferring one to the other, so that there is no pernicious enmity or hate between them that might lead to struggles or killings for this reason.

Abū Hātim is clearly arguing from an Ismaili point of view. Men are not all endowed with the same qualities; furthermore, reason is weak and fallible. This is why it is necessary to hand down authoritative teachings (*taʿlīm* – from which derives one of the names for Ismailis, *taʿlīmiti*), the first depository of which is the Prophet and, after him, the *imām* who is the Prophet's heir in that he is able to interpret the revelation both allegorically and esoterically:

> I said: Men are equal in intellect, will and natural talent, or are they not?
>
> He said (Rhazes): If they study and keep themselves active, then yes, they are equal in will and intellect.
>
> I said: To say this is to deny the evidence. On the contrary, we see and find every day that people are divided into categories. [. . .] No one can learn without a master, everyone needs a leader. No one can deny this without denying the evidence. Thus it is necessary that there is a hierarchy (*tafādul*) among men [. . .] If, therefore, it is so, there is nothing strange about the fact that God chose one people, choosing his prophets from among them, ennobling them with His revelation, in order that they should teach to other people that which they could not otherwise know, that which will lead them to what is best for them in matters of religion and in the world, giving apposite laws.[29]

If we have correctly interpreted Abū Hātim's words, it is clear how Rhazes argues as an out-and-out philosopher, exalting the absolute capacity of reason to make all people equal with one another, and maintaining that rational activity, since it grasps the deepest truth of things, makes prophecy unnecessary. Clearly, by refuting prophecy, Rhazes is apparently rejecting one of the pillars of the religion of Islam. But it would appear that the philosopher is attacking prophecy from the historical point of view at the same time as accepting the concept of a supreme intelligence that creates and orders the universe.

In al-Fārābī, prophetism consists essentially of the highest perfecting of the imaginative faculty that, predisposed to receive intelligibles through the effect of the Agent Intellect (which will be discussed more fully in Chapters 5 and 6), acquires extraordinary potential. In the *Virtuous City*, he writes:

> When it happens that the faculty of representation [the imaginative power] imitates those things [properties of the Agent Intellect] with sensibles of extreme beauty and perfection, the man who has that sight [in other words, 'understands'] comes to enjoy overwhelming and wonderful pleasure, and he sees wonderful things which can in no way whatever be found among other existents. It is not impossible, then, that when a man's faculty of representation reaches its utmost perfection he will receive in his waking life from the Active Intellect present and future particulars of their imitations in the form of sensibles, and receive the imitations of the transcendent intelligibles and the other glorious existents and see them. This man will obtain through the particulars which he receives 'prophecy' (supernatural awareness) [*nubuwwa*] of present and future events, and through the intelligibles which he receives prophecy of things divine. This is the highest rank of perfection which the faculty of representation can reach.[30] (Walzer 1985, IV 14.9: 223, 225)

Al-Fārābī is convinced that there exist different types of prophetic ability and he describes them in great detail. One of the gifts of prophecy is to be able to divine the future, whether in a waking or a sleeping state. The disposition for receiving such revelations from the Agent Intellect that make it possible to exercise the act of divination might, however, fail, in which case the subject might become convinced that he had seen things, created by the imaginative power, that in fact do not exist. This is the case of the choleric and the insane. As can be seen, al-Fārābī too sees prophecy as having an eminently natural character and one that is associated with a psychological faculty that in a privileged few becomes developed to an exceptional degree while in others it may become distorted.

Through the perfecting of his imaginative faculty, the prophet is able to speak to the masses and communicate the truths of faith with them in simple and accessible language, convincing them to follow the paths of righteousness and to act virtuously. This is, in fact, his main intention, and which is therefore a political aim. Therefore, according to al-Fārābī, the prophetic faculty is an indispensable faculty for the statesman. The ruler of the virtuous city, the *imām*, is, at one and the same time, philosopher, prophet and king:

> thus he is, through the emanation from the Active Intellect to his Passive Intellect, a wise man and a philosopher and an accomplished thinker who employs an intellect of divine quality, and through the emanation from the Active Intellect to his faculty of representation a visionary prophet [*nabī*]: who warns of things to come and tells of particular things which exist at present.

A direct relationship between prophetism and ethical-political action is established:

> [The *imām*] knows every action by which felicity can be reached. This is the first condition for being a ruler. Moreover, he should be a good orator and able to rouse [other people's] imagination by well chosen words. He should be able to lead people well along the right path to felicity and to the actions by which felicity is reached.[31] (Walzer 1985, V 15.10–11: 245, 247)

It is worth remembering here that Averroes too conceives of prophecy in a political sense. The prophet is he who performs a legislative function and, furthermore, assists in the institution of a regime that will lead to the attainment of happiness, a happiness that is deeply and intimately rooted in religion.

According to al-Fārābī, the common people are guided along the true path by a ruler who is also a philosopher and prophet. The common people do not have a knowledge of philosophy, but they need to have a knowledge of religion. But does the philosopher also need a knowledge of religion or is philosophy epistemologically self-sufficient? A reading of the works of al-Fārābī leaves us with the impression that, without actually denying the importance of religion in the government of a state and the management of the community, he sees philosophy as taking precedence over religion, not least from a temporal point of view. At the beginning of the *Book of Letters* (*Kitāb al-Hurūf*), he writes as follows:

> The dialectal and sophistical powers, together with philosophy founded on opinion or based on sophistic thought, must have

> preceded certain, which is to say demonstrative, philosophy in time. And religion too, considered as an aspect of human reality, comes later in time than philosophy in general, since its aim is to teach the masses the theocratic and practical truths than can be deduced from philosophy. This type of teaching helps the masses to understand the above-mentioned laws, either by means of persuasion or representation, or by both at the same time. The arts of theology and jurisprudence are in turn later than religion and are subordinate to it. And if religion is subordinate to a preceding philosophy, whether that based on opinion or on sophistical thought, then theology and jurisprudence, that are subordinate to religion, are in agreement with both the supreme levels of understanding, but are of a lower order.[32]

We receive the impression that, for al-Fārābī, while religion is necessary for the common people, philosophers are able to do without it, finding rational enquiry sufficient to their needs. Religion seems to be an imitation of philosophy at a lower level of complexity and cogency, even if al-Fārābī does not entirely deny that, in substance, the content of philosophy and of religion coincide. Philosophers practise a rigorous method of intellectual enquiry; they possess a superior apperception of reality and superior intellective abilities that lead the less fortunate to imitate them. A hierarchy of abilities and procedures is thus established, meaning that the least cultivated and least intelligent end up at an apparently insuperable distance from truth. The function of religion is to help the least gifted to understand more complex concepts, allowing them, as far as possible, to approach the truth.

> In the virtuous city, the sages [i.e. the philosophers] know by way of demonstration and through personal [intellectual] vision; those that follow them also know things as they exist [in reality], but by falling in with the vision of the sages [philosophers] and having faith and confidence in them; all the others know through imitative images, since their intelligence is lacking in that disposition for understanding, naturally or through habit, things as they are. These then are the two ways of knowing, of which that of the sage [philosopher] is certainly better. Of those who acquire knowledge through imitative images, some [are] from representations that are quite close [to reality], others rather more distant, other representations being very remote [from

reality]. For each community and the inhabitants of every city, things are imitated from representations that gradually become comprehensible to them; for this reason, knowledge can vary a lot or a little, depending on the community. The representations formed differ in each community from that of the others.[33] (Walzer 1985, V 15.10–11: 245, 247)

Truth is not exclusively philosophic or exclusively religious. Philosophy is more coherent and demonstratively based than religion, but religion has the support of prophecy. According to al-Fārābī, religions can vary from community to community; societies that practise a virtuous religion are virtuous, while in a virtuous society there can be different religions. Islam is the religion by antonomasia of a virtuous community, but the other religions coexisting with Islam within the virtuous society have the right to survive since they pursue the same ends and lead towards the same objective, the realisation of happiness. Al-Fārābī's liberalism is an example of how there can be harmony between the practice of religion and the speculative research of philosophy.

Averroes is another thinker who tackled the problem of the relationship between religion and philosophy in a constructive and original way, particularly in his *Decisive Treatise*. We have already referred to his ideas about the compossibility of the two orders of knowing. It should now be added that, in order to justify his own position, he puts forward a 'sociological' criterion. He affirms that, depending on their knowledge and ability to reflect and to learn, people can be divided into three basic categories: the common people, made up of the vast majority, the theologians and the philosophers. The common people lack education and any real ability to grasp the highest and most complex speculative truths and are, therefore, satisfied with images and rhetorical stories. The theologians are dialecticians in that they possess a method, but they attempt to apply it to areas and problems that lie beyond their reach. Only philosophers are demonstrative. They possess the means and the ability to understand in depth the secrets of nature and of divine things. All and any people can accept religious truths: the common people do this by hearing rhetorical speeches, the theologians by exercising dialectical disputation, the philosophers by rational demonstration. Averroes is unequivocal in his assertion that an acceptance of religion is obligatory for all. He outlines, however, a difference between those religious concepts that the common people, the theologians and the philosophers should all embrace and those religious concepts that the common people should accept literally, while philosophers can apply allegorical interpretation and rational enquiry to them. The first type of concept includes indisputable dogmas such as the existence of God, the true nature of Mohammad's prophecy, the existence of an afterlife with the rewards and punishments mentioned in the Scriptures. The second type of concept includes controversial and subtle questions such as God's essence and attributes, the significance of God's 'face' or 'hands', whether He is 'seated on the Throne', the nature of Heaven and Hell, whether and how God created the world and whether the world is eternal or not. As far as this type of question is concerned, the common people should confine themselves to the reading of the dictated Qur'an. The philosophers, on the other hand, have the right to treat the sacred text allegorically and to pursue enquiries scientifically. Such people are, according to Averroes, those who are 'well versed in science' mentioned in verse 3.7 in the Qur'an. They alone, with God (!), know the true interpretation of the ambiguous verses and abstruse and complex questions contained in the revelation and, more generally, in all areas of knowledge. To interpret the text through allegory is to go beyond the purely literal appearance of the text to reveal the speculative meanings it might contain. For example, when the Qur'an speaks of God's 'Face', it may mean His essence, with everything that this implies in terms of the philosophical analysis of God's attributes.

Averroes has effectively made a distinction that leaves no place for theologians. Although theology could be used dialectically to defend the dogmas of the faith (and this is the most genuinely Islamic definition of theology or *kalām*), it is virtually useless for a true understanding. Making clear that he considered there to be only two spheres of knowledge, Averroes writes:

> Concerning the things that are only known by demonstration due to their being hidden, God has been gracious to His servants for whom there is no path by means of demonstration – either due to their innate dispositions, their habits, or their lack of facilities for education – by coining for them likenesses and similarities of these [hidden things] and calling them to assent by means of those

> likenesses to come about by means of the indications shared by all – I mean, the dialectical and the rhetorical. This is the reason for the Law being divided into an apparent sense and an inner sense. For the apparent sense is those likenesses coined for those meanings, and the inner sense is those meanings that reveal themselves only to those adept in demonstration.[34] (Walzer 1985, V 15.10–11: 19)

God's mercy allows all people to accept religion to the degree allowed by their abilities. When theologians take it upon themselves to apply the inadequate tools of dialectical disputation to speculative problems, not merely do they make mistakes, reaching erroneous conclusions, but they can also do actual harm.

Nowhere, however, does Averroes ever enunciate the thesis of which he was accused by ecclesiastics in the Latin West, that truth is 'double', that religion and philosophy are in opposition *quasi sint duae contrariae veritates* (to quote the commission headed by the bishop of Paris, Étienne Tempier, condemning Averroism in 1277), and that, ultimately, philosophy is 'truer' than religion. In fact, Averroes asserts without a shadow of doubt that one Truth cannot conflict with another Truth, in other words that religion and philosophy are not in opposition. On the contrary, they offer reciprocal support for one another, providing evidence each to the other. Between them exists not harmony, in the sense that one can integrate itself with the other so that the two become absorbed, losing their identities in indistinct whole, but 'contact' or 'connection' (which is the meaning of the Arabic term *ittiṣāl* in the full, correctly translated title of Averroes's work: *Decisive Treatise on the 'connection' of religion with philosophy*). It is in this work that, in a complex and incisive argument, he is able to maintain that two apparently opposed propositions such as 'the world is created' (a religious truth) and 'the world is eternal' (a philosophical truth) are not in fact contradictory. The way he goes about this is by the application of a linguistic criterion: philosophy and religion speak of the same truth but using different languages. The presumption of this conclusion is explained by Oliver Leaman:

> There exist links between different applications of the same name, and these links are sufficiently strong for it to make sense to say that these uses are of the same term. Appropriate use of the terms is

> obtained thanks to their connexion with the context from which they derive their meaning, a context that is in turn rigorously justified by the way in which the world functions.

According to Leaman, in Averroes 'this variety of views is represented by the variety of language available to characterise a whole continuum of views, ranging from the entirely demonstrative to the most poetic and expressive'. Language is an instrument of the greatest flexibility and adaptability which is why the apparent conflict between the propositions of knowledge 'comes down to a stress upon different aspects of one thing, namely, the way the world really is. [Apparently contradictory views] are acceptable as different aspects of one thing'.[35] I would go further than Leaman: it is not a matter of different ways of being of a single reality, but of different ways of speaking of a single reality. Thus, for Averroes, reality is scientifically resolved on a linguistic level. As we shall discuss further in Chapter 7, Averroes is a realist preoccupied by the possibility of breaking the link between Being and thought. Given the difficulty of automatically reproducing a reality that is external to the mind within the mind itself, he is convinced of the functionality of language to translate one to the other. I do not mean that for Averroes reality is a linguistic dimension; I do mean, however, that language is the enabling link between thought and the objective world allowing thought to grasp the objective world in all its nuances and to predicate it, respecting all its nuances.

The *Decisive Treatise* is a *fatwā*, a juridical opinion with which Averroes, here wearing his jurist's hat, set out to demonstrate the lawfulness of philosophy from a religious point of view. The realisation of this project implied, however, two collateral implications: on the one hand, the radical condemnation of all those theologians who claimed to study the Scriptures, God, the cosmos, nature and man by means of dialectic rather than demonstrative and philosophical methods; and, on the other, the irrevocable prohibition for the masses to go beyond the literal meaning and attempt to allegorise. If the theologians were given free rein, or if the common people were permitted to venture beyond the prescribed boundaries, the way would be opened to misbelief and civil and religious strife. If allegorical interpretations, however correct, were made known to the common people, they would not be capable of understanding them and would perhaps reject them, just as an ignorant patient may refuse the treatment offered by a doctor. Yet – and here Averroes has the theologians in mind,

> Because of the interpretations with respect to the Law – especially the corrupt ones – and the supposition that it is obligatory to declare them to everyone, factions emerged within Islam, so that one charged the others with unbelief or with heretical innovation. Thus, the Muʿtazilites interpreted many verses and many Traditions and declared their interpretations to the multitude, as did the Ashʿarites, although they resorted less to interpretation. Because of that, they threw people into loathing, mutual hatred, and wars; they tore the Law to shreds; and they split the people up into every sort of faction.[36] (Walzer 1985, V 15.10–11: 29–30)

The defence of the elitist character of philosophy and the need for the common people to abide by the letter of the Qur'an and the sacred texts take on the character of a social prophylaxis. Certainly, Averroes can give the impression that philosophers can do without revelation, but he does not go as far as Rhazes. The philosopher will accept, like the common man, prophecy, revelation and the dictated Qur'an; but philosophy allows him to attain a more sophisticated and linguistically complex level of understanding of reality.

We can say, in conclusion, that Islamic thinkers did not approach the problem of how to reconcile reason and faith with the same urgency as that felt by the Christian and Latin medieval world. In one way or another, all the Islamic thinkers identified a role for philosophy without having to renounce or depart from their faith. The practice of religion need not restrict and, in fact, does not restrict philosophical research. This, it is true, has led to a somewhat elitist and exclusive view of philosophy. Nevertheless, philosophy does not come into conflict with dogma – the philosophers are the heirs of the message of the prophets. Ideally, philosophy can represent the most suitable means of safeguarding scientific research from any political or ideological contamination while the Islamic faith is observed as the rule for daily life and behaviour.

Chapter 3

Ways of Philosophising

It is well known that Islam is divided into two main branches: Sunni and Shia. Ninety per cent of all believers in Islam are Sunnis, while the Shiites number barely ten per cent. The schism was entirely political in origin, even if it later took on religious characteristics. From the philosophical point of view, it is possible to say that while the Sunnis adhere more closely to an exoteric reading of the revealed texts, the Shiites systematically practise esoteric allegorical interpretation. It was Henri Corbin who put forward the paradigm according to which all Islamic philosophy is prevalently Shiite in expression and has an esoteric stamp (the best-known philosopher to pursue this view is perhaps the Iranian Seyyed Hossein Nasr). Fascinating and in many ways instructive, his thesis is nevertheless overstated and one-sided.

Corbin's reasoning is consequential: since Islam is a prophetic religion, it is Shiite thought that has contributed more than any other to a philosophy of a prophetic type corresponding to a prophetic religion.[1] At the heart of Shiite prophetology is the doctrine of the celestial Adam that coincides with the metaphysical hypothesisation of the historical figure of the Prophet Mohammad:

> The human Form in its pre-eternal glory is called Adam in the true and real sense of the name (*Adam haqīqī*), *Homo maximus* (*insān*

> *kabīr*), supreme Spirit, First Intelligence, supreme Pen, supreme Caliph, Pole of Poles. This celestial *Anthropos* is invested with, and is the keeper of, eternal prophecy (*nubūwah bāqīya*), of the essential and primordial prophecy (*nubūwah aslīyah haqīqīyah*), which was disclosed before time in the celestial Pleroma. He is also the *haqīqa muhammadiyya*, the eternal Mohammadan Reality, the Mohammadan Light of glory, the Mohammadan Logos.[2] (Sherrard 1993: 41)

Corbin emphasises that, as a consequence of these metaphysical presuppositions, prophetic reality has two dimensions. The first is exoteric and corresponds to the exterior revelation that sets out the Law in all its concrete and normative dimensions. The other is esoteric, corresponding to mystical and Gnostic allegorical interpretation, the outstanding depositories of which are the Shiite *imām*. It goes without saying that it is this second esoteric dimension that translates the authentic meaning of prophecy. Corbin writes that,

> a prophetic philosophy presupposes a type of thought which does not allow itself to be bound either by the historical past, or by the letter of the dogmatic form in which the teachings of this past are consolidated, or by the limits imposed by the resources and laws of rational Logic. Shi'ite thinking is orientated by its expectation not of the revelation of a new *sharīʿah* [revealed Law], but of the plenary Manifestation of all the hidden or spiritual meanings of the divine Revelations. [. . .] Prophetic philosophy is essentially eschatological. (Sherrard 1993: 25)

The consequences of this analysis are clear. In the first place, the historic dimension of the evolution of reality and of philosophy itself is denied. Or, at the least, the evolution of human history is read in sacred terms (Corbin talks of 'hierohistory' that is, of course, of particular significance in Shiite – and especially Ismaili – circles). Philosophy has meaning only in so far as it is able to decipher sacred symbols: the authentic philosophy is theosophy. Secondly, philosophy takes on a mainly Gnostic colouration.[4] Despite the originality of its prophetic presupposition, Islamic philosophy ends up by fitting into the mainstream of 'traditional' or perennial philosophy, while drawing sustenance from hermetic sources. In the light of such a paradigm, Corbin has no difficulty in interpreting Avicenna and the Avicennan tradition mystically and esoterically. Thinkers such as al-Suhrawardī with his illuminative philosophy or Ibn ʿArabī with his doctrine of the 'Oneness of existence' become the authentic representatives of Islamic philosophy. But even in the case of a philosopher such as Rhazes who is generally considered to be 'rationalist', the alchemical and Pythagorean elements are emphasised, in addition to an eschatological concept of philosophy as the saviour of the drama of the Soul that, in its burning desire to become part of this world, becomes a prisoner of it and has to be liberated and allowed to ascend to the world of spirits. Not even Averroes is spared: Corbin firmly defines him as an 'esoteric'[5] and the unity of truth that we have resolved in a scientific and linguistic way is, of course, seen by Corbin as coming from spiritual exegesis. Corbin's greatest opponents are Ibn Taymiyya, a pious 'agnostic' believer who rejects the problems posed by philosophers, accusing them of 'rationalism', without realising that true philosophy too is anti-rationalistic, and Ibn Khaldūn, whose secularising project was unfortunately assimilated in his own time, leading to the 'cancelling out of that which had been represented by someone like Ibn ʿArabī'.[6]

Another interpretation of Islamic philosophy that has met with even greater success than that of Corbin is that put forward by Leo Strauss, particularly in relation to political philosophy. Strauss's thesis, first set out in his book *Persecution and the Art of Writing* and developed in other writings,[7] is a simple one: Arab-Islamic philosophers were normally persecuted for their ideas and their speculative daring, particularly by traditionalist theologians and the conservative establishment; this led them to disguise their true opinions either by paying lip service to religious truths or – and especially – through a technique of writing and composing designed to divert the attention of a potentially hostile reader while at the same time attracting the attention of a reader genuinely dedicated to philosophy. Thanks to devices of various kinds, analysed in great detail by Strauss, the Arab-Islamic philosophers would appear to have sought to guide the adept towards an understanding of their real ideas, while an opponent became entangled in the confusion and obscurities of their allusive and veiled writing. The two thinkers most closely studied by Strauss to support his argument are al-Fārābī and Maimonides. Several historians have followed in Strauss's footsteps, most important among them being Charles Butterworth who applied Strauss's paradigm to, for example, Averroes; B. Abrahamov and R. Frank in their study of al-Ghazālī; and especially Muhsin Mahdi who applied a similar process once again to al-Fārābī and also to Ibn Khaldūn. We will confine ourselves here to looking at the work on al-Fārābī.

Strauss examined above all al-Fārābī's *Summary of Plato's Laws*. In his introduction to the book, al-Fārābī relates the following fable:

> It is said that a holy man who had taken a vow of abstinence and who had shown himself to be worthy above all others in integrity, probity, piety and religion thought to flee from the City in fear of the tyrant. The tyrant commanded that he be found and arrested wherever he might be, so that he could not go out of any gate for fear of falling into the hands of the king's soldiers. He obtained a fool's costume, dressed himself in it, took some cymbals and at night pretended to be drunk. He arrived at one of the City gates, singing and accompanying himself on the cymbals. The guard asked who was there and he laughingly replied: 'I am the famous holy man!' The guard thought he was joking and let him pass without further ado. The holy man thus escaped without having had to utter a lie.[8]

According to Strauss, what al-Fārābī meant by this fable was that he was prepared to tell the truth even in unfavourable situations and under the threat of oppression, but only after disguising it in such a way as to render it unrecognisable, just as the holy man has done. Oliver Leaman offers a perceptive 'deconstruction' of Strauss's interpretation:

> It may be that al-Fārābī wishes his readers to think that he has disguised his views, so that only those who are capable of understanding and appreciating his teaching will recognise that he has not disguised his views at all. Such an interpretation is not as fanciful as it sounds. After all, in the story, the holy man deceives the guards by telling the truth and getting them to think that he is not telling the truth at all. Perhaps Fārābī uses the story to get people to think that he is not telling the truth, while he is expressing his real opinions after all. In that case, Strauss would be in the position of the guards, in that he naïvely assumes that when he is thus presented with the truth, he is in fact presented with a disguise.[9] (Leaman 1985: 198)

Whatever the case, Strauss's thesis is unacceptable. As can be gathered from what has been said earlier, not one of the Islamic philosophers mentioned here – not even Rhazes who may have been an 'atheist' or Averroes who is often seen as a defender of free thought – was ever persecuted for his philosophical ideas. Any persecution that did take place was for essentially political rather than philosophical reasons. Further more, it is well known that the majority of Islamic philosophers lived in powerful court circles, enjoying the sovereign's protection. By failing to take account of the historical evidence, Strauss's thesis has major historiographical implications that distort the meaning of Islamic philosophy. On the one hand, it leads to an exaggeration of the extent of the debate about and conflict in the relationship between philosophy and religion among Islamic thinkers; on the other hand, it seeks to impose a political reading on the greater part of Islamic philosophy. I would maintain that there is no doubt at all that the large majority of Islamic philosophers saw reason and revelation as peacefully coexisting without conflict, which was why there was no reason to debate the relationship between them except, occasionally, to show that in the last analysis they tend towards the same end and speak of the same truth (even leaving aside readings such as those of Corbin and Nasr who go as far as to see philosophy and religion as one and the same thing). At the same time, it is true that Islamic theological thought has an undeniable political value. It is equally true that almost all the Islamic philosophers also wrote about politics. But, strictly speaking, perhaps the only political philosophers were al-Fārābī and Ibn Khaldūn, the first giving politics a solid metaphysical basis through the connection with noetics, the second making politics central to the study of the state and of history.

It would appear, in conclusion, that Strauss's thesis is, for the most part, mistaken, even if it is true, as I have written elsewhere, that al-Fārābī engaged in a dialectical relationship with the city, a relationship that was, at one and the same time, one of involvement and exclusion. Involvement since, in the first place, as all the Islamic philosophers assert, man is a political animal; and, in the second place, because, with the exception of Avempace and Ibn Tufayl, the majority of Islamic philosophers like al-Fārābī and Averroes were convinced that the sage should live in the world and that the ordinary people were indispensable to the realisation of any of society's objectives. The aim of political association is to guarantee the attainment of happiness; since no one is capable of doing this on his own, he has need of the support of his neighbour in order to achieve this great goal. At the same time, the philosopher finds himself excluded from the city, since he is essentially uncomprehended; his knowledge cannot be communicated to any outside a restricted circle of scholars, and it is less universal than positive religion that addresses itself to the whole world and all its creatures. The truth is that the message of philosophy is not suited to simple people. The contradictory nature of this viewpoint is particularly well illustrated by Averroes. It certainly does not, however, imply persecution but, at the most, self-imposed exile (albeit only temporarily) from political life. It is perhaps possible to understand Avempace's message in this way when he exalts the 'regime of the solitary', knowing that the philosophical life and the supreme perfecting of the intellect are reserved for the 'plants', the outsiders in imperfect regimes.

Muslim and Arab scholars have similarly put forward general interpretations of the evolution of Islamic philosophy that have taken on the character of entirely hermeneutic paradigms. One of the most interesting theories is that proposed by the Moroccan philosopher Muhammad ʿĀbed al-Jâbirî (al-Jābrī) who has sought to use the analysis and interpretation of medieval Islamic philosophy to further a general ideological and political project to re-establish Arab reason. This project and its implications for contemporary Arab-Islamic philosophy and thought are of interest to our discussion of Islamic philosophy insofar as they are able to trace the line of development of medieval Islamic philosophy. Put briefly, al-Jābrī maintains that, after al-Fārābī, whom he calls 'the Arab Rousseau', philosophy was perverted by Avicenna and al-Ghazālī, becoming contaminated with Gnosticism, irrationalism and mysticism. Al-Fārābī was a rationalist who, reacting against the ramification and multiplication of doctrines and sects, called for a restoration of the unity of Islamic thought: 'the restoration of the unity of thought will mean overcoming rationalist Muʿtazilite, divisive and atomistic ideas that have shown themselves to be incapable of reconciling reason and transmission, adopting the language of "universal reason"'.[10] As for Avicenna and al-Ghazālī, they pursued a dangerous syncretism, seeking a hybrid interaction between philosophy and religion that lost sight of the autonomous meaning of 'science'. Furthermore, the significant ambiguity and duplicity of Avicenna's ideas, oscillating between an Aristotelian rationalism and the Gnostic influences of 'Eastern' philosophy, was used, paradoxically, in order to confront one Avicenna with another. This is what al-Ghazālī did when rediscovering the content of eastern philosophy, presenting Avicenna as the path leading away from perdition towards mystic salvation (as al-Jābrī paraphrases the title of a famous autobiographical work by the Persian thinker) and to a revival of the religious sciences.[11] Lastly came the Andalusian renaissance: Spain and the Maghreb, at the time of the Almohads (early 12th century to mid-13th century), witnessed the development of a tradition of thought that was to completely revolutionise Arab-Islamic philosophy, starting from the guide and founder of the Almohad movement, Ibn Tūmart, and culminating with Averroes.

Ibn Tūmart censured theology's claim to apply an analogy between the known and the unknown (*qiyās al-ghā'ib ʿalā al-shāhid*), that is, of transporting to God's plane that which we know of the human plane and thus of interpreting and explaining God in the light of human categories, which leads inevitably to anthropomorphism. Ibn Tūmart's position can be seen, according to al-Jābrī, as part of a broad project for ideological and epistemological revival, specific to al-Andalus in relation to the Muslim East, running from Ibn Hazm to Averroes and passing by Ibn Tūmart and Avempace.[12] Ibn Hazm was a Zāhirite and al-Jābrī defines his ideas as *ta'sîs al-bayân*, that is to say as the foundation of clear and evident proof. This requires the establishment of a connection between *bayān* (proof or 'indication') and rational demonstration (*burhān*), turning away from and eliminating mystic and esoteric Gnosis (*ʿirfān*). Al-Jābrī writes:

> Zāhirism represents a cultural project that is philosophic in dimension and which seeks to reconstruct 'indication' (*bayān*), the fundamental cognitive order of Sunni thought (including its Muʿtazilite and Ashʿarite forms), giving it a basis, that of demonstration (*burhān*) (the Aristotelian syllogistic method and the scientific and philosophic concepts that it brings with it) and erasing entirely any trace of Shi'ite or Sufi illuminationism.[13]

As well as reviewing the analogy between that which is open and that which is hidden, Ibn Tūmart urged a return to the sources of religion, to the Qur'an and the Prophet's *sunna* (*ryjūʿ ilā al-usūl*), exactly like

Avempace who wanted to read Aristotle only through Aristotle. Avempace shook off traditional theology, the orthodox *kalām*, and his philosophical thinking was no longer obliged to reckon with the need to reconcile intellect and revelation, *ʿaql* and *naql*. He made a clear and definitive distinction between the sphere of philosophy and science and that of religion and revelation, the latter being the preserve of the prophets. This was not pure theory, since it had an epistemological dimension with political implications: 'Just as Ibn Tūmart introduces politics into religion with the aim of modifying the political status quo, so Avempace introduces politics in philosophy with the aim of setting in motion a new intellectual occurrence (*wāqīʿ*)'.[14]

According to al-Jābrī, Averroes is – in one way or another – the heir of all these predecessors: of Ibn Hazm because of the importance conceded to the obvious reading of the text and to its immediately obvious clarity; of Ibn Tūmart both for his refusal to apply the known to the unknown and for the need to return to the sources, meaning – for Averroes – to Aristotle himself (a viewpoint shared with Avempace, even if Avempace's ideas are strongly influenced by Platonism); of Avempace also because he differentiated once and for all between the sphere of science and that of religion. The philosophic tradition in al-Andalus that culminated with Averroes stands in clear contrast to the syncretism of 'eastern' philosophers such as Avicenna and al-Ghazāli who not only mingled the divine with the human, but who also had difficulties with the problem of trying to reconcile reason and tradition. The philosophical debate in al-Andalus avoided this trap and, furthermore,

> by disencumbering itself of the eastern, Gnostic version of Neo-Platonism, was able to distinguish itself from the tendency manifested by the eastern school of philosophy of using the sciences to merge religion with philosophy and philosophy with religion. Thus, science will become again, as in the time of Aristotle, the only foundation on which philosophy can construct its edifice.[15]

Averroes's method is a rigorously scientific one, hypothetico-deductive; he rejects the tendency of analogical reasoning to assimilate the metaphysical into physical; consequently he rejects the Avicennan idea that the agent in the sphere of the unknown (metaphysics) behaves in the same way as the agent in the sphere of the known (physics). In this way, Averroes was able to return philosophy and religion each to its own sphere. Averroes can be summarised in four points: rationalism, realism, the axiomatic method and the critical approach.

Al-Jābrī's interpretation is not immune from criticism however. It is going too far, for example, to describe Avicenna as an exponent of 'a philosophy of darkness', or to consider 'eastern philosophy' as an expression of a Gnostic and esoteric inclination.[16] Nevertheless, al-Jābrī offers an original key to the reading of Averroes's philosophical and historical position, not least from the political point of view, given that Ibn Hazm and Ibn Tūmart, Avempace and Averroes are all in some ways intellectual 'militants'. And essentially militant also is al-Jābrī's interpretation; in asserting that the spirit of Averroes is relevant to our own time, he offers it as a cure for a tradition that has become doubly alienated. Doubly, because, on the one side, the integralist reading of a fundamentally anti-utopian tradition has become fossilised, nostalgic for a past that also represents the necessity of the future; while, on the other, the liberal reading of tradition, since it is indebted to European thought, exalts a 'present' that is not its own but 'from others'. Al-Jābrī asks:

> how can contemporary Arab thought recover and reinvest in a position analogous to that in which the rationalist and 'liberal' contributions to its tradition were originally invested – the struggle against feudalism, against Gnosticism, against fatalism, and the desire to install a City of reason and justice, to construct the free, democratic and socialist Arab City?[17]

This can come about through a dialecticisation of the past and the foundation of an 'authentically' Arab and Islamic present.

Part Two

Thought and Action: Some Major Themes in Islamic Philosophy

Chapter 4

Tawhīd, Pillar of Islamic Thought

Islam is intensely bound up with a burning passion for the Oneness of God or *tawhīd*. The concept of God's Oneness is therefore central to theological and philosophical speculation and, as is also the case for mysticism, is firmly rooted in the Qur'an. There are too many verses in the Qur'an that refer to God as 'One' to list them all, but we should recall first and foremost the very short *sūrah* entitled 'Oneness' (no. 112) that says: 'Say: "God is One, the Eternal God (*samad*). He begot none, nor was He begotten. None is equal to Him"'. This *sūrah* shows a clear rejection of both Christian concepts (in Islam Christ is considered to be a prophet but not the 'son' of God) and anthropomorphic concepts (none is equal to Him), while asserting God's eternity and permanence. God's self-sufficiency is proclaimed twice (2.225 and 3.2) where, in addition to Oneness ('God: there is no god but Him'), the qualifications of 'Living' (*hayy*) and 'Self-sufficient' (*qayyūm*) are also applied to Him. Divine reality in 57.3 is the alpha and omega of all that is real ('He is the First and the Last, the Visible and the Unseen') and he endures, beyond all decadence and corruption (for example, 28.88 and 55.27).

The Oneness of God is often expressed in terms of negative theology, a characteristic of very many Islamic scholars, particularly philosophers. Thus, according to the evidence of al-Ashʿarī, the

Muʿtazilites applied a systematic negation of every possible positive attribution to God:

> The Muʿtazilites are unanimous in professing that God is One and has no equals; He is wisdom and volition. He is not body, person, form, flesh, blood, substance or accident. He has no colour, taste, smell, heat, coldness, wetness, dryness, length, width, mixture or separation. He neither moves nor does He rest; He is not divisible, He does not have parts, organs, directions, right, left, front, behind, top or bottom. No place can contain him. He is not subject to time. He cannot be touched. He is neither alone nor in one place. A human quality that might imply contingence cannot be attributed to Him. He cannot be qualified as finite or infinite; nor can it be said that he has a direction. He is not limited. He is not begotten nor has He begotten. [. . .] Since eternity He has existed before all creation. He is eternally wise, powerful and living. He is a thing but not like other things. He is wise, powerful and living but not like the wise, the powerful and the living [among men]. Only Eternal, no other is eternal and there is no other god but Him.[1]

This clear attempt to affirm God's transcendence in such heightened language develops, among the Muʿtazilites, as *tanzīh*, or the 'removal' of God from any kind of contact or compromise with reality. The Muʿtazilite position is so radical that the Ashʿarites accused them of *taʿṭīl*, or of 'stripping' God of any positive attribute, making Him not only incomprehensible, but remotely distant and evanescent. In fact, like the philosophers the Muʿtazilites denied quiddity in God, whereas Ashʿarites like al-Ghazālī claim that God has quiddity and hence is a concrete being in the true sense of the word. The position of the Muʿtazilites is, nevertheless, of great philosophic interest, as can be seen if we examine one of their characteristic doctrines, that of the 'otherness' of God (*ghayr al-ashiyā*) in relation to things:

> The Muʿtazilites expressed four different points of view on the fact that God is other in relation to things:
>
> Some said, and this is the idea of ʿAbbād Ibn Sulaymān, that God is other in relation to things; and that the meaning of the expression 'God is a thing' is that He is, by His nature, unlike existing things, although not because of a dissimilarity.

Others said, and this is the opinion of al-Jubbāʾiy, that the Creator is other with respect to things and that things are other in relation to Him; for which reason God is unlike things by His nature and things are unlike God by their nature.

Yet others said that the Creator is other in relation to things because of an otherness and not by His nature, and they affirmed furthermore that such an otherness is an attribute of God that neither coincides with God himself nor is different from him. This is the opinion of al-Hilqānī.

Lastly, there were others who said that God is other in relation to things for the simple reason that He is not a thing.[2] [. . .]

On the question of whether God is a thing (*shayyʾ*):

Some said that the meaning of the expression 'God is a thing' is that He exists (*mawjūd*). This is the point of view of all those for whom there exist no other existent things but things.

Others maintained that the meaning of the expression 'God is a thing' is that He is His own will (*huwa ithbātuhu*). This is the opinion of all those who affirm that things are such before they come into being and are determined as things before coming into being; this then is the opinion of al-Khayyāt.

According to ʿAbbād Ibn Sulaymān, the meaning of the expression 'God is a thing' is that He is other [in relation to other things]; and in fact there is not a thing that is not other [in relation to other things], nor any otherness that is not a thing.[3]

It is evident from a reading of this doxographic page how Muʿtazilite theology is based on the principle that the ontological difference between God and creatures depends on a difference between their natures. The superior essence of God means that he cannot be reduced to something material. This superiority consists of the fact that he is absolute existence, since His 'quiddity' resides in being existing. The absolute existence of God means that it is He who communicates existence to creatures, for He is the transcendent eternally-creating God who gives life to the entire universe through the knowledge that He has of it.

An unusual Muʿtazilite doctrine, the most important proponents of which seem to have been al-Khayyāt of Baghdad and his disciple al-Kaʿbī, is that non-being (*maʿdūm*) is a 'thing' (*shayyʾ*), or, in other words, that nothingness is a reality because, for one thing, as has already been said, things already exist before they come into being. In fact, this Muʿtazilite concept hints at an Aristotelian idea, because it means that substances already exist, in their potential for being, before becoming actuated in existence. This principle is found clearly in the writing of two eminent Muʿtazilite thinkers, al-Jubbāʾiy and his son Abū Hāshim, when they say: 'The quality attributable to a contigency in its own right or to its species, is inherent to it right from the stage of its non-existence'.[4] Al-Shahrastānī, however, says, 'those who say that non-being is a thing, as do almost all Muʿtazilites, maintain no other stable attributes [to God] other than His existing being (*mawjūd*)'.[5] There is a super-essentiality of God in His being maximally existent, to such a degree that we find Muʿtazilites like ʿAbbād Ibn Sulaymān denying the proposition that God is a 'being', or entity (*kāʾin*), and reducing the expression 'God is existent' to the attribution to God of a 'name' (*ism*).[6] This is an extreme form of *tanzīh*, that could with some justification be accused of *taʿṭīl*. ʿAbd al-Jabbār maintained, furthermore, that God cannot be considered 'being' since He does not occupy any place in the real world. God is, rather, an 'absence' (*ghāʾib*), and His absence consists in a negative, in his non-being in relation to the world, in His irreducibility with regard to things of the world. God is existence whose essence is in total otherness, and therefore can be defined as non-being in relation to the existence of things of the world.

Thus transcendence is radically affirmed by the Muʿtazilites. There have, however, been thinkers who thought that this was not enough. The Ismaili Abū Yaʿqūb al-Sijistānī went even further down the path of such extreme rarefaction of the concept of God. He maintained that it was necessary to reject not only anthropomorphisation or *tashbīh*, obviously, but also the Muʿtazilite *tanzīh*. According to him, the theologians and philosophers are divided between those that have attributed to God a body defined in space and localised, as did the anthropomorphising Sunni traditionalists, those who, like the majority of the *mutakallimūn*, have seen God as a classifiable thing, and those who, like the philosophers, have regarded Him as a substance comparable to other substances. It was in this way that they sought to explain and define God. The Muʿtazilites and the Shiites argued using the method of the *via remotionis* (by exclusion), but to deny to God some or even all qualities is to say no more than what God is not.

However, to say that God is neither a body, nor within a body, that he is neither ignorant nor impotent, is neither in time nor outside it, and so on, nevertheless implies saying *something* about God, since it defines Him by implication as incorporeal, wise or powerful, and so on. Even if every truth is denied, the truth of the non-truth is affirmed: to deny the truth does not lead to an authentic negation of truth. To deny that God is a body could mean that God is *something other* that is not corporeal. God must remain entirely beyond all understanding or attempts at definition. God cannot be assimilated into human reason and therefore cannot be subordinate to reason. For this reason, Abū Yaʿqūb al-Sijistānī suggests that negation be denied. Not only is God not corporeal, but neither even is he non-corporeal. Not only is God not ignorant, but neither even is he not-ignorant. He writes: 'Praise to God who is adored with not and with not-not' (*al-ḥamdu li'llāh al-maʿbūd bi-lā wa lā-lā*). This is the authentic *tanzīh* and one that goes much further than that of the Muʿtazilites. 'Negation of negation is, for [al-Sijistānī], the absolute disassociation of God from intelligibility. God cannot be A nor can He be [not-A] – the item [not-A] being an intelligible idea despite its questionable ontological status'.[7]

The doctrine of negation of negation is most clearly expressed in *The Revelation of the Mystery* (*Kashf al-maḥjūb*), but it underlies other important works by Abū Yaʿqūb al-Sijistānī as well, including the *Book of Wellsprings* (*Kitāb al-Yanābiʿ*). Despite his profession of transcendence, the author clearly cannot manage without 'speaking' of God and referring to Him in some way. It is common in Ismaili theology to find God defined as the 'Initiator' or 'Innovator' (*al-mubdiʿ*), or He who creates from nothing (how this relates to cosmology will be explained in Chapter 5). But neither does the negation of negation mean a divine ipseity, a being God coinciding with itself. In the Book of *Exodus* the divine ipseity is revealed by the definition – so profound from the metaphysical point of view – that God gives of Himself: 'I am that I am'. In Arabic, a language in which the verb 'to be' is not copulative, the equivalent expression might be *Allāh huwa huwa*, or 'God [is] himself' or 'God is God'. In the *Book of Wellsprings* al-Sijistānī attempts, albeit in a somewhat convoluted way, to explain the divine ipseity in the light of the non-intelligibility of the First:

> Pure ipseity that relates to the First Initiatior (*al-mubdiʿ*) – which transcends all that can be affirmed or denied about Him – is the act of

> being of the first being as act of being of the creative foundation that is in it. [. . .] So it is not that the First has existing ipseity or non-existing ipseity beyond that which is revealed and manifest to the First Intelligence [the first being created anew by the First] through its same act of being, since the First is neither the being about which one can affirm that it is, as one does for the ipseity of the existing things installed by it in being, nor the non-being about which it can be said negatively that it is not, as one does for the negative ipseities of installed existences. No, its ipseity is the notification of the fact that it is necessary to deny both the ipseity and the absence of ipseity of the First.[8]

If it is not possible, in the name of the necessity of the double negation, to identify exactly what is divine ipseity, one can perhaps conclude, with Corbin, that for Abū Yaʿqūb al-Sijistānī 'the first being is, according to the essence of causing-to-be (*hast-kardeh*). The *mubdiʿ* cannot be a being; He is however the causing-to-be (*hast-kardan*)'.[9] God is not intelligible in essence but at least His existence is perceptible through acts. Actions do not exhaust essence, nor do they explain it, but they allow humankind to identify a chink through which they can become aware of God and of His beneficent and caring actions.

Similar in inspiration to the Ismailis, the Brothers of Purity too liberate God from an intelligibility that might seem too much like the Aristotelian categories:

> Know that of Him who initiates essences, that gives being to quiddities, who originates quantities, who forms qualities, who selects the where, who orders quantifications and [is] the reason for whys, we should not say: what is He?, nor ask: how, how much, which, when or why is He? In fact, of these problems and questions there are but two and no more that are possible and permissible about Him and for Him and they are: Is He? and Who is He? as has been said, He is He who acted in such and such a way, and He who decreed this thing and that. [. . .]The [Quraishite] polytheists and their adversaries asked this of the Prophet – praise be upon Him – saying: 'We worship our idols and our gods and we can see them, we have direct evidence of them and we know them, therefore tell us of your God whom you worship, what is He?' and God sent down his word: 'Say: He, God, [is] One' (Qur'an, 112.1). Then they said: 'We do not

understand and we do not comprehend'. They wanted [to understand] the quiddity of His essence, if He [is] substance or accident, light or darkness, body or spirit, internal or external, standing or sitting, free or occupied, and similar problems and questions that are not proper to His Lordship. God is far above that which is said by the unjust.[10]

The fact that the only thing that can be asked of God is 'Who is He?' is a further underlining of the importance of ipseity in the (tentative) definition of the divine. When the Prophet repeats the Qur'an ('God is One'), the misbelievers say that they do not understand because they seek erroneously to entrap God in the meshes of categories. But God is 'far above all that': Oneness and unpredictability are the mirror in which divine ipseity finds its reflection. This God is not a quiddity, any more than is the Muʿtazilite God opposed by al-Ghazālī.

The theme of negative theology is also closely linked to the existence of God in the work of philosophers like al-Fārābī, whose theories clearly owe something to Muʿtazilite ideas. In setting out his own theology, al-Fārābī adopts a rigorously philosophical vocabulary and, when speaking of God, rarely uses the word *Allāh*, preferring the locution 'First Being'. 'The First Existent is the First Cause of the existence of all the other existents', he writes in the *Virtuous City*[11] (Walzer 1985, I 1.1: 57), while in the *Book of Political Science* he uses more nuanced words: 'The First [Being] (*al-awwal*) should be believed to be "God" (*al-ilāh*), which is to say the direct cause (*sabab*) of the existence of the second [causes] and of the Agent Intellect'.[12] It will be seen that, in this second text, the God of the philosophers is explicitly identified with the God of revealed religion, while in the *Virtuous City* al-Fārābī seems to be speaking as a 'pure' philosopher. However, in the first chapters of the treatise, he offers a description of God that is clearly inspired by Muʿtazilite theology and which is not unaware of the traditional language of *kalām*.

God is unlike all other things, he does not exist in potentiality, he does not possess a cause, He is neither material nor is He contained in any substratum. He has no associates, neither can He be multiplied, since, even if it were admitted that there were two gods,

that in which they differed would not be the same as that which they shared, and thus that point of difference between the two would be a

> part of that which sustains the existence of both, and that which they have in common the other part. Thus each of them would be divisible in thought, and each of the two parts of the First would be a cause for the subsistence of its essence; and it would not be the First but there would be another existent prior to it and a cause for its existence – which is impossible.[13] (Walzer 1985, I 1.2: 61)

God does not have opposites, since if He did have an opposite it would be subject to corruption; He is indivisible and indefinable. He possesses positive attributes, however, and these are mentioned in the Qur'an itself and recognised by theology: He is knowing (*ʿālim* – and 'its knowledge of its essence is nothing else than its substance. Thus the fact that it knows and that it is knowable and that it is knowledge refers to one essence and one substance' (Walzer 1985, I 1.2: 73), which is to say that, as for the Muʿtazilites, the attribute coincides with the essence[14]); He is wise (*hakīm*); true (*haqq* – the term is one of the most important of the 'beautiful names' of God and is linked to reality, since *haqq* means both 'true' and 'real'); He is living (*hayy*); great (*ʿazīm*); majestic (*jalāl*); glorious (*majīd*).

Of all the qualifications of God or the First Being, however, the most characteristic are existence and intelligence. Although they can be found in the Qur'an, these qualifications have a solid basis in philosophy. According to al-Fārābī, existence is that which distinguishes God from creatures:

> That which is 'perfect' means the thing apart from which no other existent of its species can exist. [. . .] If, then, the First has perfect existence, it is impossible that any other existent should have the same existence. Therefore the First alone has this existence and it is unique [*wāhid*] in this respect'.[15] (Walzer 1985, I 1.2: 61, 63)

The Oneness of God consists in the perfection of existence that makes Him, in His transcendence, irredeemably different from every other existing thing. But that would not be sufficient to determine the absolute divine otherness; for this reason, al-Fārābī personalises the Muʿtazilite principle of the inherent nature of attributes in essence, connecting the attribute of existence directly to essence: 'The First is that from which everything which exists comes into existence (*wujūduhu li-ajli dhātihi*)'[16] (Walzer 1985, I 1.2: 89). At the beginning of Chapter V of the *Virtuous City* we find a very clear definition that, if translated literally from Arabic, is as follows: 'the existence it has, by which it is distinguished from all other existents, cannot be any other than by which it exists in itself (*alladhī huwa bihi fī dhātihi mawjūd*)'[17] (Walzer 1985, I 1.2: 69). In other words, the existence of God cannot consist in anything other than in his being existent through essence.

Although essence and existence coincide, this does not mean that existence is exclusive to Him alone. Al-Fārābī says that beings that derive from God are endowed with real existence. God communicates his existence to other beings by emanation: 'The genesis of that which comes into existence from it [God] takes place by way of an emanation [*fayd*], the existence of which is due to the existence of something else, so that the existence of something different from the First emanates from the First's existence'[18] (Walzer 1985, I 1.2: 89). Given life by emanation, other beings are structures according to a hierarchical scale (exemplified in the gradations of the cosmos) according to which 'every existent gets its allotted share and rank of existence from it'[19] (Walzer 1985, I 1.2: 95). The existence of other beings adds nothing to the perfection of the First in whom essence and existence, and substantiality and causality (since it is part of the substance of the One, the First Being, to also be the First Mover) coincide: 'Therefore that existence of it through which existence emanates to something else than it, is in its substance and in that existence of it through which its essence has substance identical with that existence of it through which everything else comes into existence from it'[20] (Walzer 1985, I 1.2: 93).

Lastly, God is intelligence. God 'understands Himself with Himself'; He understands his own essence for Himself; what Aristotle calls a thought of [a] thought:

> And when a thing exists without being in need of matter, that very thing will in its substance be actual intellect; and that is the status of the First. It is, then, actual intellect. In order to be intelligible the First is in no need of another essence outside itself which would think it but itself thinks its own essence. Thus it is intellect and intelligized and thinking, all this being one essence and one indivisible substance.[21] (Walzer 1985, I 2.1: 71)

The intellection that God has of Himself perfects His substance in such a way that in Him, the activity of thinking, the passivity of being thought of and the object itself of the thought become one and the same thing.

It is in the work of al-Fārābī that we first encounter the solution via emanation being clearly put forward as an argument for God's transcendence. It is one that obviously owes much to the Neo-Platonic concept of the cosmos, and particularly that of Plotinus. But the Transcendence of the One is seen in Islamic terms while the arrangement of the emanative system (which we shall examine in greater depth in the next chapter) is an innovation introduced by the Islamic thinkers. Emanation is then linked to the process of intellection, of how God understands Himself and how other emanated beings understand God. Al-Fārābī taught all this to Avicenna. But he also hints at another of Avicenna's doctrines, one that was to prove particularly fruitful: that of the distinction between essence and existence and between the necessary and the possible. Although it is possible to trace this theory back to al-Fārābī, it was only developed in a systematic and orderly way by Avicenna. And it was thanks to Avicenna that it made its mark on the development of western medieval metaphysics. It is through the works of this philosopher, therefore, that we shall examine it.

Avicenna takes as his point of departure the definition of 'necessary', 'possible' and 'impossible'. The 'necessary' is that whose non-existence implies a contradiction. The 'possible' is that whose existence or non-existence does not imply a contradiction. The 'impossible' is that whose existence implies a contradiction. The necessary is, therefore, that which must necessarily exist; the possible may exist or not exist; the impossible will never exist. This raises the question, how can the possible, that, as such, can exist or not exist, come into existence? The answer is, thanks to the intervention of a Necessary Being which is existent in itself and necessary for itself. Such is God, in whom essence and existence coincide. The Necessary Being – God – which possesses existence through His essence, transfers it in turn to the possible, the essence of which is to be contingent and which is without existence in the face of the Necessarily Existing. Made to exist by the external intervention of the Necessary Being, however, the possible is no longer merely contingent, but becomes in its turn necessary insofar as it exists. This necessity is, however, not 'for itself' but 'for the other'. Thus, while the Necessary Being is necessary in itself, the possible in itself becomes necessary for 'the other'. This determines the ontological difference between the Necessary Being and the possible and the ontological subordination of one to the other.

This doctrine has two interesting consequences. The first is that all that which is possible must be translated into existence, otherwise it would be impossible and would never exist. In other words, the possible can only exist or not exist in theory, because, in reality, if it did not exist it would be impossible, which is why it must of necessity exist. All that which is possible must, therefore, exist: Avicenna prefigures here what came to be known later as the 'principle of fullness'. If all that which is possible exists, our world is the only world that can exist and it is not possible to think that other worlds might exist or other beings outside it. All this has important theological implications. Avicenna can, in the *Metaphysics of the Book of Healing* for example, assert that God is the efficient cause (and not only the motive cause) of reality thus safeguarding the Qur'anic view of creation. Nevertheless, such an efficiency is necessitated: God must cause all possible things to exist in action, the only alternative being their absolute inexistence (and hence the inexistence of the world itself). Ours is the only world of all possible worlds (although not necessarily the best); and God has had no element of choice in 'creating' it. Avicenna's view conflicted with Averroes's firm statement that it is absurd to distinguish the possible 'in itself' and the necessary 'from another'. An existing thing is necessary and that is all. It no longer contains within itself any dimension or particle of possibility. On the one hand, 'in absolute non-existence there is not potential of any kind',[22] meaning that non-existence can never give way to existence. On the other hand, in reality only the necessary exists, but not the possible, whereas Avicenna attempted to preserve, potentially at least, the dimension of contingence and of essential inexistence of the beings 'created' in order to reserve for God the total perfection of essence. It should be noted, however, that Averroes arrives at basically the same conclusions as Avicenna: all that which can exist, exists in fact, while that whose existence is impossible will never exist. Not even God can make the impossible exist, since this is a logical contradiction.

The second consequence is that, in Avicenna, existence appears incidental to essence, in the sense that it is essence that determines the ontological difference between beings. God, Necessary Being, is superior to all creatures since, in his essence, existence is fully in action, while in creatures existence is a mere possibility, actualised 'from outside'. The primacy of essence over existence has been challenged in various ways in the history of philosophy, in favour of the primacy of existence over essence (as happens in Thomas Aquinas). An important question to consider is whether Avicenna regards the accidental nature of existence as being purely logical or, on the contrary, as being ontologically real. The problem is a knotty one, but scholars including Amélie Goichon and Afnan incline to the view that there is a real distinction.

The logicality or, rather, the inevitability of the distinction between essence and existence may derive from a linguistic difficulty in Arabic, and one that has obvious philosophical implications. As L. Goodman reminds us,

> Graham notes that 'a verb "to be" which serves both as copula and as indicator of existence is confined almost exclusively to Indo-European languages," that "a concept of Being combining essence and existence is confined to philosophies developed in the languages of the Indo-European family" [. . .] "In the two major philosophical traditions which developed outside this family, Arabic *wujūd* and Chinese *yu* are not "being" but existence. . . . It was in Arabic, which sharply separates the existential and copulative functions, that the distinction between existence and essence emerged".[23]

It is interesting to remember that L. Gardet and G. Anawati have asserted that this difficulty of predicating being may lie at the origins of a certain 'weakness' of Islamic metaphysics compared with Christian metaphysics.[24] If we accept the thesis put forward by J. Jolivet, however, their opinion might seem less well founded. According to Jolivet, Avicenna's distinction between essence and existence does not derive from a reworking of Greek philosophy but from the theological discussions of the Muslim *kalām*,[25] which would confirm the placing of this important philosophical distinction within the context of a culturally distinctive debate.

Existence is a qualifying attribute of God's essence and it reflects onto the things of the world. Avicenna sought, through his profound meditations on metaphysics, to determine how this comes about. His ideas seem to have had a degree of influence on al-Ghazālī, particularly where the latter speaks of a being that has existence in itself and of beings that draw their existence from the First Being. Of all his metaphysical works, the one that most significantly tackles these problems is probably the *Niche of Lights*, a text that stands midway between a philosophical treatise and mystical speculation and that has sometimes been thought to be apocryphal. It is true that a superficial reading gives the impression that the *Niche of Lights* is permeated by a spirit of Gnosticism not very different from that which we encounter, a generation later, in the work of post-Avicennan thinkers such as al-Suhrawardī whose esoteric interpretation of the theme of light resulted in a re-reading of the entire metaphysics of Avicenna, Iranian angelology and Islam itself. But al-Ghazālī's point of departure remains the Qur'an and the hierarchy he prefigures does not anticipate al-Suhrawardī's rays of latitudinal and longitudinal Lights.

In the magnificent verse 24.35 of the 24th sūrah of the Qur'an ('Light'), God's existence is likened to a Light (*nūr*) that looks down over the heavens and the Earth:

> God is the light of the heavens and the earth. His light may be compared to a niche that enshrines a lamp, the lamp within a crystal of star-like brilliance. It is lit from a blessed olive tree neither eastern nor western. Its very oil would almost shine forth, though no fire touched it. Light upon light; God guides to His light whom He will.

It is not difficult to understand how the mysterious symbolism of this verse gave rise to a multitude of philosophical and mystical interpretations, including that of al-Ghazālī. He provides a commentary to this Qur'anic verse in his *Niche of Lights*. The whole of the first part of the treatise, however, is dedicated to a philosophical discussion of the existence of God in relation to that of creatures. A systematic summary of his vision is well set out in the following passage:

> Existence can be classified as the existence that a thing possesses in itself, and that which it possesses from another. When a thing has existence from another, its existence is borrowed and has no support in itself. When the thing is viewed in itself and with respect to itself, it is pure nonexistence. It only exists inasmuch as it is ascribed to another. This is not a true existence [. . .]. Hence the Real Existent is God, just as the Real Light is He.
>
> From here the gnostics climb from the lowlands of metaphor to the

> highlands of reality, and they perfect their ascent. Then they see – witnessing with their own eyes – that there is none in existence save God and that 'Everything perishes except His Face' [Qur'an 28.88]. [It is] not that each thing is perishing at one time or at other times, but that it is perishing from eternity without beginning to eternity without end. It can only be so conceived since, when the essence of anything other than He is considered in respect of its own essence, it is sheer nonexistence. But when it is viewed in respect of the 'face' to which existence flows forth from the First, the Real, then it is seen as existing not in itself but through the face adjacent to its Giver of Existence. Hence, the only existent is the Face of God.
>
> Each thing has two faces: a face towards itself, and a face toward its Lord. Viewed in terms of the face of itself, it is nonexistent; but viewed in terms of the face of God, it exists. Hence nothing exists but God and His face [. . .].[26] (Buchman 1998: 16–17)

In this passage, al-Ghazālī uses words from the Qur'an to explain a notion derived from Avicenna, that of being 'in itself' and being 'from another'. His vision seems to imply that God is the only truly existing reality, while other beings are reduced to pale shadows and reflections of the supreme divine existence. Things draw their existence from God who is the One truly existing being and those who understand all this see only the One in existence. A similar idea is also found in al-Ghazālī's *Revival of the Religious Sciences* (particularly in the book entitled *Faith in Divine Unity and Trust in Divine Providence*). There are four types of people:

> The first type of man affirms the Oneness of God in words alone and this is enough to protect him in this world from swords and spears. The second, in affirming the Oneness of God, links the spirit of his words to his heart, believing sincerely in their meaning. [. . .] The third type affirms the Oneness of God in the sense that he contemplates a single agent. When the Truth has revealed to him what it is, he sees no more than a single [being], the essential reality having been revealed to him as it is. This is the rank of ordinary men and theologians. In fact, the theologian is no different from the ordinary man in terms of his religious belief, but only on account of his activities in theological interpretation designed to guard against the tricks of the innovators. As for the fourth type, he affirms the Oneness of God in such a way

> that, in his contemplative vision, the only thing present is the One and he does not see the whole as a multiplicity but, it too, as a single thing. This is the extreme limit of *tawhīd*.[27]

Al-Ghazālī's thoughts on this matter have led some scholars to see the Persian philosopher and theologian as anticipating the doctrine of the 'oneness of existence' (*wahdat al-wujūd*) formulated by the Andalusian Ibn ʿArabī. According to this doctrine, there is nothing in existence but God. Ibn ʿArabī's concept is set out fairly straightforwardly in the following passage:

> In the name of God, the Merciful, the Compassionate, and Him we ask for aid: Praise be to God before whose oneness there was not a before, unless the Before were He, and after whose singleness there is not an after, except the After be He. He is, and there is with Him no after nor before, nor above nor below, nor far nor near, nor union nor division, nor how nor where nor when, nor times or moment nor age, nor being nor place. And He is now as He was. He is the One without oneness and the Single without singleness. He is not composed of name and named, for His name is He and His named is He. So there is no name other than He, nor named. And so He is the Name and the Named. He is the First without firstness and the Last without lastness. He is the Outward without outwardness, and the Inward without inwardness. [Allusion to the Qur'an, 57.3: 'He is the First and the Last, the Visible and the Hidden'.] I mean that He is the very existence of the First and the very existence of the Last, and the very existence of the Outward and the very existence of the Inward. So that there is no first or last, nor outward nor inward, except Him, without these becoming Him or His becoming them.[28]

In the past, Ibn ʿArabī was often accused of pantheism and the doctrine of *wahdat al-wujūd* seen as dangerously leaning towards pantheism. The passage quoted above might lead one to reject such an interpretation. Nevertheless, other texts by Ibn ʿArabī are much more ambiguous as can be seen from the following extract summarising several pages of the *Fusūs al-hikami* (*The Pearls of Wisdom*):

> Know therefore that so-called non-divine reality, which is to say the world, relates to God as a shadow relates to a person. Thus the world is the shadow of God; this is the way in which being (*wujūd*) is

> attributed to the world. Since a shadow belongs unequivocally to the order of the senses, on condition however that there is something for this shadow to project itself onto; so that, if you could remove all supports from the shadow, it would not longer exist in sensible terms but only as something intelligible. [. . .] The essences of possibilities do not shine because they are non-existent; they are unchanging, but they cannot be qualified as being or existence; in fact being is light. [. . .] You do not know the world except insofar as you can know shadows. It is the divine name 'Light' of which we speak, and it is that which is made real in the visual order, since shadows do not exist in the absence of light. All that which you see is nothing more than the being of God in the permanent essences of possibilities; the ipseity (*huwiyya*) [of that which you see] is God, it is He that is in being. In its existential oneness, the shadow is God Himself, since God is the Unique (*wāhid*), the One (*ahad*); and from the point of view of the multiplicity of sensible forms, it is the world. In fact, reality is such that we can say that the world is illusory (*mutawahham*).[29]

Even though the similes used here seem to suggest that Ibn ʿArabī considered physical reality as a mere reflection of the one effective reality which is divine reality (in which nature is ultimately swallowed up and disappears), today such pantheistic interpretations have been mainly, if not entirely, abandoned. As A. Ventura has written:

> The doctrine of the oneness of existence (*wahdat al-wujūd*) never sought to reduce reality simplistically to a single principle, nor did it teach that the objects of creation are God or that God resides substantially in things. [. . .] Things are real insofar as we see them as part of that existence that is the beginning of everything, and unreal insofar as we perceive only their qualified and transitory existence. To say that the world is illusory does not, therefore, mean asserting its unreality in an absolute way, but only relatively: the world and things are real in that they are the 'abode' of an eternal manifestation of God, but if we exclude this manifestation they are inexistent (*maʿdūma*), evanescent and false.

Some Muslim theoreticians have proposed, in the place of the 'oneness of existence', the notion of *wahdat al-shuhūd*, the oneness of 'vision' or 'perception'. To quote Ventura again, this view,

> teaches that it is a mistake to believe that it is existence that is one: oneness is not in *wujūd*, or reality, but in *shuhūd*, which is the perception that we have of reality. In other words, it cannot be said that when the light of the Sun hides the stars from us that they do not exist, because, on the contrary, we know very well that they are only momentarily absent from our view. The same happens in the case of transcendent Reality: when he attains an understanding of the One, man is so overwhelmed by this perception that he can see nothing but Him and this is what is meant by the oneness of vision (*wahdat al-shuhūd*), although this does not in any way mean that Reality can be reduced to a single real principle.[30]

With these remarks in mind, it would seem that al-Ghazālī's position in the *Niche of Lights* comes closer to the idea of *wahdat al-shuhūd*. This enables him to distance himself from the risks of pantheism (risks that are, in my opinion, nevertheless present in the doctrine of the 'oneness of existence') and yet assert the principle of divine Oneness. In Book XXXIX of the *Revival of the Religious Sciences*, entitled 'On Meditation', al-Ghazālī writes:

> All the beings in this world are an effect of the power of God the Highest and a light of His essence; indeed, there is no darkness blacker than non-existence, nor light more bright than existence, and the existence of all things is a light of the essence of He who is the Highest and Most Holy, since the basis of the existence of things is in the essence of He who exists in Himself, just as the basis of the light of bodies is in the light of the Sun that illuminates of itself.[31]

Here, creatures are 'based' in God and draw their light from the Light of God, but their existence is established without doubt, whereas 'non-existence' is pure darkness for creatures as well.

In fact, in al-Ghazālī, the profession of Oneness is very much better expressed by the definition of divine ipseity, where totality itself is 'seen' in its unity in relation to God as the light with the Sun that emanates it:

> Thus the face of every possessor of a face is toward Him and turned in His direction. 'Whithersoever you turn, there is the face of God' [Qur'an 2:115]. Hence, there is no god but He. For 'god' is an

expression for that toward which a face turns through worship and becoming godlike. Here I mean the faces of the hearts, since they are lights. Indeed, just as there is no god but He, so also there is no he but He, because 'he' is an expression for whatever may be pointed to, and there is no pointing to anything but Him. Or, rather, whenever you point to something, in reality you are pointing to Him. If you do not know this, it is because you are heedless of 'the Reality of realities' that we mentioned.

One does not point to the light of the sun but, rather, to the sun. In the obvious sense of this example, everything in existence is related to God just as light is related to the sun. Therefore, 'There is no god but God' is the declaration of God's unity of the elect, since this declaration of God's unity is more complete, more specific, more comprehensive, more worthy, and more precise. It is more able to make its possessor enter into sheer singularity and utter oneness.[32] (Buchman 1998: 20)

Al-Ghazālī makes the daring assertion that this identification of Oneness with divine ipseity represents the authentic meaning of the phrase in the Qur'an where God is called 'the Light of the heavens and the Earth' and Totality is one of His Lights.

As for the other symbols in verse 35 of the *sūrah* called 'Light',[24] in the *Niche of Lights* (and unlike the interpretation in *Faith in Divine Unity and Trust in Divine Providence* mentioned earlier) al-Ghazālī explains them as meaning the gradation of human 'spirits' or of the faculties of understanding. The sensitive spirit that receives information by means of the five senses is the niche. The imaginative spirit that registers the information acquired through the senses and safeguards it in order to present it, when needed, to the intellective spirit is the crystal. The intellective spirit by means of which concepts that are beyond the sense are acquired is the lamp. The reasoning spirit that takes the simple concepts of the intellect and combines them together, deducing higher notions from them, is the olive. The oil represents the holy prophetic spirit (*rūh qudsī nabawī* in an echo of Avicenna's analogy *ʿaql qudsī* or 'holy intellect'), which is that of the prophets and whence the Tables of the Invisible One give forth their light and which contains the innermost secrets of the Kingdom of the heavens and the Earth.[33]

Speculation on the Oneness of God by Muslim philosophers resulted in their adoption of a wide range of different positions. Their interpretations of the Qur'an led them far away from the simplicity of the sacred words. Theologians like Ibn Taymiyya argued that it was possible to speak of God using no other expressions than those found in the Qur'an, without distortion, without negation, without seeking to understand how, and without having recourse to comparisons.[34] This literalism made it possible, despite everything, to stand apart both from a crude anthropomorphism and from an excessive spiritualism that, as in the case of Muʿtazilite theology, led to a negation of God's attributes. It can be argued that the philosophers' view both spiritualised God and, at the same time, simplified His essence in an ipseity in which essence and existence coincide. In this way, the idea of God appears phenomenologically simplified as pure essence appearing to humankind as a given that may not be questioned. But the world must derive from God and it is how the world derives from God that is the object of the metaphysical reflection of the philosophers.

Chapter 5

The Structure of the Cosmos

The concept of Oneness is resolved in a transcendence of God that, as we have seen, has been interpreted in many different ways. This transcendence must, for many philosophers, be safeguarded even at the cost of separating God from any 'physical' contact with reality. For this reason, even if al-Kindī, for example, aligns himself with the theologians in hypothesising creation *ex nihilo*, a significant number of Islamic philosophers accepted an emanationist vision of the structure of the cosmos with the implied hierarchisation of beings that it imposes. Such a hierarchy does not, however, imply contact between the unattainable divine transcendence and the created material world; for this reason, in Islamic philosophy the predominant principle was that which stated that only one can come from One (*ex uno non fit nisi unum*). This principle was, however, applied in different ways.

It was al-Fārābī who set out the emanationist view of the cosmos. The first presupposition of his construct is obviously the hierarchisation of beings. Here we should quote in full from a previously-mentioned passage in the *Virtuous City*:

> The existents are many in number, and in addition to their being numerous, they vary in excellence. The substance of the First is a substance from which every existent emanates, however it may be, whether perfect or deficient. But the subject of the First is also such

> that all the existents, when they emanate from it, are arranged in an order of rank, and that every existent gets its allotted share and rank of existence from it.[1] (Walzer 1985, I 2.1: 95)

Having established the presupposition of a hierarchy, al-Fārābī goes on to describe the emanationist structure in detail:

> From the First emanates the existence of the Second. This Second is, again, an utterly incorporeal substance, and is not in matter. It thinks of (intelligizes) its own essence and thinks the First. What it thinks of its own essence is no more than its essence. As a result of its thinking of the First, a third existent follows necessarily from it; and as a result of its substantification in its specific essence, the existence of the First Heaven follows necessarily.
>
> The existence of the Third, again, is not in matter, its substance is intellect [*ʿaql*], and it thinks its own essence and thinks the First. As a result of its substantification in its specific essence, the existence of the sphere of the fixed stars follows necessarily, and as a result of its thinking of the First, a fourth existence follows necessarily.
>
> This again is not in matter. It thinks its own essence and intelligizes the First. As a result of its substantification in its specific essence, the existence of the sphere of Saturn follows necessarily, and as a result of its thinking the First, a fifth existence follows necessarily.[2] (Walzer 1985, I. II.3, 1–3: 101)

This reasoning is repeated in identical form until it reaches the tenth Intelligence or eleventh Being that corresponds to the Agent Intellect, whose essential role it is, according to al-Fārābī, to intervene to actualise the human intellect and to represent the goal of the ascent to human intellective perfection (as will be seen in more detail in the next chapter). It is useful to see al-Fārābī's cosmic system in diagrammatic form:

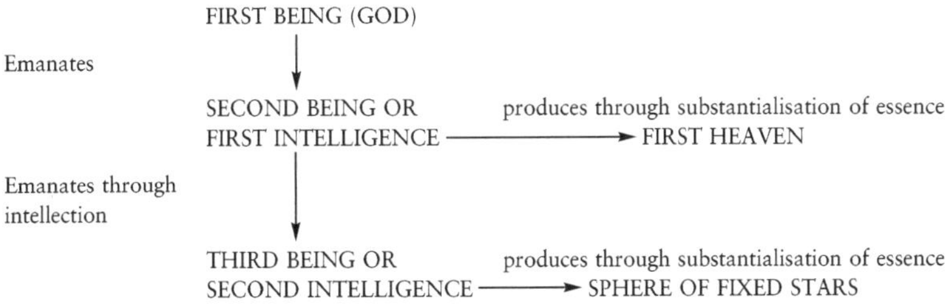

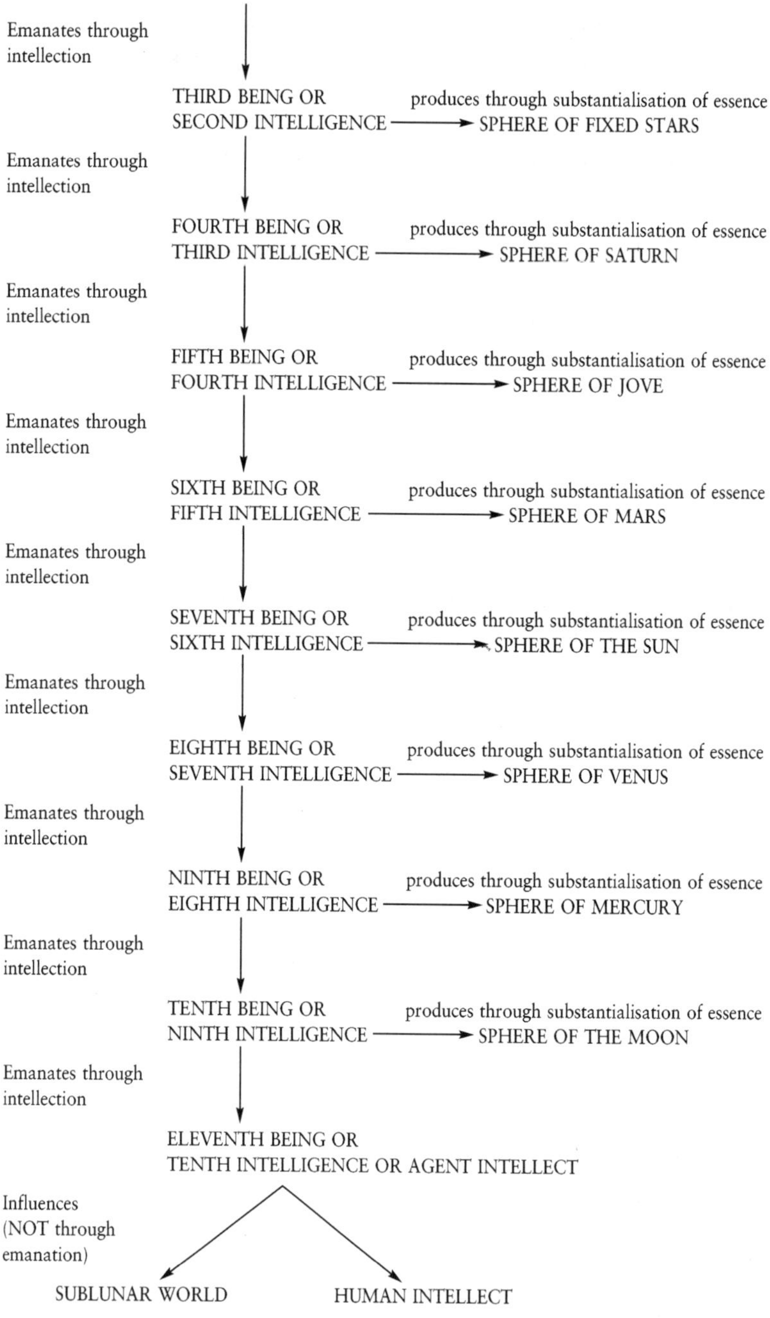
Emanates through intellection
THIRD BEING OR SECOND INTELLIGENCE
produces through substantialisation of essence
SPHERE OF FIXED STARS
Emanates through intellection
FOURTH BEING OR THIRD INTELLIGENCE
produces through substantialisation of essence
SPHERE OF SATURN
Emanates through intellection
FIFTH BEING OR FOURTH INTELLIGENCE
produces through substantialisation of essence
SPHERE OF JOVE
Emanates through intellection
SIXTH BEING OR FIFTH INTELLIGENCE
produces through substantialisation of essence
SPHERE OF MARS
Emanates through intellection
SEVENTH BEING OR SIXTH INTELLIGENCE
produces through substantialisation of essence
SPHERE OF THE SUN
Emanates through intellection
EIGHTH BEING OR SEVENTH INTELLIGENCE
produces through substantialisation of essence
SPHERE OF VENUS
Emanates through intellection
NINTH BEING OR EIGHTH INTELLIGENCE
produces through substantialisation of essence
SPHERE OF MERCURY
Emanates through intellection
TENTH BEING OR NINTH INTELLIGENCE
produces through substantialisation of essence
SPHERE OF THE MOON
Emanates through intellection
ELEVENTH BEING OR TENTH INTELLIGENCE OR AGENT INTELLECT
Influences (NOT through emanation)
SUBLUNAR WORLD
HUMAN INTELLECT

The system functions thanks to a dual process of emanation, from the First to the Second and so on until the Eleventh, and of intellection from the Eleventh to the Tenth and so on as far as the First. The emanative process descends while the intellective process ascends. The process is necessary, and so must be presumed to be eternal, insofar as the Second necessarily (and for eternity) emanates from the First, the Third from the Second, and so on. Although al-Fārābī does not say so explicitly in the text, the emanation from the First (God) to the Second Being must occur through the intellection that God has of Himself. 'Creation' seems therefore to resolve itself in the necessary effect of an act of awareness that, following Aristotle, the First Being has of Himself. The Second Being is 'single' – thus safeguarding the principle of *ex uno non fit nisi unum* – but already within it multiplicity appears. With this multiplicity appearing only with the Second Being, the absolute transcendence of the First and its non-compromise with material reality is guaranteed.

The system of heavens reproduces the cosmic structure of Greek astronomy, with a first heaven that contains and surrounds all the others. This is followed by the sphere of fixed stars, the spheres of the planets and ends with the sphere of the Moon, below which, placed in the centre of the cosmos, is the Earth. In this way, al-Fārābī effects a correction to the image of the world held by Aristotle and a considerable number of late Greek philosophers such as Alexander of Aphrodisias. They did not put forward the idea of a first heaven, suggesting instead that the sphere of fixed stars was the outermost sphere. It is likely that al-Fārābī was influenced by Ptolemy, an indication of the extent of his scientific knowledge. The system of heavens is explained as the product of the process of emanation-intellection thanks to a 'substantialisation of the specific essence' (*bi-mā huwa mutajawhar bi-dhātihi allatī takhussuhu*) of the Intelligences. This phrase is not entirely clear but appears to mean that the production of bodies and celestial spheres is not the result of a 'physical' act, but of a 'metaphysical' act.

Al-Fārābī's concept seems, not surprisingly, to derive fairly directly from Neo-Platonism, with which it shares, in particular, the concept of hierarchy. Nevertheless, if we look at the details of the structure of material and nature that underlies the celestial system, we see that the Muslim philosopher is also profoundly indebted to Aristotle. Scholars such as Gutas have gone so far as to call him an Aristotelian.

Certainly, al-Fārābī's doctrine cannot be considered to be Neo-Platonic in an absolute sense. In outlining the emanative process, he does not respect the One-Intellect-Soul triad described by Plotinus. An Ismaili thinker, Abū Yaʿqūb al-Sijistānī would have acquired elements of Neo-Platonic ideas, possibly via al-Fārābī, but he must also have been aware of the need to respect Qur'anic creationism. The transcending idea of the One and the idea of a hierarchy seem particularly suited to Islam, but the emanative system also implies a sort of participation by God in nature and creatures, a participation that a theology such as that of the Ismailis energetically rejects. For this reason, Abū Yaʿqūb al-Sijistānī outlines an emanative scheme that, while retaining the substance of Plotinus's triad, removes God from reality, reserving for Him a purely creative function:

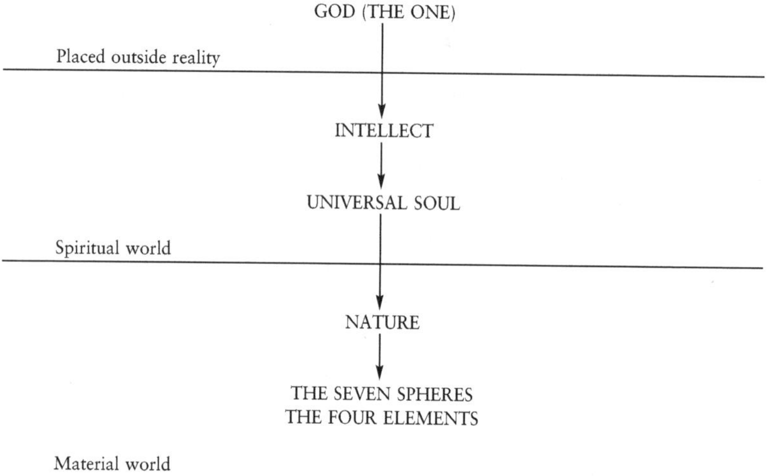

The distance between God-One and nature is filled by the Intellect and the Universal Soul, notions that clearly reproduce Plotonius's hypostasis. But the Intellect does not emanate from God as in al-Fārābī, and as it will subsequently in Avicenna: God 'creates' the Intellect through an act of innovation *ex nihilo* (*ibdāʿ*). The *ibdāʿ* brings the Intellect in existence in a single moment and, together with it, the flow of emanation that results from it. The world is thus brought into complete existence through the creative act. Creation *ex nihilo* is the product of God's 'order' (*amr*) with which Abū Yaʿqūb al-Sijistānī explains the birth of the cosmos, making reference to a concept taken directly from the Qur'an ('The Spirit is at my Lord's command', 17.86). The Universal Soul then emanates from the Intellect, even if the term used by the philosopher to express this process is not *fayd*, as in al-Fārābī, but *inbiʿāth*, a word expressing the idea of 'emission'. From the Universal Soul there then emanates in turn material and natural reality, but here too the process is called *inbijās*, meaning 'effusion'. Abū Yaʿqūb al-Sijistānī does not follow the system of Intelligences found in al-Fārābī. Instead, Intellect and Universal Soul are used to represent concepts and realities of the Qur'anic revelation. The Intellect, called 'the Preceding' (*sābiq*) is identified with *kursī*, the Throne of God of verse 2.255 of the Qur'an: 'His throne is as vast as the heavens and the earth'. The Soul, called 'the Following' (*tālī*), is identified with the *ʿarsh*, once again the Throne or 'Seat' of God, as in verse 7.54 of the Qur'an: 'God, who [. . .] ascended the throne'. And again, the Intellect is the 'Pen' (for example, verse 96.4 in the Qur'an), while the Soul represents the Imperishable Tablet (85.22) on which the heavenly eternal text of the holy Book is written. It would seem that just as the 'Pen' inscribes God's decrees on the Imperishable Tablet, so does the Intellect 'emit' the Soul, stamping it with the divine Order. Finally, 'the Preceding' and 'the Following' seem to allude to two central figures in Ismaili theology: the speaking Prophet bearer of the revelation, often referred to as 'he who precedes', and the *imām*, esoteric interpreter of the revelation and 'he who follows'.

It is possible to trace a parallelism between the concept of the cosmos as held by the Ismailis and that of the Brothers of Purity, who were almost certainly Shiite in inclination. The Brothers' cosmology could, at first sight, be mistaken for a Neo-Platonic system, but it has a number of important elements that differ from the structure of being put forward by those following in the footsteps of Plotinus. First and foremost, reality is arranged in a hierarchy, divided into nine descending levels, the first four being outside nature and the last five corresponding to the material world:

1. at the top, obviously, is the Creator, One and absolutely simple;
2. then comes the Intellect (or Intelligence), innate and acquired;
3. next, the Soul identifiable in three types: vegetable, animal and rational;
4. then primary Matter
5. from which derives Nature that includes celestial and elemental nature.

6. Below Nature is the Body, determined in space;
7. then the Sphere that contains the seven planets,
8. and below this, the four elements with their accompanying qualities (hot, cold, wet and dry).
9. Lastly, the beings of this world, minerals, plants and animals.

The Brothers maintain that God 'created' the cosmos instantaneously, or at least that He produced the first three levels of the cosmic hierarchy instantaneously: Intellect, Soul and Matter. The process is described as follows in a passage from the *Epistles* (or *Encyclopaedia*):

> Know, O brother, that the first thing which the Creator originated and invented from the light of His unity was a simple essence called the Active Intellect, just as He produced two from one by repetition. Then He created the Universal Celestial Soul from the light of the Intellect, just as He created three by the addition of one to two. Then He created Prime Matter from the movement of the Soul just as He created four by adding one to three.[3]

Although the Brothers' Intellect and Soul correspond to Plotinus's hypostasis, the process described above is not strictly speaking emanative. Similarly, the hypostatic rank given to Matter is clearly not Plotinian. It seems to consist not so much of emanation as of a numerical multiplication, consistent with the markedly Pythagorean tendency of the sect. On the other hand, Prime Matter, although remote from the One, is neither understood in an Aristotelian way as pure potentiality nor in a Plotinian way as mere negativity, appearing rather as a positive spiritual principle.

Another element characteristic of the Brothers' cosmology is the analogy drawn between the universe and the human body, to the extent that some scholars have spoken of a 'giant man' universe:

> Know, O Brother, that by the Universe (*ʿalām*) the sages (*hukamā ʾ*) mean the seven heavens and the earths and what is between them of all creatures. They also call it the great man (*al-insān al-kabīr*) because it is seen that the world has one body in all its spheres, gradation of heavens, its generating elements (*arkān*) and their productions. It is also seen that it has one Soul (*nafs*) whose powers run in all the organs of its body, just like the man who has one soul

> which runs into all of his organs. We desire to mention in this treatise the form of the world and describe the composition of its body as the body of man is described in a book of anatomy.[4]

There is a close correspondence between micro- and macro-cosmos; a secret harmony links the heavens and the earth and man's substance is projected in a spiritual and all-embracing vision.

Like Abū Yaʿqūb al-Sijistānī, Avicenna also describes a structure of the cosmos in which, compared to al-Fārābī, the Neo-Platonic model is mainly retained. In fact, in order to guarantee the absolute transcendence and oneness of God, the Necessary Being, and in order to avoid entirely any suggestion that He might be multiple, Avicenna hypothesises that with the first being emanating from God, which the philosopher calls the 'First Intelligence' (*al-ʿaql al-awwal*), multiplicity is not produced immediately. Through the pure intellective act of knowing Himself, God emanates only the First Intelligence. The First Intelligence, in turn, knowing God, emanates the Second Intelligence and nothing else. It is only now, with the Second Intelligence, that multiplicity begins. At this point, Avicenna finds it necessary to apply the previously defined principle of the distinction between the necessary and the possible. The Second Intelligence, aware of being merely possible in relation to God, produces the body of the sphere of the First Heaven; then, aware of being nevertheless necessary on account of the external intervention of God, the absolutely Necessary Being, it produces the soul that moves the sphere of the First Heaven. Meanwhile, of course, knowing God, the Second Intelligence emanates the Third. In this way, only one derives from the supreme One. As in al-Fārābī, this scheme is then repeated for each of the seven spheres of the planets until the Tenth Intelligence or Agent Intellect that governs the sub-lunar world is reached. The Third Intelligence, knowing God, emanates the Fourth; aware of itself as possible in relation to God, it produces the body of the sphere of the fixed stars and, knowing itself to be necessary in that it have been brought into existence by God, produces the soul that moves the sphere of the fixed stars. The hierarchy continues. Avicenna also calls the last one, the Agent Intellect, the 'giver of forms' (*wāhib al-suwar*), a locution that was rendered literally into Latin by medieval philosophers as *dator formarum*. Avicenna's system can be summed up diagrammatically as follows:

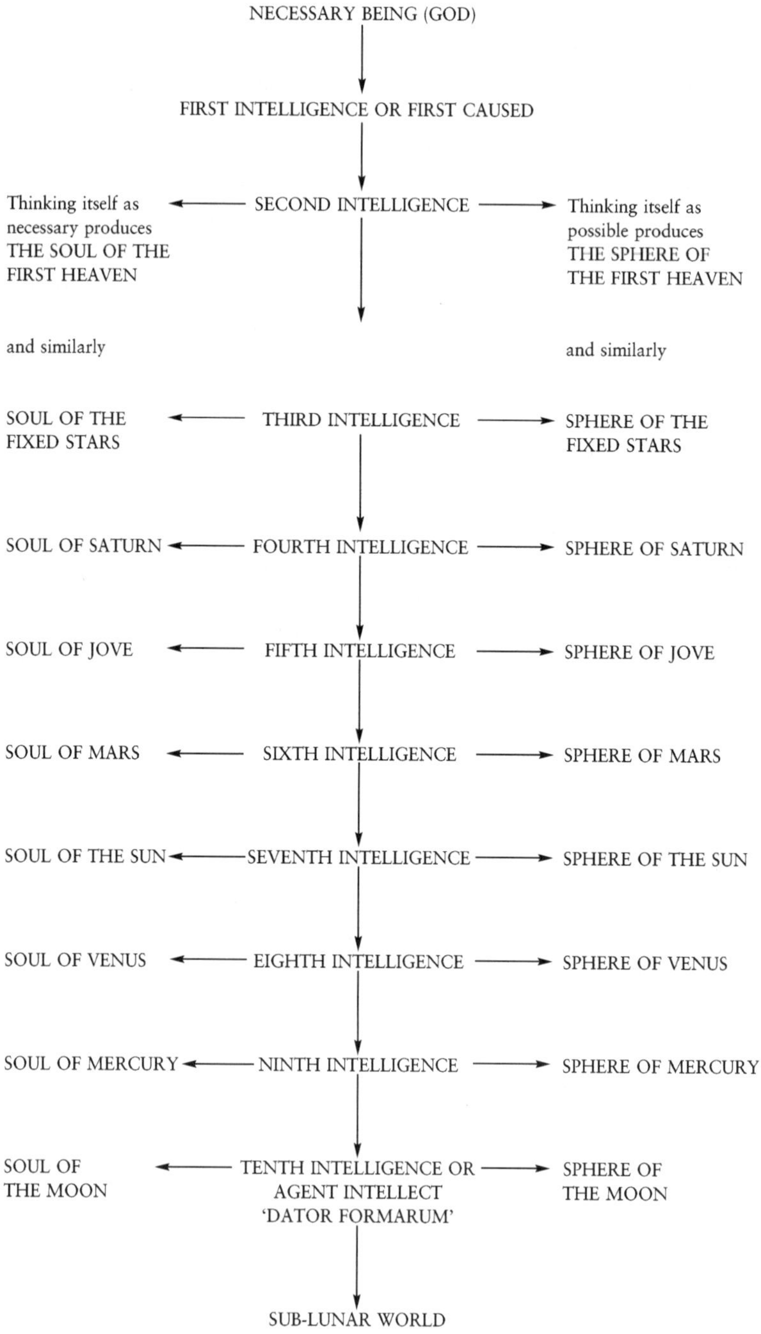
NECESSARY BEING (GOD)
FIRST INTELLIGENCE OR FIRST CAUSED
SECOND INTELLIGENCE
Thinking itself as necessary produces THE SOUL OF THE FIRST HEAVEN
Thinking itself as possible produces THE SPHERE OF THE FIRST HEAVEN
and similarly
and similarly
THIRD INTELLIGENCE
SOUL OF THE FIXED STARS
SPHERE OF THE FIXED STARS
FOURTH INTELLIGENCE
SOUL OF SATURN
SPHERE OF SATURN
FIFTH INTELLIGENCE
SOUL OF JOVE
SPHERE OF JOVE
SIXTH INTELLIGENCE
SOUL OF MARS
SPHERE OF MARS
SEVENTH INTELLIGENCE
SOUL OF THE SUN
SPHERE OF THE SUN
EIGHTH INTELLIGENCE
SOUL OF VENUS
SPHERE OF VENUS
NINTH INTELLIGENCE
SOUL OF MERCURY
SPHERE OF MERCURY
TENTH INTELLIGENCE OR AGENT INTELLECT 'DATOR FORMARUM'
SOUL OF THE MOON
SPHERE OF THE MOON
SUB-LUNAR WORLD

Avicenna's argument presents several interesting and also contradictory points. Firstly, although the First Intelligence derives from God thanks to an emanation consequent on the awareness the Necessary Being has it itself, Avicenna defines this process as 'creation' and calls the First Intelligence the 'first created' (*al-mubdaʿ al-awwal*). This might seem strange in the light of the fact that Avicenna speaks of the permanence of matter. In reality, however – and this idea was also arrived at by al-Kindī – creation means simply existence after non-existence. So God 'creates' in the sense that He gives beings, starting with the Intelligences, an existence that is not inherent in their essence. Secondly, the Intelligences are explicitly identified with the angels and the Tenth Intelligence specifically with the archangel Gabriel. In this way, Avicenna connects the philosophical construction of the cosmos with the Islamic religion: 'the spiritual angels that are Intelligences occupy the highest place, being called by the philosophers active Intelligences and they correspond to those things that in the language of religion are presented as the angels closest to God and entirely united with Him'.[5] Thirdly, it is not entirely clear whether, in addition to governing the sub-lunar world, the Tenth Intelligence or Agent Intellect also governs the sphere of the Moon. As A. Badawi notes, 'it is difficult to know whether, for Avicenna, the Agent Intellect or active Intelligence, which presides over the regulation of the terrestrial world, is the Intelligence of the sphere of the Moon or a separate intelligence. Avicenna's writings are not clear on this point'.[6] Finally, even if al-Fārābī's Agent Intellect corresponds for the most part to that of Avicenna, the latter's performs a much more complex function. Al-Fārābī's Agent Intellect, particularly in the *Virtuous City* and the *Philosophy of Aristotle*, seems to be mainly occupied with the illumination and actualisation of the human intellect, where it is the combination of heavenly influences that conditions the world of generation and decay. Avicenna's Agent Intellect, by contrast, has direct responsibility for the direction of the changeable material world. The difference is discussed by Davidson who writes:

> As Alfarabi did in *al-Madīna al-Fādila* [*The Virtuous City*] and *al-Siyāsa al-Madaniyya* [*Political Science*], Avicenna connects the uniformity and diversity within the lower world to uniformity and diversity within the heavens. But for Avicenna, the heavens are only an auxiliary cause of what exists in the lower world; the active

intellect is the primary cause. In an unexplained way the uniformity of celestial motion helps the active intellect to emanate the eternal matter of the sublunar world. [. . .] While Alfarabi's *Risāla fī al-ʿAql* [*Epistle on Intellect*] had represented the active intellect as the agent that emanates natural forms above the level of the four elements, Avicenna goes beyond the *Risāla* too, for he understands the active intellect to be the cause of the matter as well as the forms of the sublunar world, and to be the cause of the four elements as well as the forms of more complex beings.[7]

In Avicenna, the Agent Intellect carries out precisely the ordering role of God, which is kept well beyond material reality; in al-Fārābī, the Agent Intellect is the mediator between human reality – and the human intellect – and the unattainable world of the divinity.

When Averroes began to think about the structure of the universe,[8] he had therefore to contend with a consolidated tradition that, while containing Aristotelian elements and also Aristotle's planetary system of spheres and Intelligence, bears the stamp of Neo-Platonic ideas about emanation and hierarchy. But Averroes set out to construct a system based on Aristotelian foundations, which was why he could not descend to using an emanative model. In the *Incoherence of Incoherence*, Averroes briefly but clearly sets out his definitive opinion. The vertical ascension of the system of causes leads to the postulation of the existence of a first cause:

> Since, in their [the philosophers] opinion, causes cannot endlessly follow on from one another, they have presupposed the existence of a first cause and permanent agent. Some have maintained that this cause coincides with the heavenly bodies; others that it is a separate Principle but one that accompanies the heavenly bodies; yet others that it is the First Principle [God]; finally, there are those that believe that it is a [agent] inferior to the First.[9]

Averroes naturally accepts the opinion that the First Principle and First Cause is God. Below it is the cosmic system of the heavenly bodies that 'the philosophers agree [. . .] are conditions for the generation of [sub-lunar bodies] in that they are remote efficient causes'. The cosmic system of the heavenly bodies echoes exactly that of ancient astronomy: beyond the Earth is the Moon; then Mercury, Venus, the Sun, Mars, Jove and Saturn. Averroes, however, doubting that a ninth sphere beyond the sphere of fixed stars could exist, does not postulate nine spheres, but only eight.

According to Averroes, 'the heavenly bodies possess movers thanks to which and by which they are moved. From their investigations, it appeared to them [the philosophers] that such motor principles are neither corporeal bodies nor forces inherent in bodies'. These movers are pure Intelligences. Thus God appears as the Prime Mover, imprinting movement on the Intelligences that, in turn, move the heavens. The heavens, in their turn, move and govern the sub-lunar world. Averroes calls God the Prime Mover, in the knowledge that, as is made clear particularly in Book VIII of the *Large Commentary on Physics*, this is the only rationally and philosophically possible way of demonstrating the existence of God. Opposing Avicenna, who maintained that a metaphysical demonstration was possible, Averroes maintains that only a physical demonstration was possible, the central argument for which states that a corporeal force can produce only a finite movement; but the movement of the heavens is infinite, therefore the force that moves the heavens, the Prime Mover, is incorporeal. As well as being the Intelligence that moves the outermost sphere of the universe, Averroes calls the Prime Mover 'pure act' and First Form in the hierarchy of separate Intelligences. In this sense, Averroes clearly goes beyond the emanative vision of the cosmos held by al-Fārābī and Avicenna, not least because emanation is related to efficient causes, whereas the First Cause is not an efficient cause.[10]

Averroes, nevertheless, feels the need to identify a hierarchical arrangement in the Intelligences: 'The order and structure [of the First] are the cause of the orders and structures that are evident in the realities below Him. The Intelligences have reciprocal degrees of excellence in relation to the state of nearness or distance from Him'. Furthermore, like al-Fārābī and Avicenna, Averroes seems to conceive the process of derivation of the Intelligences from God as being a process of intellection and awareness. Similarly, the act of intellection by the Intelligences is the cause of the process of derivation from them to all the rest of reality:

> that which the First understands of its essence is the cause of all existing things; that which each of the Intelligences below Him understands is the cause both of that which existing things

> individually derive from that Intelligence and from its creative capacity, and of its own essence, or the human intellect in its universality.

In this sense, for Averroes God is not merely a mechanical and unknowing Prime Mover, for He preserves some of the characteristics of the Islamic God.

God is the cause through the intellective act, but He is also the finalistic cause. How can the finalism of the world be expressed? For Averroes, intellection is not a cold, pure act of understanding as it might appear in al-Fārābī. Intellection implies loving; understanding implies desiring. In his commentary on Book Lambda (XII) of Aristotle's *Metaphysics*, Averroes asserts that, on the one hand, the intellective appetite induces the movers of the heavenly bodies (which is to say, the Intelligences) to move the heavenly bodies; and, on the other, that the Prime Mover, God, moves the beings below Him in the same way that the loved one moves the lover. On the one hand,

> it appears in all clarity that these celestial bodies have souls and that of the powers of the soul. They have only the intellect and the faculty of desire [. . .] the movers of the celestial bodies are movers in both ways without being multiple. Insofar as these intelligibles are their [the movers] forms, they [the celestial bodies] impart motion as efficient causes; insofar as they are their ends, these are moved by them [the movers] by means of their desire.[11]

The efficient causality of the movers of the heavenly bodies, the Intelligences, is determined by the actualisation in them of intelligibles. As the Intelligences turn to the intelligibles, and naturally to the highest of them all, which is God, they impart to the bodies a movement that is the product of their desire to know the intelligibles and God. On the other hand,

> This first mover imparts motion, without being moved, to the first object moved by it, just as the beloved moves his lover without being moved itself, and it imparts motion to what is below its first moved by means of the first moved. By its first moved, he [Aristotle] means the celestial body, and by all the other moved, that which is below the first body, namely all the other spheres and that which is subject to

> generation and corruption. The first heaven is moved by this mover by means of its desire for it, I mean because it imitates it according to its ability as the lover is moved to [imitate] the beloved. All the other celestial bodies are moved by their desire for the motion of the first body.[12]

That is to say, the Prime Mover moves insofar as it is loved without being in its turn in movement (the Prime Mover is physically and metaphysically immobile); furthermore, it is the object of the desire of the creatures in an ascending scale of pleasures and appetites the basis of which is intellection.

> Having explained that the first mover is eternal, substance, pure actuality and free from matter, that it imparts motion without being moved but as object of desire and pleasure and that the principle of all motion is from something and towards something, he [Aristotle] wants to tell what the principle of this motion in the object moved is and what the object towards which there is motion is and says: 'the principle is the intellectual representation', meaning: the principle of this motion in the celestial body is intellectual representation.[13]

Averroes's Prime Mover is certainly something more spiritual than Aristotle's Prime Mover; furthermore, unlike the One of the Ismailis, it is not outside creation, nor does it have, as in Avicenna, an isolated intermediary between it and creation. This once again excludes emanation, but it does not exclude the existence of a close relationship between God and creation.

Chapter 6

The Human Intellect

The attempt to characterise and explain human intellect has been one of the constant concerns of Islamic philosophy. The exaltation of the role of the intellect as an instrument of understanding and as a vehicle of human perfection was not confined only, as might be expected, to those who were, strictly speaking, philosophers. Theologians too – such as al-Ghazālī – sought to do the same, but from an explicitly religious point of view. God made the intellect the instrument of the ordering of the cosmos. Furthermore, intellect makes man the authentic interpreter of God's words, and for this reason understanding is the noblest activity that he can pursue.

The doctrine of intellect in Islamic philosophy has a particularly irregular and stormy history. One undoubted cause of these difficulties lay in the fact that Islamic philosophers had to contend with an Aristotelian doctrine of the intellect that, as is well known, is particularly obscure and ambiguous. The main Aristotelian text is the Book III of *De Anima*, particularly Chapter V, where Aristotle speaks of a possible intellect and an active intellect: the first is analogous to matter and becomes all things; the active intellect is separate, pure and impassive and produces all things. The very general nature of Aristotle's formulations has naturally led later commentators to elaborate at length on what he really meant. The main commentators of antiquity were Alexander of Aphrodisias and Themistius, both of whom had an important role in the development of this theme in Islamic philosophy.

The first to set out a coherent theory of the human intellect was al-Kindī. He was the first Islamic philosopher to distinguish four types of intellect or Reason (*ʿaql*): 'the first is Reason which is always in act; the second is Reason which is in potentiality and is in the Soul; the third is the Reason which has passed from the state of potentiality in the soul to that of actuality; and the fourth is the Reason which we call the manifest'.[1] The first intellect, the intellect that is always active, is separated from matter and from the human body. It is possible that al-Kindī identifies it with the Neo-Platonic cosmic intellect, but it has not been possible to reach a definite conclusion in this matter. The potential or passive intellect is clearly considered to be part of the soul. When it receive intelligibles, it passes from being potential to being active. Thought arises, in particular, when the soul 'makes contact [*bāshara*] with intellect, that is, with intelligibles containing neither matter nor imagination'. The first intellect 'supplies' that which the soul 'acquires' and the product is 'intellect acquired (*al-ʿaql al-mustafād*) by the [human] soul from the first intellect'.[2]

Al-Fārābī deals with the question of the intellect in several of his works, the most important of which being the *Epistle on the Intellect* and *The Virtuous City*, and in doing so he discusses al-Kindī's ideas in depth. It is almost certain that the *Epistle* was written at an earlier date than the *Virtuous City*, the conclusions of which are mainly returned to in the *Book of Political Science*. In the *Epistle*, al-Fārābī seems basically to be commenting on Aristotle and explaining what the idea of the intellect means for the Greek philosopher. Apart, obviously, from the active intellect or Agent Intellect, he divides the human intellect into three kinds: the potential intellect, the active intellect and acquired intellect.

> The potential intellect is a certain soul or kind of soul or one of the soul's faculties, or a certain thing whose essence has been prepared or which is ready to abstract the quiddities and the forms of all the existing [beings] from their matter. [. . .] If the forms of the existing [beings] are produced [in that essence that is potential intellect], this essence becomes active intellect. [. . .] When the active intellect grasps the intelligibles that are, for it, forms insofar as they are grasped

> actively, [this] intellect that we said before was active intellect becomes now acquired intellect.[3]

Like al-Kindī, al-Fārābī sees the potential intellect as being part of the soul and the substrate of intellection; the active intellect is when that which is potential receives intelligibles, again as in al-Kindī. By contrast, the concept of acquired intellect seems to be different, appearing in al-Fārābī as a further perfecting of the active intellect in that it does not limit itself to receiving and actualising the intelligibles, but 'understands' them as such, grasping them as actual forms. The Agent Intellect is that which emanates illumination to the potential intellect – in itself passive and inert – thereby bringing about its activation and transformation into active intellect and then acquired intellect. Al-Fārābī uses the unoriginal but effective metaphor of the Sun and the eye:

> The relationship of the Agent Intellect to the potential intellect is like the relationship of the Sun to the eye, which is potential sight as long as it remains in the dark. When light is realised by the sight, in the air and in things of the same type, it becomes sight, through the light that is realised in it, active sight, and colours become actively seen. And we say that sight has become active sight not only because active light and transparency [that is, the means by which light spreads] have reached it, but also because, when active transparency reaches the sight, the forms of visible objects are realised in it.[4]

The Sun is the Agent Intellect; the eye before seeing is the potential intellect; the eye that sees, which is to say, sight in action that has received the light of the Sun, is the active intellect; sight where the forms of the objects seen are realised is acquired intellect.

While in the *Epistle*, al-Fārābī is perhaps confining himself to interpreting Aristotle, it is certainly his own view on the function of the intellect that he is expressing in *Virtuous City* in Chapter XXII on rational potential (corresponding to Chapter XIII in Walzer's edition) and Chapter XXVII on the dominant organ (Chapter XV in Walzer's edition). The two descriptions do not entirely correspond with one another, the second seeming to be an extension of the first. In the first, in Chapter XXII, al-Fārābī identifies three types of intellect: the material, potential or passive intellect, the active intellect and the

Agent Intellect. He says, 'But the human intellect which arises in man by nature from the very outset is a disposition in matter prepared to receive the imprints of the intelligibles, being itself potentially intellect [and "material intellect"] [. . .].'[5] (Walzer 1985, IV 13.1: 199). The potential intelligibles 'become actual intelligibles when they happen to be intelligized by the intellect in actuality'[6] (Walzer 1985, IV 13.2: 199). That is to say, the potential intellect is activated by receiving intelligibles. This occurs as a result of the intervention of the Agent Intellect, for the potential intelligibles

> are in need of something else which transfers them from potentiality to a state in which [the intellect] can make them actual. The agent which transfers them from potentiality to actuality is an existent. Its essence is an actual intellect of a particular kind and is separate from matter.

It is thus that the Agent Intellect operates in this context, exactly as in the *Epistle*, like the Sun in relation to sight. The relationship of the Agent Intellect to the material intellect 'is like the relation of the Sun to the eye'[7] (Walzer 1985, IV 13.2: 201). There is no mention here of acquired intellect which is discussed instead in Chapter XXVII. This time al-Fārābī is precise:

> Indeed any man whose Passive Intellect has thus been perfected by all the intelligibles and has become actually intellect and actually being thought, so that the intelligible in him has become identical with that which thinks in him, acquires an actual intellect which is superior to the Passive Intellect and more perfect and more separate from matter than the Passive Intellect. It is called the 'Acquired Intellect' and comes to occupy a middle position between the Passive Intellect and the Active Intellect, nothing else being between it and the Active Intellect. The Passive Intellect is thus like matter and substratum for the Acquired Intellect, and the Acquired Intellect like matter and substratum for the Active Intellect. [. . .].[8] (Walzer 1985, V 15.8: 243)

The place of acquired intellect is between the Agent Intellect and the passive, material or hylic intellect. It is a form of the passive intellect but a substrate of the Agent. Therefore the acquired intellect is the active intellect (that which has been received by the intelligibles and which is therefore the form of the passive intellect made ready to receive the intelligibles) projected towards a higher and transcendent sphere. When a man has realised and perfected acquired intellect, he finds himself in conjunction with the Agent Intellect: 'this man holds the most perfect rank of humanity'[9] (Walzer 1985, V 15.11: 245). We shall return to this conjunction below. First it is necessary to note that the context makes it impossible to decide unequivocally whether the acquired intellect is unique and found only in the philosopher-*imām* or whether it is a quality that can be extended to all human beings. The fact that al-Fārābī speaks about acquired intellect only here and not in Chapter XXII inclines me to the view that the level of maximum perfection of the active intellect, that is transformed into acquired intellect and is conjoined with the Agent, is reserved for the few, while for ordinary human beings there are only two sorts of intellect, potential and active. The way to perfection is selective, just as the immortality of the soul is selective. The argument developed in the *Virtuous City* presupposes that immortality is reserved for those who attain the rank of acquired intellect. This, since it can unite with the Agent, separates itself from material things, thus attaining a state of everlasting happiness. Only in this case is it possible to talk of individual immortality. Otherwise, immortality is associated with that kind of universal soul into which all the souls of the dead are drawn in an indeterminate unity.

Sticking firmly, as can clearly be seen, to the idea of the specificity of the Agent Intellect, Avicenna increases the number of gradations of the human intellect. He identifies four types: the material intellect which is potential without qualifications and therefore relates to all members of the human race; the intellect *in habitu* (*bi'l-malaka*), which is defined as 'possible potential' and represents the actualisation of thought that occurs when the intellect receives the first intelligibles; the active intellect which, for Avicenna, is not possible intellect that has become actualised after receiving intelligibles, but another kind of potential, 'complete' potential which allows intelligible forms, that is the propositions and derived concepts, to be received in addition to the first intelligibles; lastly, acquired intellect that properly occupies the place reserved by other thinkers for the active intellect, since it corresponds to the phase in which the intellect has received or acquired from outside intelligible forms that are absolutely active. As can be seen, Avicenna introduces a number of new elements into the schema constructed by al-Kindī and al-Fārābī. Furthermore, according to H. Davidson, in addition to changes in the definitions of active and acquired intellects, he gives even more importance to the influence of the Agent Intellect in activating human intellect:

> In Alfarabi, the term acquired intellect designated the highest stage of human intellectual development, and Alfarabi's choice of the term was problematic, because the highest stage in his scheme of intellect is not in fact acquired from an external source but rather fashioned from below and within, by human effort. Avicenna's acquired intellect is, literally, acquired from the active intellect [the Agent Intellect].[10]

In other words, while in al-Fārābī, the acquired intellect is the product of a spontaneous perfecting of the active intellect, in Avicenna it is made to be such by the intervention of the Agent. This intervention by the Agent is compared once again to the light of the Sun. As the light of the Sun, combining with the human capacity to see, makes colours that are potentially visible actually seen, so the power of the Agent Intellect is directed towards the potential intelligibles in the imaginative faculty with the aim of making them actually intelligible and of transforming the potential intellect into actual intellect.

The pre-eminent role reserved for the Agent Intellect can be justified in the light of the fact that Avicenna, particularly in his late works, imposes a metaphysical reading on the reality of the human intellect and the active intellect, interpreting a passage in the Qur'an allegorically as a revelation of this sort of 'transcendent psychology'. This is the section 24.35 in the *sūrah* entitled 'Light', al-Ghazālī's commentary on which in relation to God's essence has already been mentioned. Avicenna takes up this subject in two works, in the *Book of Directives and Remarks* and in the *Epistle on Prophecy*. In the first treatise, after distinguishing the practical intellect (the faculty that chooses what things must be done in order to achieve particular ends) from the speculative intellect, he writes:

> Among the faculties of the soul, there is that which it possesses to enable it to perfect its own substance, making it active intelligence. It is a faculty that prepares it to turn towards the intelligibles; some people call it material intellect and it corresponds to the niche. This is

> followed by another faculty that comes to the soul during the activation in it of the first intelligibles. With this new faculty, [the soul] is ready to acquire the second [intelligibles]; either, if it remains weak, by means of reflection – which is the olive – or through intellectual intuition – which is the oil – if intuition is stronger than reflection. This [second faculty] is called the intellect *in habitu* and it corresponds to the crystal. A noble and mature faculty is a holy faculty, 'in which the oil will shine'. A little later, an active faculty and perfection reach it. Perfection consists in the fact that the intelligibles are given [to the soul] actively, in an intuition that represents them to the spirit, and is 'Light on Light'. The faculty consists in that which realises the acquired intelligible, thus brought to its completion, as it is the object of the intuition, without needing to acquire it, and it is the lamp. This perfection is called acquired intellect and this faculty is called active intellect. It is the Agent Intellect that causes the intellect to pass from being *in habitu* to being active, and also the material intellect to being *in habitu*, and this corresponds to the flame.[11]

Avicenna's exposition is anything but simple but may perhaps be interpreted as follows. The intellects are contained one within the other, or rather they are not different species of intellects but different forms of a single intellect. Within the niche (the material intellect) is the lamp (the active intellect), which is in turn contained in the crystal (the intellect *in habitu*). This corresponds in fact to a hierarchy of perfection. Reflection and intellectual intuition are the instruments (the olive and the oil) by means of which the intellect *in habitu* prepares to perfect itself through the actualisation of the intelligibles. The perfection thus attained is the acquired intellect and the actualised intelligibles are 'Light on Light'. The Agent Intellect is the flame that lights the oil and kindles the flame of intellection within the human intellect.

The question of intellection thus often leads Muslim philosophers to project themselves into a mystic dimension. This occurs in the case not only of Avicenna, but also of Avempace, a thinker who, in some of his works (such as the *Regime of the Solitary*) seems to abandon entirely any religious dimension in favour of a severe intellectualism. The intellectual mysticism of the *Regime* can, however, be detected in all Avempace's other works, although it is sometimes veiled or conveyed in entirely transcendent terms. In the *Treatise on the Union of the*

Intellect with Man, for example, Avempace first of all distinguishes between the active intellect (*al-ʿaql biʾl-fiʿl*) and the Agent Intellect (*al-ʿaql al-fāʿil*). The active intellect is the mover of man (section 5: 'the prime mover of man is the active intellect that is also the active intelligible; in fact, the active intellect is the active intelligible'); if it were one all men would be numerically one without any distinction between one individual and the next (section 6: 'if this intellect were numerically one in every man, it would follow that all men, present, past and future would be numerically one, but this conclusion is absurd and impossible'). The active intellect is therefore a property of each single individual. The Agent Intellect is what triggers off the intellective process. To use the usual metaphor, the Agent Intellect performs the same function, in the relationship between intellect and intelligibles, that is performed by light in the relationship between eye and seen object (section 16).[12] The Agent Intellect confers on man the knowledge of universal intelligibles and converts the potential intellect into acquired intellect. It is this acquired intellect that represents the highest level of man's intellective perfection and that connects and joins with the Agent Intellect. Although Avempace is not clear on this point, it would seem that he is concluding that the Agent Intellect corresponds to God.

Avempace then goes on to distinguish between three levels of understanding: that of the common people; that of the intellectuals (in other words, the solitary man and the 'plants' of the *Regime*); and that of those 'happy ones' who have attained total separation from the body (the intellective mystics of the *Regime*). This distinction is expanded on in section 15 of the *Treatise on the Union of the Intellect with Man*. The first category is that of the common people whose intellect is attached to material forms. Secondly, there is the level of speculative understanding which represents the highest attainment of human nature. In the third place, there is the level of those happy men who 'see' things in their true essence. Avempace explains this hierarchy by referring to the Platonic myth of the cave (section 17). The common people are chained up in the cave and cannot see the light of the Sun; they see existing things as obscure shadows. The category of speculative people go out of the cave and are able to seize the colours and light of the Sun. The truly happy are those who, by perfecting their nature to the furthermost limits, become similar to the Sun and to the seen object (*ammā al-suʿadāʾ . . . yasīrūna hum al-shayyʾ*). This third state of intellection is bestowed by God on the most worthy of his servants who, becoming similar to the Sun become united with the Agent Intellect (section 19). The intellect becomes like a light among lights (section 7). Avempace says that 'this intellect, that is one, is a gift and a grace that God bestows on the most beloved of his servants' (section 7). Here there is no longer, as in the *Regime of the Solitary* (also known as *The Hermit's Guide*), an exclusively intellective realisation, but a realisation that, while still intellective, results from an explicitly divine intervention. This state obviously makes it possible to attain that level of beatitude defined in *sharīʿa* as belonging to saints and prophets. This state of intellection is single and those who share it, as for al-Fārābī, are part of a single soul and not subject to suffering or corruption (section 20).

As with cosmology, when Averroes turns his mind to a consideration of intellect and intellection, he finds himself confronted with an established and well-developed tradition. He therefore borrows arguments and technical terminology from his predecessors. It would, however, be impossible to attempt to summarise Averroes's ideas in the space of a few pages. There is a simple reason for this: over a period of forty years or more of speculative study and writing, Averroes's ideas on the subject underwent a profound evolution and modification. The viewpoint outlined in the *Medium Commentary* of Aristotle's *De Anima* are not those of the *Large Commentary* (*tafsīr*). Here I shall attempt to chart as coherent a course as possible, drawing chiefly on the *Large Commentary* which, being composed quite late in his career (probably around 1190), best represents, I believe, the author's definitive views.

Averroes starts by giving the Agent Intellect a central and pre-eminent role in the intellective journey. It is the Agent Intellect that produces intelligible forms by actualising them within the psycho-gnoseological process. 'The intelligibles that have entered naturally into our possession come from something that is in itself intellect and is separated from materiality – which is to say from the Agent Intellect'.[13] Again it is the Agent Intellect that acts on the material intellect 'conjoining' it with intelligible forms. The way in which this occurs is described in the usual way:

> You must know that the relationship of the Agent Intellect with this [material] intellect is like the relationship of the light with

> transparency and that the relationship of the material forms with this intellect is like that of colour with transparency. Just as light perfects transparency, so the Agent Intellect perfects the material intellect.[14]

As the light of the Sun, by actualising the means (the air) also actualises visible objects, allowing the eye to see them, so the Agent Intellect actualises the potential intelligibles making them acquirable by the human intellect.

The material intellect is also called the intellect *in habitu*, in the sense that it has the capacity to think and conceive intelligibles according to the intention of the thinking subject.[15] This type of intellect in Averroes is similar to that described in Avicenna as 'possible potential', or as the intellect that contains all the primary intelligibles. According to De Libera, the *intellectus in habitu* (al-ʿaql bi'l-malaka) is in fact understood here in the Avicennian sense of first perfection of man as man, acquired naturally with the emanation of the first intelligibles through the intervention of the Agent Intellect.[16] The acquired intellect or *adeptus* is the material intellect once it has become united or *copulatus* with the Agent Intellect.[17] The speculative intellect (*intellectus speculativus*) is, by contrast, more or less the same as that which, in earlier thinkers, corresponded to the active intellect. Before going any further, we need to examine the material intellect a little more closely, given that Averroes's doctrine on this subject (the doctrine of the single material intellect, separate and eternal) was widely known and discussed by medieval philosophers in the Latin West.

Averroes's concept of the material intellect thus underwent such radical revision that, if examined at the beginning or the end of his career, it will seem almost unrecognisable:

> At an early stage of his thought, we can conclude with a fair degree of confidence, Averroes followed Ibn Bājja [Avempace] and construed the material intellect as a disposition in the imaginative faculty of the soul. Somewhat later [. . .] he construed the material intellect, with Alexander [of Aphrodisias], as a disposition in the soul without specifically locating it in the imaginative faculty. Still later, he arrived at the intermediate theory that an individual material intellect is engendered whenever the active intellect joins the inborn disposition awaiting it in an individual human soul. At what we can presume was

> the crowning stage of his thought, he construed the human material intellect as a single eternal substance shared by all men, consisting in the quasi matter that analysis can discover in other incorporeal beings and standing immediately below the active intellect in the hierarchy of existence.[18]

In the *Large Commentary* Averroes is explicit:

> He who supposes that the material intellect can be generated and is corruptible, cannot, it seems to me, find any natural way by which we can unite ourselves (*continuari*) with separated intelligibles. Indeed, the intellect must be identical to the intelligible from all points of view, and even more so in things free of matter.[19]

The material intellect is not generated and cannot be corrupted, which is to say it is eternal: this is the first presupposition. The intellect 'makes' things 'known to itself': to learn the intelligibles means to be 'intelligent' and to 'become' the intelligibles. This identity between intelligence and object intellect derives naturally from Averroes's realistic conviction: for him the structures of the mind and the structures of reality are like mirror images of one another.

There are two basic reasons – and these can easily be reduced to one – why Averroes hypothesises a single and separate material intellect. On the one hand, material intellect that was mere potential and which was tightly united to the human body would not be able to receive incorporeal intelligible forms; the nature of intelligibles is, furthermore, such that they cannot be received a single individualised material intellect, for otherwise the intelligibles would become individualised and would lose their universality. On the other hand, if the material intellect can receive all intelligible forms, this means that, originally, it was entirely without such forms. Whichever way it is understood, we are bound to conclude that the material intellect is incorporeal. Following inevitably from this is its separateness in relation to the human body; and following from its separateness is its oneness.

> How can that which is corruptible think that which it is not? [. . .] To we who have supposed that the material intellect is eternal and that the material intellect contemplates both material forms and separate

> forms, it is clear that the subject of the speculative intelligibles and of the Agent Intellect is one and the same, that is, the material [intellect].[20]

The material intellect is therefore, like the Agent Intellect, unique, eternal and separate. As is well known, Averroes's conclusion was repugnant to the Christian Church because, like all of Averroes's noetics, it appeared to deny the individual immortality of the soul, immortality being guaranteed exclusively to an intellect that, once separated from the body, has lost all the memories, specificity and capacities of that single individual human being to whom it had been connected. In my view, in the light of his definitive opinion, Averroes would certainly not have rejected this interpretation, given that he is concerned to discover new paths that might guarantee the immortality of individuals, something that is also part of the Islamic religion. Whether such a definitive opinion correctly interprets Aristotle is open to doubt; it is likely, in fact, that Averroes departs somewhat from Aristotle's admittedly cryptic ideas.

We must, therefore, turn to the speculative intellect. It is this that makes up the disposition of the concrete individual. The speculative intellect represents a sort of composite whole, the material of which is supplied with the material intellect and the form of the Agent Intellect. The text that perhaps most clearly sets out these ideas is the following:

> This is why it is necessary to assert – as has already become clear from Aristotle's discourse – that in the soul there are two parts to the intellect. One is receptive, the being of which we explain here, the other is agent. This has the effect of making the intentions contained in the imaginative faculty into active movers of the material intellect after having been potential movers, as Aristotle's discourse will also show. These two parts are neither generable nor corruptible. The relationship of the receiver to the Agent is like that of matter to form.
>
> This is why Themistius says that we are the Agent Intellect and that the speculative intellect is nothing other than the conjunction of the Agent Intellect with the material intellect. But things are not as he believed. We need, rather, to imagine that the intellect has three parts: one is the receiving intellect, the second is the efficient intellect and the third [speculative intellect] is product. Of these three, two are eternal, that is the agent and the receiving intellects. As for the

> third, it is in a sense generable and corruptible and in another sense eternal.[21]

Having established that the material intellect and the Agent Intellect can similarly be neither generated nor corrupted, Averroes goes on to define the speculative intellect as the product of their unification. In this case, it seems clear how the speculative intellect connects the corporeal dimension of intellection with the transcendent dimension. We need to ask, therefore, if it is mortal or immortal, whether it perishes with the body or not. We have just read that Averroes maintains that the speculative intellect is partly generated and corruptible and partly not.

The problem is a thorny one: since it is not possible to locate the basis of individual human immortality in the material intellect – which is, however, a tenet of Islam – where should we look to find it? The fact is that Averroes, at least when he speaks as interpreter of and commentator on Aristotle in the *Large Commentary*, does not seem to leave space for any kind of individual immortality.[22] In his complex analysis of the intellect, he also speaks of a passive intellect (clearly different from the material intellect), but, believing that he is representing the authentic opinion of Aristotle, he says that this is the imaginative faculty: '*intendit per intellectum passivum virtutem imaginativam*'.[23] Commenting on Aristotle's text (no. 33, 'he thinks in fact as if he were seeing things through the imagination'), during the last phase of his noetic thinking, Averroes locates the authentic individual cognitive power in the imaginative faculty. The fact is that 'Aristotle says that the cognitive virtue that he calls possible intellect is also generated and corruptible'.[24] This seems to leave little room for doubt: the cognitive faculty in close relationship with the imaginative virtue dies with the death of the body. Therefore there is no individual immortality with the material intellect since it is single and separate; there is no individual immortality in the imaginative and cognitive faculties because they perish with the corruption of the body.

It seems in fact that only the speculative intellect can guarantee some form of immortality, but in a very particular way. In that it is not generated or corruptible, the speculative intellect resembles closely the kind of general intellect proposed by Dante in the *Monarchia*, where understanding belongs, not so much to isolated beings (al-Fārābī's *imām*-philosopher or Avempace's solitary), as to humanity in general, through whom knowledge and philosophy will always – and certainly sooner or later – be realised somewhere. According to Averroes:

> Since this discourse has led us to the conclusion that the material intellect is one for all humankind, and that, from this, we have also been led to consider the human species to be eternal, [we assert now] that, necessarily, the material intellect cannot be deprived of the natural principles common to all humankind, which is to say the first propositions and first simple concepts common to all [mankind]. These intelligibles are single according to the receiver, but multiple according to the intention received. Therefore, according to the modality by which they are single, they are necessarily also eternal. [. . .] This is why, when, from the fact of its relation to an individual, one of the first intelligibles finds itself corrupted following the corruption of the subject thanks to which it has united itself to us and it is true, this intelligible is necessarily not corruptible in the absolute sense, but only in relation to the individual. And this is the reason why we can say that the speculative intellect is one in all [humankind].
>
> Since wisdom exists in a particular way characteristic to men, just as different sorts of artefacts exist according to ways particular to men, we consider it impossible that the whole inhabited Earth should be without philosophy, exactly as it is impossible that it be without natural arts. If, in fact, a certain part [of the Earth] were to be without, meaning the arts, for example the northern quarter of the Earth, the other quarters would not be without, since it is established that it is possible to inhabit both the southern and the northern parts. Consequently, philosophy will be able to exist in all times in the greater part of the subject just as man exists thanks to man, and the horse thanks to the horse. Thus, in this way, the speculative intellect is neither generable nor corruptible.[25]

The conclusion that can be drawn at this point from Averroes's reasoning is somewhat disturbing: the intellect continues to think in the human species, which is eternal as the intellect is eternal, even if single individual humans disappear. *Thought is, as it were, hypothesised and separated from the individuality of the thinking subject. It is not single human beings who think, but separate intellects that think through humans. Since intellects never cease from thinking, there will always be, thanks to them, humans who think. This guarantees the eternity of the human species but not, of course, the eternity of the single individual.* Individual immortality is, however, possible if it is accepted that the speculative intellect, insofar as it is a faculty available to the concrete individual, is always in activity, this thanks to the intervention of the Agent Intellect, and is to be separated from the bodily corruption of single individuals. The speculative intellect is immortal, and with it the single individual human being, since it participates in the whole complex mechanism of the universal intellection. The Agent Intellect is always active, continually actualising the speculative intellect from the material intellect, and thus actualising intelligible forms. Thanks to this actualisation of the function of thought, even the individual speculative intellect can become eternal and participate in the beatitude of the Agent Intellect. This is the conclusion reached by the Aristotelian Averroes even if, not surprisingly, in his theological works (the *Decisive Treatise* or the *Unveiling of the Methods of Proof*) he claims to accept the traditional Islamic dogma of the immortality of the individual soul.

We have already referred several times to the notion of 'conjunction' or 'contact', a key element in Islamic speculation on the intellect. If the Agent Intellect represents the light that illuminates the intelligibles and intervenes on the intellect so that it can acquire them and if the Agent Intellect is form while the human intellect is matter then it is clear that there is contact between the Agent Intellect and the human intellect. This connection, called *ittiṣāl* in Arabic, was rendered as *continuatio* or *copulatio* in Latin. This conjunction represents the highest level of human perfection and, at the same time the source of truest happiness. Naturally the primary source drawn on by the Muslim philosophers is Aristotle, through the mediation of commentators such as Alexander of Aphrodisias and Themistius. But their viewpoint goes beyond that of Aristotle since, for them, conjunction constitutes the moment when man (the philosopher) attains, during his life, direct perception of God. While generally being only the last of the separated Intelligences, the Agent Intellect is, however, the only portal through which man (the philosopher) can gain entry to the world of divine sovereignty, insofar as it is granted to him and it is possible given the absolute transcendence and distance of God-One. Intellectual happiness is, therefore, the earthly enjoyment that the philosopher draws from his relationship with God. The human intellect, received from the cosmic context, does not limit itself to contemplation (as may be deduced from Aristotle) but participates actively in the harmony of the universal order.

Al-Kindī had already conceived the possibility of a connection of the human soul with the transcendent Intelligence that takes place when intelligible forms contained in the human soul become one with Intelligence. In this way, the human soul becomes intellectually active and actualised. It is once again al-Fārābī, however, who hypothesises a degree of refinement and development of the human intellect raised to such a pitch that the Agent Intellect takes up residence in it:

> And when the natural disposition is made the matter of the Passive Intellect which has become actually intellect, and the Passive Intellect the matter of the Acquired Intellect, and when all this is taken as one and the same thing, then this man is the man on whom the Active Intellect has descended.[26] (Walzer 1985, V 15.9: 245)

Al-Fārābī speaks of 'infusion' or of 'inherence', using the verb *halla*, a word of significance also in Muslim mysticism where the term *hulūl*, derived from *halla*, is used to refer to God's 'inhabitation' of the mystic, almost the incarnation of God in the mystic. This state of perfection and bliss appears to be attainable by every philosopher, even if, when speaking of the philosopher-*imām*-prophet-king on the same page of the *Virtuous City*, al-Fārābī seems to give him direct contact, since 'his soul is perfect and united to the Agent Intellect'. (In his edition of the Arabic text, Richard Walzer interpolates a *ka*, thus making the sentence more hypothetical: 'his soul is perfect and *as if* united with the Agent Intellect'.) What is beyond doubt is that, for the mature al-Fārābī, conjunction is a given fact. In the last period of his writing, however, and particularly in the *Commentary on the Nichomachean Ethics*, al-Fārābī seems to have changed his mind entirely. This work has not survived but the evidence of other authors, particularly Averroes, tells us that, at the end of his life as a philosopher, al-Fārābī dismissed his belief in the possibility of conjunction, asserting that it was nothing more than 'an old wives' tale'. A certain scepticism seems to have taken over when he states that the only and ultimate happiness possible for human beings is political happiness resulting from the perfecting of human faculties and opportunities within the framework of social life.

While in al-Fārābī, at least in the *Virtuous City*, the process of conjunction seems to imply a kind of spiritual perfecting, Avicenna and Avempace consider *copulatio* in more intellectual terms. For Avicenna, 'conjunction with the external active element is not a miraculous ecstatic element, but a technical constant of the logical-abstractive process that is repeated every day, lodging the resulting abilities (but not the intelligibles) in the intellect *in habitu*'. For Avempace, 'knowing and identifying itself with the intelligibles in itself the speculative intellect unites itself at the same time with the Agent Intellect that produces them'.[27]

Averroes, on the other hand, is a convinced upholder of the facticity of conjunction. In the *Large Commentary on De Anima*, he says that the Agent Intellect and the material human intellect unite in such a way as to be, at one and the same time, individual and unified: 'They are in fact two because of the diversity of their action; the action of the Agent Intellect is to generate while that of the material intellect is to be informed. But they are also one since the material intellect is perfected by the Agent and so understands it'.[28] This conclusion leads the Averroes of the commentaries, the purely Aristotelian Averroes, to identify the path to immortality as lying in the conjunction between the material intellect and the Agent Intellect. As Davidson says:

> Like Aristotle and philosophers standing in the Aristotelian tradition, Averroes rules out the immortality of the non-intellectual parts of the human soul. He further rejects the immortality of theoretical human thought linked in any way to perceptions of the physical world, his grounds being that such thought depends upon non-intellectual parts of the soul, which perish with the brain. The only aspect of man capable of immortality, in Averroes' view, is therefore the material intellect. In works where he construes the material intellect as a disposition for thought in the human organism, and where he defends the possibility of the material intellect's conjoining with the active intellect, he recognises the immortality of material intellects that achieve conjunction.[29]

It is the general nature of the eternal and separate material intellect that guarantees the immortality of humanity as a species and, as was seen above, guarantees that the intellect, actualised by the Agent Intellect, will continue to think even after the death of the individual. Conjunction comes about, therefore, thanks to that part of the material intellect that is contained within every human being and which, when it unites with the Agent Intellect, continues on beyond the death of the individual.

Chapter 7

Necessity or Freedom in Divine Action

Theories advanced on the subject of the Oneness of God and the cosmic system deriving from it pose a number of important and interesting questions. First and foremost, the absolutely transcendent God of the philosophers seems to conflict with the Qur'anic image of an omniscient and omnipresent God. The God of the philosophers seems remote and separate, knowing little of and little involved with either the functioning of nature or human passions. The knowledge He has of himself seems to prevent Him from knowing the minutiae and details of anything that happens below Him (it is significant that one of the most direct criticisms of the philosophers made by al-Ghazālī is that they deny that God has knowledge of individual things). The emanation structure proposed by al-Fārābī and Avicenna (and also Averroes's idea of the Prime Mover) exclude creation *ex nihilo*, something that is strongly affirmed by the Qur'an, and require divine action. The effect of this requirement is to hamper and limit God's omnipotence.

It was in this context, and prompted by the fear that philosophy might damage or nullify the tenets of faith, that al-Ghazālī spoke out against the philosophers, invoking an absolute and extreme theism where God, although still transcendent, is the only creator and the only agent. Al-Ghazālī sets out to demonstrate that philosophy is not capable of supporting as much as it boldly claims. Not because philosophy is insincere, for it too believes in the need to profess the Oneness of God and His ability to create the world, but because the tools of philosophy are not sufficiently refined to allow them to penetrate into the innermost secrets of a God who, in any case, remains unyielding to human understanding. Al-Ghazālī pursues this aim by attacking philosophy with philosophical tools, challenging the philosophers on their own ground and revealing their *incoherence*. Averroes in far away al-Andalus responds, anxious to explain how philosophy is perfectly able to satisfy the requirements of reason and dedicated to revealing the *incoherence of the incoherence* of the opponents of the philosophers. In my opinion, the debate between al-Ghazālī and Averroes marks the high point in medieval Islamic philosophy for two reasons: not only does it question the overall meaning of the system of causes and hence of the natural order of things, but it also brings to the fore the dialectic of reason seen from a markedly Islamic viewpoint.[1]

Before examining the crux of the debate, therefore, it is vital to take a brief look at the epistemological attitudes of the two opponents. Perhaps surprisingly, al-Ghazālī considers mathematics to be a rigorous science offering certain and solid theorems: 'it deals with irrefutable things based on proof'.[2] On the other hand, far from denying the usefulness of the tools of reason, he defends the cogency of Aristotelian logic and maintains that demonstration leads to true conclusions. M. Marmura has commented on the paradoxical nature of al-Ghazālī's position that embraces the deductive and demonstrative rigour of science while, at the same time, denying the causal connection of phenomena:

> in his writings, al-Ghazālī does not deny the claim that demonstration can give us a certain knowledge about the natural order. [. . .] He seems for the most part to be reproducing the essentials of the Aristotelian demonstrative theory [athough] in one section he reaffirms his rejection of necessary causal connection in nature. [. . .] This, then, is al-Ghazālī's unqualified rejection of essential efficient causality in nature. Just as unqualified, however, is his defence of demonstrative science, which for Aristotelians involves the causal theory he rejects. Hence the paradox.[3]

The apparent contradiction may, perhaps, be resolved if we remember that, for al-Ghazālī, as a Muslim thinker, the only true necessity is ontologically divine will, to which nature is subject. Therefore, even if human beings are capable of establishing valid and rigorously argued *a priori* schema of reasoning, this does not mean that they can immediately grasp the logic of God's voluntary actions. It must be said that it is not immediately clear in al-Ghazālī that thought corresponds to reality. Thought functions on a different plane from reality, where the action of God that is inscrutable is explained.

Averroes, on the other hand, establishes a very close link between reality and thought. This link is well described by Miguel Cruz Hernández:

> [For Averroes] there can be no demonstration unless it is supported by the ontological structure of reality, starting from the fundamental pillar of the principle of non-contradiction. The thing that allows the formal reality of nature to convert itself into the formal reality of the human intellect is the relation of fundamental consubstantiality that exists between the ontological and the gnoseological worlds.[4]

The *Incoherence of the Incoherence* is unequivocal on this subject: 'for truth (*sādiq*), as it has been defined, is the agreement of what is in the soul with what is outside the soul'[5] (Van Den Bergh 1954: 60). It continues, approaching from the opposite point of view: 'Existence in the nature of things is a logical concept which affirms the conformity of a thing outside the soul with what is inside the soul'[6] (Van Den Bergh 1954: 179). Therefore, 'true knowledge is the knowledge of a thing as it is in reality'[7] (Van Den Bergh 1954: 325). These different epistemological stances explain how it is that al-Ghazālī and Averroes are able to develop two different concepts of causality. An examination of the problem of causality, arguably the key element of the dispute, can more usefully take place within the broader framework of a consideration of creation. Whereas al-Ghazālī asserts that the world is produced by God with an act of volition whereby the universe exists in time, the philosophers, including Averroes, maintain that the world is eternal. The two adversaries conceive of creation in different ways. For al-Ghazālī it is the result of the intervention of God who acts, as creator, in three main ways:

> *Al-Khāliq* – the Creator, *Al-Bāri'* – the Producer, *Al-Musawwir* – the Fashioner. It might be thought that these names are synonymous, and that they all refer to creating and inventing. But it does not need to be that way. Rather, everything which comes forth from nothing to existence needs first of all to be planned; secondly, to be originated according to the plan [intended]; and thirdly, to be formed after being originated. God – may He be praised and exalted – is creator [*khāliq*] inasmuch as He is the planner [*muqaddir*], producer [*bāri'*] inasmuch as He initiates existence, and fashioner [*musawwir*] inasmuch as He arranges the forms of the things invented in the finest way.[8]

Thus creation consists essentially of two stages: firstly the drawing of existence from non existence according to a rational programme; then the determination of existence according to a specific form and its own laws. In Averroes, by contrast,

> Creation must [has to] be understood in a distributive rather than collective sense[9]

Creation, then, is the continuous production of contingent, generated and corruptible beings within a cosmos that is in substance ungenerated and incorruptible. This continuous production is upheld in the *Incoherence of the Incoherence* as the authentic form of creation, the authentic way of attributing eternity to the cosmos and the most worthy of being attributed to God. On the one hand, '[the philosophers] do not mean by the expression 'eternal' that the world is eternal through eternal consituents, for the world consists of movement. [. . .] Therefore the term 'eternal becoming' (*hudūth dā'im*) is more appropriate to the world than the term 'eternity' (*qidam*)'[10] (Van Den Bergh 1954: 193–204). On the other hand,

> if the meaning of 'eternal' is that it is in everlasting production and that this production has neither beginning nor end, certainly the term 'production' is more truly applied to him who brings about an everlasting production than to him who procures a limited production. In this way the world is God's product and the name 'production' is even more suitable for it than the word 'eternity'.[11] (Van Den Bergh 1954: 96–7)

It will be noted that Averroes uses the word 'emanate', the same term that al-Fārābī used, even if the communication that exists between God and the world is mediated by movement. Here, as also in the *Decisive Treatise*, he very clearly anticipates the general idea of the eternal nature of the cosmos even if not in every detail: God, who has no cause for His existence, is authentically eternal; contingent, generable and corruptible beings are authentically created; the world in general is a kind of intermediary, that is neither generated nor corruptible, but which nevertheless has an eternal cause for its existence and is therefore eternal in that it is eternally caused or produced.[12]

The debate about whether or not the world is eternal takes up the greater part of the *Incoherence of the Incoherence*. The arguments put forward by Averroes in support of its eternity are certainly consistent. First and foremost, he makes use of the philosophical 'prejudice' according to which *ex nihilo nihil*. To derive existence from non existence is not only a physical impossibility, but also a logical one: that which is inexistent can never exist (for Averroes, as we have seen, it is absurd to speak of something in itself 'possible'). Secondly, the doctrine of creation from nothing and in time introduces significant contradictions in the idea of God. Why would God have chosen, in the course of the infinite passing of time, one particular moment to create rather than another? There are only two possible answers: either He acted upon whim, without any particular motive, and thus appears imperfect since He is swayed by unjustifiable caprices; or else He acted because induced to act by some need or lack. In this case He appears equally, if not more, imperfect because constrained by necessity or driven by desire or lack, both incompatible with his perfection and absolute completeness. Consequently, it is logical to deduce that God created or produced the universe in eternity, escaping in this way from the constraints of temporality. Thirdly, if the world had been created in time, there would have been an infinite time *a parte ante* before finite time *a parte post*, which is absurd. Finally, Averroes anticipates a question that was to be formulated a few centuries later by Giordano Bruno to justify the infinity of the universe: how can we imagine a God who for an infinite time was idle and inactive before starting to act? It is not possible to impose aims or terms on the Creator's omnipotence: 'When one imagines an eternal entity whose acts are not delayed after its existence – as indeed must be the case with any entity whose existence is perfect [. . .]'[13] (Van Den Bergh 1954: 72).

As we said above, to be the agent of a continuous production is more appropriate to God than to be the agent of a discontinuous and interrupted production. Averroes seeks to safeguard the ontological superiority of God with regard to creation: even if the universe is 'eternal', in the sense of being eternally produced, it is nevertheless caused and its cause, God, is obviously superior and antecedent to it.

We do not know, of course, how al-Ghazālī would have answered Averroes's arguments. Nevertheless, in all probability the confrontation would not have been able to continue given the radical differences between the philosophical presuppositions that were the starting points for the two thinkers. Above all, there is the fact that al-Ghazālī conceives God as a free agent who wants to choose between compossible models of the universe, creating one rather than another according to His judgement – but without being confined by any necessity or having to obey a particular aim. To explain what he means, he puts forward an unusual but not entirely convincing metaphor:

> How then will you refute those who say that rational proof has led to establishing in God a quality the nature of which is to differentiate between two similar things? And, if the word 'will' does not apply, call it by another name, for let us not quibble about words! We only use the term 'will' by permission of the Divine Law. It may be objected that by its conventional meaning 'will' designates that which has desire, and God has no desire, but we are concerned here with a question not of words but of fact. Besides, we do not even with respect to our human will concede that this cannot be imagined. Suppose two similar dates in front of a man who has a strong desire for them, but who is unable to take them both. Surely he will take one of them through a quality in him the nature of which is to differentiate between two similar things. All the distinguishing qualities you have mentioned, like beauty or nearness or facility in taking, we can assume to be absent, but still the possibility of the taking remains.[14] (Van Den Bergh 1954: 21)

Averroes seems to have no difficulty in responding that al-Ghazālī's example does not stand up:

> For, when one supposes such a thing, and a willer whom necessity prompts to eat or to take the date, then it is by no means a matter of distinguishing between two similar things when, in this condition, he takes one of the two dates. It is nothing but the admission of an equivalence of two similar things; for whichever of the two dates he may take, his aim will be attained and his desire satisfied. His will attaches itself therefore merely to the distinction between the fact of taking one of them and the fact of leaving them altogether; it attaches itself by no means to the act of taking one definite date and distinguishing this act from the act of leaving the other (that is to say, when it is assumed that the desires for the two are equal); he does not prefer the act of taking the one to the act of taking the other, but he prefers the act of taking one of the two, whichever it may be, and he gives a preference to the act of taking over the act of leaving.[15] (Van Den Bergh 1954: 23)

So, for Averroes, the choice with regard to God is not between the creation of one world and the creation of another compossibile with the first, but between creation and inactivity. Given that it would be inconceivable for God to be inactive, he deduces from this that the world is eternal. For al-Ghazālī, the eternity of the world implies the incapacity of God to act freely and to choose the best and most functional model of universe; for Averroes, if the world were merely contingent, the infinite power of God would be negated by this ontological limitation.

In any case, by specifying that the man who chooses between the two date trees is starving, al-Ghazālī puts forwards a false example. Hunger implies constraint and if God were that man, it would mean that his choice between one world and another compossible one was constrained by an external factor that induced him to make the distinction. But, on the other hand, Averroes is wrong to confuse similes with opposites. According to al-Ghazālī, God is faced with a multiplicity of equivalent choices rather than with the dilemma of choice. Shifting the problem to that of a clear alternative between opposites, Averroes is entirely right in asserting that will in itself cannot imply choice between two homologues: if I am hungry, eating from one date tree rather than another is not significant from the point of view of my satisfaction and I will pay no attention to whether one date tree is more mature than the other or has fruit that are easier to pick. In doing this, however, Averroes is unfaithful to al-Ghazālī's example and changes the rules of the game; since al-Ghazālī too is right in maintaining that, if God is omnipotent, His will does not relate to two contraries, but to two equivalents, since either of the possibilities are identical for him.

This failure to understand one another is not surprising: the two adversaries held concepts that are opposed from many points of view. There are four aspects to be examined, relating to the concepts of time; possibility, action/agent and, lastly, cause.

In the first place, for al-Ghazālī, time begins with creation. Before the world was created time did not exist, given that God is outside time:

> The objection to this [the philosophers' argument] is: Time is generated and created [*ḥādith makhlūq*], and before it there was no time at all. The meaning of our words that God is prior to the world and to time is: He existed without the world and without time, then He existed and with Him there was the world and there was time. And the meaning of our words that He existed without the world is: the existence of the essence of the Creator and the non-existence of the essence of the world, and nothing else. And the meaning of our words that He existed and with Him there was the world is: the existence of the two essences, and nothing else. (Van Den Bergh 1954: 38)

Once again, al-Ghazālī minimises the importance of the contingent existence of the world compared to the absolute existence of God who, philosophically, is made to coincide with His essence. For Averroes, on the other hand, time is the measure of movement and of things which is why it is a property inherent to the existence of the universe: 'there are two kinds of existence: one in the nature of which there is motion and which cannot be separated from time; the other in the nature of which there is no motion and which is eternal and cannot be described in terms of time' (Van Den Bergh 1954: 38).

Averroes concedes to al-Ghazālī that God is outside time, but maintains that temporality is a natural characteristic of being: 'It is not of the nature of the Creator to be in time, whereas it belongs to the nature of the world to be so; and for this very reason it is not true that He is either simultaneous with it or prior to it in time or causation'[17]

(Van Den Bergh 1954: 37–8). If time is a natural characteristic of reality, it is easy to conclude that such a reality is eternal, since according to Aristotle time is infinite. If on the other hand time is an accident created by God, the universe is liberated from any dimension of continuity and hence can be created.

Turning to the question of the possible, according to al-Ghazālī, while only God is necessary, possibility is ontologically inherent in substances (an idea not all that distant from Avicenna's view). The mere possibility and not the necessity of possible beings can be demonstrated by their being contingent and transient. The possible corresponds essentially to the contingent; and that which exists is 'determined' (*maqdūr*) by the power (*qudra*) of God, the absolute Determiner. This is to consider the question ontologically. Seen from an epistemological viewpoint, however, possibility is a pure judgement of the intellect and the intellect is not in any way obliged to admit existence or non-existence. Unlike in Averroes, it is not obligatory to consider only those things that exist:

> The objection is that the possibility of which [the philosophers] speak is a judgement [*qaḍā'*] of the intellect, and anything whose existence the intellect supposes, provided no obstacle presents itself to the supposition, we call possible [*mumkin*] and, if there is such an obstacle, we call it impossible [*mustaḥīl*] and, if we suppose that it cannot be supposed not to be, we call it necessary [*wājib*]. *These are rational judgements which need no real existent which they might qualify.* [. . .] *And this shows that the intellect in order to decide whether something is possible need not admit an existing thing to which the possibility can be related.*[18] (Van Den Bergh 1954: 60–1)

Thus, for al-Ghazālī, the intellect is capable of studying possibility and contingency without being constrained by the obligation to reproduce that which exists outside the mind. On the other hand, the Islamic concept of the Oneness of God forbids the understanding of Him. Consequently, in the Islamic vision which al-Ghazālī entirely shares, it is permissible to trace a parallel relationship between God and the world in terms of reciprocal understanding and necessity. It is possible to have an understanding of that which in itself is neither necessary, nor ontologically consistent or real, while that which is truly necessary in itself and ontologically real – which is to say, God – eludes scientific perception. It is possible to have an understanding of that which is not necessary in itself insofar as it is an act of God; indeed, it is possible even to have an understanding of non-existence in that it is God that determines it, just as He does existence. It would appear that we must hypothesise in al-Ghazālī a division between mind and reality that would make him nothing less than an anticipator of so-called 'weak thought'. The world of understanding is a world that is neither foreseeable nor necessary (not foreseeable because God could occasionalistically decide to change the rules of functioning of reality in mid-stream). The world's unforeseeability and non-necessity have the effect of making the world plural (God could have created different types of worlds, having had the faculty of choosing between compossible models). But if that were the case, men would have had knowledge of that which God cannot create, even if such knowledge is only subjective. Long before Heidegger, al-Ghazālī demolishes the belief that truth consists in conformity between thought and objective being.

The concept of the possible for Averroes is not in any way connected with the existing substance (as was discussed earlier, in Chapter 4, the possible for Averroes is obligatorily necessary because otherwise it would be impossible):

> we cannot think of regarding what is described by 'possibility' and 'change' as identical with the actual, i.e. which belongs to the becoming in so far as it is actual, for the former [possibility] again vanishes and the latter must necessarily be a part of the product. Therefore there must necessarily be a substratum which is the recipient for the possibility and which is the vehicle of the change and the becoming, and it is this of which it is said that it becomes, and alters, and changes from non-existence into existence.[19] (Van Den Bergh 1954: 62)

Averroes, following Aristotle, understands the possible as potential:

> This is evident from the definition of the possible that it is the non-existence which is in readiness to exist or not to exist. This possible non-existent is possible neither in so far as it is non-existent nor in so far as it is actually existent. It is only possible in so far as it is in

> potency, and for this reason the Muʿtazilites affirm that the non-existent is a kind of entity.[20] (Van Den Bergh 1954: 61)

If the possible is only potential, the necessary is also actual. All that which is possible necessarily exists and all that which is potential is also actual. This model serves to delineate a concept of the world that is complete and closed, where that which is truly possible is also actual and that which is realisable is automatically intelligible, given that there is a direct correspondence between that which is outside the mind and that which is inside it.

A third element where the views held by al-Ghazālī and Averroes diverge is in the definition of act and agent. For al-Ghazālī, action implies will and power on the part of the agent. To be an agent does not simply mean being the cause of something (for example, man in relation to his shadow), but rather a conscious intervention of free will directed towards a particular end.

> We say: 'Agent' means someone from whom there proceeds an act with the will to act according to choice and with the knowledge of the object willed. But according to the philosophers the world stands in relation to God as the effect of the cause, in a necessary connexion which God cannot be imagined to sever, and which is like the connexion between the shadow and the man, light and the sun, but this is not an act at all. On the contrary, he who says that the lamp makes the light and the man makes the shadow uses the term vaguely, giving it a sense much wider than its definition, and uses it metaphorically, relying on the fact that there is an analogy between the object originally meant by it and the object to which it is transferred, i.e. the agent is in a general sense a cause, the lamp is the cause of the light, and the sun is the cause of luminosity; but the agent is not called a creative agent from the sole fact that it is a cause, but by its being a cause in a special way, namely that it causes through will and through choice.[21] (Van Den Bergh 1954: 89)

In this sense, natural causality appears to be merely metaphorical and the only authentic agent is God, since natural action is evidently unreflecting and therefore cannot properly be defined as an action; while human action is not the product of free will but is created by God. Al-Ghazālī accuses the philosophers of understanding the causative capacity of God by analogy with natural capacity: God acts by necessity just as the Sun by necessity emanates light. On the contrary, God acts freely and decides freely to create the world. Therefore, the philosophers do not know how to demonstrate that God is the Maker of the world: because they do not make Him a being with volition, whereas God is the agent of that which He wishes; and because they tie up the world to God with a relationship of emanation (al-Ghazālī obviously has Avicenna in mind). According to Averroes, action means transformation from potential to action. Therefore, in an absolute and general sense, God is the agent, but so too are natural substances when they carry out the operation of translating potentiality into actuality. There are metaphorical actions (such as when one says that a wall falls) and natural actions (such as when one says the fire burns the wood), and actions that imply the separation of agent from action. This last describes the action of God in relation to the world. God produces the world from eternity, while at the same time remaining separated from it and ontologically superior to it. Averroes regards the presupposition of the theologians and al-Ghazālī according to which God must be held to possess 'volition' as being ambiguous. In fact, the First Agent transcends the attribute of will since he who wishes lacks what he wishes for, and God cannot be lacking in anything. As we have already said, if God had created the world in a determined moment in time, that would have meant that He was lacking something, that He was impoverished, and that would have implied that He was not perfect. God does not, therefore act voluntarily – or at least not in the way that we understand it in reaction to human will. Man can be a voluntary agent, since, if he is thirsty, he wants to drink. But God lacks nothing which is why it is illogical to maintain that He acted as the result of an impulse of volition similar to a human impulse, even if He is endowed with a will specific to Him. But God's actions are not even natural, since natural action is unreflecting, whereas God acts through His wisdom. Clearly, just as God's will cannot be compared to human will, nor can His wisdom. Human wisdom is a derived wisdom, the effect of existing things; divine wisdom, by contrast, is creative, the cause of existing things.[22] God produces the world with His wisdom, but we cannot explain 'what' this wisdom is like. And yet, nevertheless, God's action is not merely the automatic product of a movement in the way that fire automatically burns the wood with which it comes in contact.

Therefore, God's action is neither strictly speaking natural nor voluntary. To sum up:

> the philosophers certainly believe that God is separated from the world and according to them He is not to be classed with this kind of natural cause. Nor is He an agent in the sense in which any empirical agent, either voluntary or involuntary, is; He is rather the agent of these, drawing forth the Universe from non-existence to existence and conserving it, and such an act is a more perfect and glorious one than any performed by the empirical agents.[23] (Van Den Bergh 1954: 90)

Al-Ghazālī gives the metaphorical nature of natural action further support when arguing against the effectuality of secondary causes. This well-known argument has been compared in recent times to that advanced by Hume. Like Hume, al-Ghazālī refuses to establish a necessary causal chain between phenomena:

> According to us [the theologians] the connexion between what is usually (*ʿāda*) believed to be a cause and what is believed to be an effect is not a necessary connexion; each of two things has its own individuality, and neither the affirmation nor the negation, neither the existence nor the non-existence of the one is implied in the affirmation, negation, existence, and non-existence of the other.[24] (Van Den Bergh 1954: 316)

Again like Hume, al-Ghazālī maintains that causality is a mere impression deriving from the habit of seeing phenomena as being linked one to the other: 'We [theologians] only profess that these things [causal relationships] are not necessary, but that they are possible and may or may not happen, and protracted habit time after time fixes their occurrence in our minds according to the past habit in a fixed impression'[25] (Van Den Bergh 1954: 324). The fact is that, since God is the only agent because God is the only being endowed with free will and with effective volition, it is He in fact who creates the connection (and here, obviously, we are departing from Hume):

> For the connexion in these things is based on a prior power of God to create them in a successive order, though not because this connexion is necessary in itself and cannot be disjoined – on the contrary, it is in

> God's power (*taqdīr*) to create satiety without eating, and death without decapitation, and to let life persist notwithstanding the decapitation, and so on [. . .].[26] (Van Den Bergh 1954: 316)

Life and death are nothing other than accidents created within the body by God.

According to al-Ghazālī, philosophers have no other proof to support the necessity of the causal connection than empirical observation: they see that fire placed against cotton will burn it and deduce from this that fire is the cause of the burning of the cotton. In reality, it is God who gives fire the potential to burn and the cotton the potential to be burned. If God wishes, He could arrange things so that fire does not burn and water does not extinguish nor the Sun give out light. As the Qur'an reveals, at times God has indeed done such things: for example, he permitted the flames not to kill Abraham (21.68–9). God is free to create the world as He wishes and to change the rules of the functioning of reality, that are, therefore, merely possible. What might seem surprising, given the premises, is that al-Ghazālī's position is not, after all, that of a sceptic. On the contrary, he takes a positive view of reality. On the one hand, in fact, he does not entirely deny secondary causes. Al-Ghazālī is not mad: he would not for a minute suggest that fire does not burn or water not extinguish. He confines himself to saying that natural things do not have necessary properties, inherent in their essence and independent of God's direct intervention. On the other hand, existing things, dependent on God and determined (*maqdūrāt*) by His omnipotence, are absolutely real even if transient. The existence of nature is not metaphorical: if He wishes, God could destroy it in a twinkling of the eye, but since He does not do this, nature is absolutely concrete and functions in obedience to precise rules.

Despite this, Averroes's anxiety with regard to al-Ghazālī's views is manifest. As a good Aristotelian, he naturally propounds the existence of secondary causes and of a necessary causal connection between phenomena. The denial of efficient causes implies going against the evidence of the senses and the mind and denying the obvious philosophical principle that every effect must have an agent. Furthermore, not only does al-Ghazālī's view upset the necessary causal order that rules the universe and which is the product of God's knowing intervention, it also calls into question the very intelligibility of the universe.

> Now intelligence is nothing but the perception of things with their causes, and in this it distinguishes itself from all the other faculties of apprehension, and he who denies causes must deny the intellect. Logic implies the existence of causes and effects, and knowledge of these effects can only be rendered perfect through knowledge of their causes. Denial of cause implies the denial of knowledge, and denial of knowledge implies that nothing in this world can be really known, and that what is supposed to be known is nothing but opinion, that neither proof nor definition exist, and that the essential attributes which compose definitions are void. The man who denies the necessity of any item of knowledge must admit that even this, his own affirmation, is not necessary knowledge.[27] (Van Den Bergh 1954: 319)

The relationship of close connection established between the mind and reality means that Averroes cannot abandon the necessary order of reality without at the same time abandoning the necessary order of intelligibility. Knowledge depends on the stability of the universe.

In concluding this brief analytical discussion of the *Incoherence of the Incoherence*, I believe it is possible to trace a precise epistemological and ontological contrast between al-Ghazālī and Averroes. *Al-Ghazālī's cosmos is a cosmos where divine freedom is expressed, in which many worlds exist and many possible realities. Knowledge is plural and being is a flexible concept, metaphysically weak. The breaking of the chain of cause and effect, in fact, not only opens the possibilities of God's intervention, but also of human freedom and the plurality of knowledge. Averroes's cosmos is a cosmos of divine necessity, where there exists a single possible world (that is therefore also real) and where the principle of necessity obliges reality to be as it is and not otherwise. Knowledge, in Averroes's view, is one, and corresponds to the structures of reality and the concept of being is rigid, metaphysically strong.* It is probably pointless to ask which of these two visions of reality and knowledge is the more authentically Islamic. It would appear that al-Ghazālī ought to win the argument. Both thinkers, however, use metaphysical arguments to discuss causes with the aim of establishing a coherent vision of God, which is the most important question from an Islamic point of view. What should be stressed, rather, is that a theistic concept such as that of al-Ghazālī does not necessarily lead to an impoverishment of the philosophical viewpoint. His theistic ideas are just as philosophical as the Aristotelian ideas of Averroes. Indeed, they can, perhaps paradoxically, be seen to open the way to a plural rationality, offering the human mind broader vistas of unfettered speculation and enquiry.

Chapter 8

Ethics and Politics

Almost all the Islamic philosophers who have concerned themselves with politics have followed Plato and Aristotle in maintaining that man is a political animal and that society is man's natural environment. A clear formulation of this view is set out in the writings of Ibn Khaldūn who says at the beginning of the first chapter of the *Muqaddima*:

> Human social organisation [*ijtimāʿ*] is something necessary. The philosophers expressed this fact by saying: 'Man is "political" (*madanī*) by nature'. That is, he cannot do without the social organization for which the philosophers use the technical term 'town' (*polis*) [*madīna*].
>
> This is what civilisation [*ʿumrān*] means. (The necessary character of human social organization or civilisation) is explained by the fact that God created and fashioned man in a form that can live and subsist only with the help of food. He guided man to a natural desire for food and instilled in him the power that enables him to obtain it.[1] (Rosenthal 2005: 45)

The need to feed and defend themselves leads humans to cooperate with one another, since 'Through co-operation [*taʿāwun*], the needs of a number of persons, many times greater than their own number, can be satisfied'[2] (Rosenthal 2005: 45). Human nature is, however, fundamentally aggressive and violent which is why a 'moderating curb' is required. This moderating curb is the sovereign, since the origins of monarchy lie in humankind's need for an effective power that will prevent them from fighting amongst themselves.[3] This is the presupposition, not dissimilar from Hobbes, of the birth of the state. As was mentioned in the 'Introduction', Ibn Khaldūn then identifies group feeling as being the motor that leads to the organisation of state and political organisations. A weakening of this sense of group feeling, combined with the triumph of luxury and corruption in urban civilisations, brings about the decadence of the state which, in turn, triggers off the cyclical process of the birth, growth and death of a society.

Ibn Khaldūn's analysis is coldly pessimistic and realistic. Earlier, al-Fārābī and Avempace had discussed a corollary that almost inevitably leads to the conviction that man is a political animal: the aim of life in society is the procurement of happiness. Happiness is not, therefore, exclusively a matter beyond this world, being above all natural. The philosophers' analysis is not, however, realistic, aiming as it does rather at identifying in political science the instrument for obtaining the greatest harmony in society and the greatest degree of individual realisation for philosophers and sages. Al-Fārābī and Avempace are two profoundly different thinkers with differing political viewpoints. Al-Fārābī is perfectly convinced that the destinies of man and of the sage lie within the social world to which humans must belong in order to cooperate and support themselves. Avempace, on the other hand, develops the idea of the regime of the solitary man: in imperfect cities the wise man has the right and the duty to turn his back on it and to seek spiritual perfection on his own. The different interpretations given by the two writers to the metaphor of the 'plants' is indicative: while Avempace, as we saw in Part I, maintains that the 'plants' are the virtuous people in an imperfect city and who represent the only hope for a possible reform of a corrupt society, for al-Fārābī the 'plants' are the rogue elements within a perfect society, or, literally, the weeds that need to be eradicated. Admittedly, the essential concepts of political science are the same in al-Fārābī and Avempace. These concepts are understanding, virtue and happiness. The wise man is also virtuous and only he who knows and understands is perfectly happy. The goal of political science is to procure and guarantee men's happiness and hence to promote understanding and virtue. For this reason, apart from what he says about the *imām*, al-Fārābī does not describe in any way the structures and institutions of the virtuous city. He is more concerned with the 'ideas' and the 'opinions' of the virtuous city. The virtuous city is one in which upright opinions are professed and it is enough that its citizens apply understanding, philosophy and virtue for it to enjoy harmony and continuity. Avempace, meanwhile, asserts that a perfect society needs no judges or doctors but, like al-Fārābī, he does not describe the characteristics of the ideal society, confining himself to a discussion of the wise man's path to perfection.

Al-Fārābī makes an explicit connection between politics and happiness with his presupposition of the natural sociability of human beings in the treatise on the *Virtuous City*:

> In order to preserve himself and to attain his highest perfection every human being is by his very nature in need of many things which he cannot provide all by himself; he is indeed in need of people who each supply him with some particular need of his. Everybody finds himself in the same relation to everybody in this respect. Therefore man cannot attain the perfection, for the sake of which his inborn nature has been given to him, unless many (societies of) people who co-operate come together who each supply everybody else with some particular need of his, so that as a result of the contribution of the whole community all the things are brought together which everybody needs in order to preserve himself and to attain perfection.[4] (Walzer 1985, V 15.1: 229)

Happiness, in the context of the Virtuous City, is presented above all as a theoretical happiness which leads the wise man to abandon entirely and renounce material things: 'Felicity means that the human soul reaches a degree of perfection in (its) existence where it is in no need of matter for its support, since it becomes one of the incorporeal things and of the immaterial substances and remains in that state continuously for ever'[5] (Walzer 1985, IV 13: 205, 207). Through the perfecting of his own intellect and by detaching himself from material things, man makes himself similar to the celestial Intelligences, as we have seen in relation to conjunction.

If, in the *Virtuous City*, al-Fārābī seems to posit an exclusively theoretical happiness, in other works he seems to take up a different point of view. In the *Attainment of Happiness*, for example (although it is not certain whether this treatise precedes or follows the *Virtuous City*), a view of happiness is proposed that is both theoretical and political. Al-Fārābī says that 'The human things through which nations and citizens of cities attain earthly happiness in this life and supreme happiness in the life beyond are of four kinds: theoretical virtues, deliberative virtues, moral virtues, and practical arts'.[6] Theoretical virtues are obviously those developed by the philosopher who practises science, and they make it possible to perceive moral virtues. Deliberative virtues are those that make it possible to translate things 'into actual existence by the will at a determined time, in a determined place, and when a determined event occurs'.[7] Finally, practical arts are those that enable sovereigns and *imām* to govern, for example through the persuasion of the masses. Thus, both theoretical and strictly practical and political elements come together in the attainment of happiness. Happiness is attained within society through the simultaneous action of intellectual perfecting and wise government. Subsequently, in the *Commentary on the Nichomachean Ethics*, al-Fārābī appears to favour the view that happiness is only possible in the political sphere. This would fit in with the more sceptical and disenchanted tone that he takes, in the last years of his life, with regard to the possibility of conjunction. It would seem to be natural (but here we have to speculate since the text has not survived) that happiness that is solely political would require the need for the existence of the virtuous city.

On the other hand, according to al-Fārābī, happiness need not only be sought within the virtuous city. This is also the view of Avempace who, in the *Regime of the Solitary*, informs us that he has written a book *On Political Science* where he discusses the goals appropriate to men and philosophers in a just society ruled by an *imām*. As for the aims to be pursued in an imperfect city, 'since he [the solitary] is an integral part of it, they derive from the actions that are appropriate to him precisely because he is solitary'.[8] These are, of course, exclusively intellectual actions, relating to thinking and reasoning, by means of which the solitary man and the philosopher 'make themselves divine'.

Through the practice of science and reason, the philosopher can acquire happiness even within an imperfect society. Happiness can be acquired by the solitary man who cultivates his own soul; within the state, wise government will balance and direct associative relationships.

The question of the relationship between virtue, happiness and society is also raised by Averroes in his *Commentary on Plato's Republic*. In particular, he returns to al-Fārābī's idea, set out in the *Attainment of Happiness*, of the four possible types of virtue with the greatest importance being given to the intellectual virtues:

> It has been explained in the first part of this science [meaning in the theoretical part of the political science] that the human perfections are, in general, of four kinds: speculative virtues, intellectual virtues, ethical virtues and practical conduct, and that all these perfections exist only for the sake of the speculative ones and as a preparation for them.[9]

Thus, in a more decisive and unequivocal manner than al-Fārābī – and perhaps influenced by Avempace – Averroes subordinates all the other virtues to the speculative virtues. He goes on to say that even the speculative virtues can only be practised in society, and this for the reason that man is a political animal:

> It has also been explained that it is either impossible for one person to be distinguished in all these virtues or, if it were possible, that he would be hard to find. Rather is it possible that it [i.e. perfection] exists mostly in many individuals [together]. It is likewise seen to be impossible for one person to make [even] one of these virtues his own without the help of other persons; man is in need of others in acquiring his virtue. Therefore, he is a political being by nature.[10]

Averroes does not betray the original idea according to which philosophers have need of the masses in order fully to develop their activities. The practice of virtue leads to the pursuit of happiness which is defined as 'an action belonging to the rational soul [performed] with virtue'.[11]

The practice of virtue and the pursuit of happiness are one of the goals of philosophical activity. How then should a philosopher behave in an imperfect society? Averroes is aware that, in moments of crisis (and he maintained that his time showed evidence of a profound crisis in the Muslim states), the philosopher could be tempted to live the life of a solitary, as urged by Avempace. Averroes, however, comes to the conclusion that Avempace's position is incorrect. Man can achieve his goal only insofar as he is part of the state, given that he can only exist insofar as he is part of the state. If he chooses to live as a solitary, he will not attain the highest level of perfection and hence will not be able to achieve happiness.[12] As also in the *Decisive Treatise*, a central role is given to upbringing. A good mind that receives a bad upbringing will become corrupted and harmful. We see here a third version of the metaphor of the 'plants', differing from those given by al-Fārābī and Avempace: 'Similarly seeds of the best plants when they cannot find proper soil and nourishment are transformed into the very worst of the bad kinds. So it is with those excellent natures when they grow up in these States and are badly educated. These men alone are the cause of the greatest evils in these states'.[13] The perversion of one nature, even when originally good, reflects negatively on the character of society.

From the views discussed above, it will appear that the Islamic philosophers' preoccupations are entirely theoretical and this has the risk of isolating philosophy from concrete social praxis. An analysis of the concept of justice, to which is linked that of good government, leads political science back to its practical concerns.

Justice is the basis of the ethical and political doctrine of Islam. Even if al-Fārābī, curiously, does not explicitly discuss justice in the *Virtuous City*, it is the guarantee of the functioning of the ideal society and, indeed, of the very Community (*Umma*) of Muslims. There are two types of justice: God's justice and human justice. God's justice, theodicy, is understood in very different ways by the Muʿtazilites and the Ashʿarites and relates to their attitude to the fundamental matter of God's omnipotence. The Muʿtazilites assert that not only does God do no evil, but also that He is incapable of so doing – an assumption that seems clearly to limit His omnipotence. Since it is evident that evil exists in reality, then it must be imputed exclusively to man, who is responsible for his own actions. God's freedom ends where human freedom begins. But the Muʿtazilites also circumscribe God's actions in another way by saying that, as an inevitable and direct consequence of the principle according to which God does no evil, He must do 'the best' for living creatures, since otherwise he would be unjust. This conclusion is vigorously attacked by al-Ghazālī who relates an effective fable on the subject:

> He, the Most High, does with His servants what He will and is not bound to do 'the best' for his servants, since as we have already said He is not bound to anything; thus it is not possible to understand how there can be obligation with regard to Him. I would much like to know how the Muʿtazilite, when he asserts in the matter presented here that God is obliged to do 'the best', would reply. Let him imagine a dispute in the Beyond between two dead Muslims, one a boy and the other an adult. God gives greater consideration to the adult and places him before the boy because he, grown to adulthood, has excelled himself in faith and good works and for this, according to the Muʿtazilite, God is supposed to be obliged to him. Now, if the boy should say: 'Lord, why have You placed the adult in a higher position than me?', He would reply: 'Because he did many good works'. And if the boy replied: 'You caused me to die as a child; You should have kept me alive so that when I grew up I could have done good works; therefore you departed from justice, favouring the adult by prolonging his life more than mine; why then did you prefer him?', God would reply: 'Because I knew that you, when you became an adult, would have been a polytheist and would have rebelled; better for you to have died in childhood', and in this way the Muʿtazilite would explain God's action. But then the misbelievers would cry out from the depths of hell: 'Lord, did you not know then that, when we reached adulthood we would be polytheists? Why then did You not cause us to die in childhood? We would have been content to be placed in a position even below that of the Muslim boy.' How do we answer this question? We must simply assert that divine matters are too high by virtue of God's majesty to be weighed in the Muʿtazilite's scales.[14]

In reality, according to al-Ghazālī and the Ashʿarites, God is free to do what He wants:

> It is possible for God – on Whom be praises – to oblige creatures to do things that they are not capable of, contrary to what the Muʿtazilites say. [. . .] God the Great and Powerful can make

creatures suffer and torment them without previous sin and without subsequent reward, contrary to what the Muʿtazilites say, because He may freely dispose of His kingdom, nor is it possible to imagine that it is unjust that He disposes of His kingdom, since injustice lies in usurpation in the domain of another, without his permission, which is absurd for God the most High.[15]

In acting in this way, God remains, nevertheless, 'just', since God's justice cannot be defined or measured in relation to human justice. Justice and injustice are meaningless when applied to God. God, master of His realm, cannot be judged to be either just or unjust: Quite simply, He is God and 'None shall question Him about His works, but they shall be questioned' (Qur'an, 21.23).

This does not, for all that, mean that God acts under the impulse of irrational whim. Al-Ghazālī, while anxious to assert absolutely God's omnipotence, ends up by admitting that ours is the best of all possible worlds. In the *Revival of the Religious Sciences*, for example, he states that

It is according to the necessarily right order, in accord with what must be and as it must be and in the measure in which it must be; and there is not in possibility anything whatever more excellent, more perfect, and more complete than it.[16]

Similarly, in the Book on the Forty Principles of Religion, we read:

He who is certain of the truth of the secrets will not be surprised by the actions of God the Highest, but rather by his own failure [to recognise them]. And he will not torment himself about why or how God created his heavenly kingdom [*malakūt*]. Thus four aspects emerge: complete knowledge of the perfection of divine generosity (*jūd*) and wisdom (*hikma*) and of the functioning of causes necessitating the caused; knowledge of the inchoative decree (*al-qadā' al-awwal*) that happens in the twinkling of an eye; the knowledge of predestination (*qadar*) which is the evident cause of the translation in detail of the decree (*tafāsīl al-qadā'*). In truth, all these things are set up in the best and most perfect of ways and it is not possible that there could exist anything better or more perfect, since if it did exist [. . .] God would spare Himself [in creating], and then He

> would not be generous, but miserly, and thus impotent (*ʿajz*) and that would be a contradicition of His power (*qudra*).[17]

Theodicy does not mean that there is no providence and foresight in God. Al-Ghazālī relates an interesting story in his *Counsel for Kings*:

> Moses, God bless him, addressed a prayer to God on High. 'O Lord God', he prayed, 'show me your justice.' 'O Moses', He said, 'cannot you be patient?' 'O Lord', he replied, 'with Your help I can.' 'Arise,' He commanded, 'and go to such and such a spring and sit there hidden.' Moses went and did so. A rider came unto the well, drank water, performed the ablutions, took a purse from his girdle, left it there, and went. Then a boy came and took the purse and went. Then a blind man came and performed the ablutions and stood in prayer. Suddenly the rider came back. 'I left a purse here,' he said to the blind man, 'and you have come but nobody else has been here during this last hour. Give back the purse!' 'I am blind', answered the man; 'I have not seen any gold.' The rider grew angry and drew his sword and killed the blind man; then he searched for the gold but did not find it and went. Moses said, 'O Lord God, I know what the facts are.' Then Gabriel came down and said: 'God the Strong and Glorious has commanded me (to tell you this). 'I know things which you do not know. As regards the boy who took the purse, that purse was his own property. The gold (in it) belonged to his father, who was a labourer in the service of this rider. All that he had accumulated through his labour for the rider was in that purse, and this boy has now recovered his family's rightful substance. As regards the blind old man, before he went blind he had killed this rider's father, and now the rider has taken vengeance on him. Behold, O Moses! Such is Our justice!'[18]

So, in al-Ghazālī's 'orthodox' interpretation, it is for God to decide what is good and what is bad. Good and evil do not exist in their own right, but things are good or bad when God has declared them so. It is pointless to impute to God those ills that may happen to us in life. These can be 'good' when seen from a different viewpoint or providentially. It is for this reason that the ethics of 'orthodox' theologies such as that of the Ashʿarites are fundamentally 'subjective' and based on a voluntaristic principle of God's omnipotence. In his

Unveiling of the Methods of Proof concerning the Principles of Religion, Averroes comments ironically on the consequences of this 'orthodox' point of view:

> It is the height of absurdity! In this case, in fact, there would be nothing that was in itself good, nor anything that was in itself bad. It is immediately obvious, indeed, that that which is just is good and that which is unjust is bad. [For the theologians] associating [divinity with God] would not in itself be unjust or wrong, but [it is so only] insofar as the Revelation affirms it. Thus, if the Revelation declared that it was obligatory to believe that [God] has an associate, that would be just! Similarly, if the Revelation told us that we must disobey Him, that would be just! All this is formally contradictory with traditional assumptions as well as with reason.[19]

So, as Averroes's words make clear, the Muslim ethics of the Muʿtazilites and the philosophers are, on the contrary, 'objective': good and bad exist in their own right to which God himself adapts His own actions. Human action is free and capable of distinguishing between good and evil. Therefore, for the Muʿtazilites and for philosophers such as al-Miskawayh, God's prescriptions have a rational goal: pilgrimage and prayer, for example, were prescribed in order to stimulate the natural human tendency to be sociable. For al-Ghazālī, on the other hand, it is essentially impossible to understand the reason for divine commands which must be believed not because they are rational but because they are the product of the divine order.

As part of this same viewpoint, al-Ghazālī says that man is not responsible for his own actions; God creates them and man confines himself to 'acquiring them':

> God – may He be praised! – is the only one to 'invent' men's movements. He does not mean that these actions may be the object of human capacity by way of 'gain' (*kasb*), for God the Highest has created together both the capacity (*qudrah*) and its object, and He has created together volition and its object; as for capacity, it is assigned to man and created by the Lord.[20]

The acquisition of actions does not mean that in man there should not be an intention (*niya*) to act well; but, even if man would wish to act well, he cannot if God does not allow him to do so by creating his actions and making him 'acquire them'. Similarly, even man's evil and sinful actions are in a sense 'allowed' by God (not wanted, but permitted), although He has the power to judge them after death and reward or punish them. And this too is part of God's justice. The position taken by al-Ghazālī (and the Ashʿarites) is a 'moderate' one, seeking a middle way between those Islamic theologians (such as the Jabrites) who espouse complete and total predestination and the Muʿtazilites who believe in complete and total freedom.

As for Averroes, he attempts to safeguard the Qur'anic principle according to which God is the only creator of all things and men's capacity to act:

> It seems clear that God – the blessed and Most High – has created powers [faculties] in us thanks to which we are able to acquire things that are contrary to us. But since the acquisition of these things does not occur for us except through the action of the causes that God procures for us from outside, and the cessation of that which opposes it, it results that the actions attributed to us happen thanks to both the one and the other [i.e., the faculties inherent in man and the extrinsic causes]. Things being thus, the actions that are attributed to us happen in fact thanks to our will and insofar as extrinsic actions are concordant with them: these are given the name of 'divine decree'.[21]

God's decree is, therefore, the system of causes within which man acts, even if his actions are inevitably conditioned and limited by these causes. M. Geoffroy correctly observes that, for Averroes,

> the contradiction between the affirmation of human liberty and of predestination which is supposed by the absolute prescience and omnipotence of God, is resolved by the universal determinism of efficient causes. Man is 'surrounded' by causes that are continuously in action, and his free will is one element in this causality that governs the functioning of the universe.[22]

God is 'just' in His sphere, as men should be 'just' in theirs. Justice is an essential attribute of caliphs and kings. For example, al-Ghazālī writes that:

> As you will hear in the Traditions, 'the Sultan is God's shadow on earth', which means that he is high-ranking and the Lord's delegate over His creatures. It must therefore be recognized that this kinship and the divine effulgence have been granted to them by God, and that they must accordingly be obeyed, loved and followed. To dispute with kings is improper, and to hate them is wrong; for God on High has commanded (Q. iv.62) 'Obey God and obey the Prophet and those among you who hold authority' which means [. . .] Everybody to whom God has given religion must therefore love and obey kings and recognize that their kingship is granted by God [. . .]. The Sultan in reality is he who awards justice, and does not perpetrate injustice and wickedness, among God's slaves; for the unjust Sultan is ill-starred and will have no endurance, because the Prophet stated that 'sovereignty endures even when there is unbelief, but will not endure when there is injustice'.[23]

Al-Ghazālī's position is a traditional one in Islam and implies, on the one hand, the duty of subjects to obey and, on the other, the duty of the sovereign to be just and to further the well-being of the population.[24]

In the *Muqaddima*, Ibn Khaldūn outlines a view of the function of monarchy and sovereign power that is closely linked to economic reality. His presupposition is that the state is like a vast market in which, as in a melting pot, civilisation develops with all its multiple elements, social, political, cultural and economic. Justice is the axis that allows this complex mechanism to function. It obeys precise rules that derive from a need to determine boundaries by the holder of highest authority. The sovereign must be strict, he must know how to impose his own power (using force if necessary), but, above all, he must be fair and just. His authority is first and foremost executive and must obviously be subject to the authority of the Law (most importantly, divine law but also sanction in the field of positive law). Good government consists in acting in the public interest of the subjects and is synonymous with moderation. To exercise power prudently and act in the interests of the people as a whole it is necessary, on the one hand, to refer to wisely drawn-up political laws that enjoy the consensus of the population (the positive law that is the foundation of a rational regime) and, on the other, to rely on a revealed religious Law useful in both this world and the next. The sovereign should not impose too many taxes because an excess of taxation prevents the accumulation of wealth and discourages private initiative. The sovereign should, rather encourage trade and free initiative. Private property is a necessity that must be protected and promoted. Ibn Khaldūn seems almost to anticipate some of the theories of classic economics when he asserts not only the productive importance of the middle or bourgeois class (the economy is, of course, based on agriculture, but the wealth produced from agriculture is introduced into the productive cycle of commerce), but also that profit consists of the (quantity) of work required to produce a product that can then be sold: 'The value realised from all such labour becomes part of his profit (*al-makāsib qiyam al-aʿmāl*)'[25] (Rosenthal 2005: 304). The direct relationship between work, profit and wealth is established again elsewhere: 'the capital a person earns and acquires, if resulting from a craft, is the value realized from his labour'[26] (Rosenthal 2005: 298). Ibn Khaldūn seems to have an almost libertarian and capitalist view of the economic functioning of the state. The sovereign must not monopolise the market, nor must he have conflicting interests in economic activities. A sharp distinction is made between the public and private spheres: the private sphere of the sovereign should not interfere with the public sphere; the sovereign's private interests should not damage or impede public interests. If the sovereign takes up trade or other money-making activities,

> It causes harm to the subjects in many ways. First, farmers and merchants will find it difficult to buy livestock and merchandise. [. . .] Furthermore, the ruler can appropriate much of the agricultural produce and the available merchandise by force [. . .]. Thus he will be able to force the seller to lower his price.'[27] (Rosenthal 2005: 304)

Lowering prices too much can result in a crisis in economic activity and lead to poverty. One of the effects of this is that injustice triumphs and injustice is the determining cause of the fall of dynasties and the crisis of civilisation.

This brief look at the different approaches to the concept of justice would not be complete without a brief consideration of Averroes's strictly philosophical view of justice in a broader political framework as expressed in the *Commentary on Plato's Republic*. Political problems do not occupy a central place in Averroes's speculative thinking, unless we are to interpret his doctrine of the three ways to truth and his measures for the prevention of disease and intellectual hygiene as described in the *Decisive Treatise* in a political sense. The *Commentary on the Republic*, however, contains a number of interesting points. Following Aristotelian tradition, Averroes sees politics as consisting of a theoretical and a practical side. The theoretical side is found in the *Nichomachean Ethics*; the practical side in Aristotle's *Politics*. While Averroes was very familiar with the *Nichomachean Ethics*, writing as he did a commentary on it, he knew nothing about the *Politics* that, as he himself mentions, had not reached al-Andalus. It was for this reason that he decides to 'substitute it' with Plato's *Republic*. He makes no attempt, however, to reconcile the two great philosophers of Antiquity, being entirely aware of the differences between them. It is his opinion, nevertheless, that Plato's *Republic* performs the same function as Aristotle's *Politics* in that it deals with the practical aspect of political science.

In the first book of the *Commentary on Plato's Republic*, Averroes sets out to discuss the characteristics of the state, the ruling class of the guardians and the *imām* although he gives less importance and space to this latter topic than does al-Fārābī. Extrapolated from their Platonic context, these elements have a clearly propaedeutic and pedagogical role intended, in all probability, for the Almohads and designed to provide a philosophical education for the Almohad ruling class. Averroes's text is, indeed, composed from the viewpoint of the Almohad political plan. The perfect state is either a monarchy or an aristocracy and is based on four ethical and moral pillars: wisdom, courage, temperance and justice. The discussion of justice is of central importance and the concept takes as its starting point a quotation from Plato: '[justice] consists in no more than every citizen following the activity for which he is best qualified by nature'[28], and again: 'Justice consists in every one of its citizens doing only that for which he is destined individually'.[29] This concept has, however, aspects that, even if originally inspired by Plato, take on a rather different meaning in the circumstances of the political situation of Islam. Averroes says, in fact, that, in order to ensure the governance of the state, it may be useful at times to lie: the ruler has the right to lie to his subjects if to do so will benefit the prosperity of the system. Justice and virtue can be taught to the masses by rhetorical and poetic means, but justice may also be imposed by force.

> But in the State which we describe in this treatise such a practice (I mean, education by coercion) is rare. But in other nations outside, this is a necessity; nor can coercion for obdurate nations take any other form but war. In our divine Law, the same is true of laws which follow (the pattern of) human laws, for the ways which lead in it to God are two, one by persuasion and the other by war.[30]

Persuasion through education and struggle against religious deviations were two important political instruments used by the Almohads.

Averroes goes on to list the Platonic qualities the guardians of the ideal city should possess. They should eat in moderation and practise music and gymnastics; they should be strong and courageous; they should disdain material pleasures and pleasures of the flesh; they must be lovers of truth and science. In short, as in Plato, they should be philosophers. The head of the state or *imām* is, as in al-Fārābī, a philosopher, legislator and king even if not necessarily a prophet, since, in any case, the gift of prophecy would derive from a seeking after perfection and not from a necessity. Averroes says that a succession of enlightened sovereigns (like the Almohads) has an influence on the state and leads to good government. The influence can be of two types: on actions and on convictions. It is clear that a genuinely virtuous sovereign, who is also a philosopher, will exercise a greater influence through convictions; but, 'in our time', the management of power by the sovereigns (the Almohad caliphs) is more likely to lead to good actions (orthopraxis) than to good convictions. The Almohad sovereigns should, therefore, combine philosophy with wise government in such a way that orthopraxis may combine with orthodoxy. Averroes exhorts the Almohad sovereigns to make philosophy the basis of their social reform inspired by religious principles.

At the beginning of the third part of the *Commentary*, Averroes identifies six types of constitution: two good ones, which are monarchy and aristocracy, and four degenerate ones, namely timocracy, oligarchy, democracy and tyranny. This scheme is Platonic but Islamic elements become apparent in the examination of the characteristics of the virtuous sovereign and upright government. The sovereign has five qualities: wisdom, intelligence, the persuasive ability to speak to the masses (the rhetorical abilities required for al-Fārābī's philosopher-legislator-prophet), imagination, and the ability and physical integrity to wage war (like the Sunni caliph, even if in this case Averroes does not seem to be thinking of *jihād* as understood in religious terms). These five qualities can be found united in a single person – who would then embody the perfect sovereign – or in five different people who are then, together, entitled to govern in collaboration. This happens in theory, but Averroes is aware that the reality of the Muslim states is different. He stresses, however, that a knowledge of the Law and an ability to wage war – the functions of the judge and the soldier – are the two indispensable qualities for a sovereign who wishes to rule according to the Law. They are qualities that are identified by classical political doctrine in the ideal governor: they can, however, be associated with the figure of the caliph (the legal expert who knows the Law) and that of the sultan, who is the person who wages war. This is the situation of 'many of the Muslim kings',[31] even if the Almohad caliphs could be capable of carrying out both functions.

Averroes then moves on (still following Plato) to a discussion of states that are not virtuous, beginning with timocracy or a state of honour. This he judges to be the best of the imperfect states since it can still lead to notable and virtuous actions. Democracy is the system in which the people, feeling free from bonds and constraints, abandon themselves to pleasures and desires. In a democracy, the heart of society and the very goal for which the state exists is the family; there are laws, but a powerful majority betrays the multitude and a state of war and violence, stimulated by human passions, gains the upper hand. Averroes notes that the majority of the states of his time are democratic and that the aristocratic elite tends to be tyrannical. The Almohad regime should fight against tyranny which is one of the greatest ills that can affect politics. A tyrannical regime is an unjust regime, the very antithesis of the virtuous state where reigns a perfect harmony between governor and governed. 'The masses serve the masters in that whereby the aim of philosophy is fulfilled for them, while the masters serve the masses in that which leads them to their happiness'.[32] The philosopher-kings, the ruling class, cannot do without the masses (this concept too is, as we have seen, found in al-Fārābī); the masses achieve happiness in a state that is wisely guided and governed.

The art of government represents one of the major topics of classical Islamic political thought. It is interesting to note, however, how the rules and principles of good government are not always or necessarily deduced from religious presuppositions. It is the case that an important current of political thought developed in Islamic culture, leading to the production of *specula principium* (mirrors for princes), books of advice, stories and maxims that might be of use to sovereigns in the management of power, the court and the state. Works of this kind were not Islamic or even Arab in origin, but Persian. Influenced by the Iranian tradition, they draw heavily on anecdote, literature and traditional wisdom. The two most important texts of this type are the *Book of Politics* or *Siyāsat Nāma* by the Seljuk grand vizier who was al-Ghāzālī's patron Nizām al-Mulk, and the *Advice to Kings* or *Nasīhat al-Mulūk* by al-Ghāzālī himself. Although the premises of these books claim to refer to Islamic truths, the advice offered to sovereigns draws to a large extent on a pre-Islamic tradition of oriental kingship and particularly, as has been said, that of Persia. The principles of just administration, wisdom and moderation with regard to their subjects, provision for the needs of the state and, most importantly, its military needs, are supported by examples that do not come from the usual Islamic tradition. Ibn Khaldūn, too, often refers to the wisdom of the Iranian kings and their Zoroastrian ministers, as for example when he cites Anushirvan and the circle of virtue existing between the sovereign, the subjects and the instruments of power, the axis of which is justice (*ʿadl*).

> 'The religious law [*sharīʿa*] persists only through royal authority. Mighty royal authority is accomplished only through men. Men persist only with the help of property. The only way to property is through cultivation. The only way to cultivation is through justice. Justice is a balance set up among mankind. The Lord set it up and appointed an overseer for it, and that overseer is the ruler'.
>
> There is also a statement by Anôsharwân to the same effect: 'Royal authority exists through the army, the army through money, money through taxes, taxes through cultivation, cultivation through justice, justice through the improvement of officials, the improvement of officials through the forthrightness of wazirs, and the whole thing in the first place through the ruler's personal supervision of his subjects' condition and his ability to educate them, so that he may rule them and not they him'.

In the *Book on Politics* that is ascribed to Aristotle and has wide

> circulation, we find a good deal about our subject. The treatment, however, is not exhaustive, nor is the topic provided with all the arguments it deserves, and it is mixed with other things. In the book, the author referred to such general ideas as we have reported on the authority of the Môbedhân and Anôsharwân. He arranged his statement in a remarkable circle that he discussed at length. It runs as follows: 'The world is a garden the fence of which is the dynasty. The dynasty is an authority through which life is given to proper behaviour. Proper behaviour is a policy directed by the ruler. The ruler is an institution supported by the soldiers. The soldiers are helpers who are maintained by money. Money is sustenance brought together by the subjects. The subjects are servants who are protected by justice. Justice is something familiar, and through it, the world persists'.[33] (Rosenthal 2005: 40–1)

The reference to pre-Islamic Iranian tradition alludes to the universal value of justice and political wisdom, even though, for Ibn Khaldūn, and certainly more than for Nizām al-Mulk even though he was a fervent Sunni, the ethical pillars of justice are established by the Qur'an and the *hadīth*. Thus the art of government correctly finds its place again in an Islamic context, not least because, for Ibn Khaldūn, the most urgent political question from the theoretical point of view (but not from the practical point of view, as we shall see) remains that of the caliphate.

The question of the caliphate is central to the political doctrine of Sunni Muslims. Doctrinal elements on the orthodox view of the caliphate can already be found in the *Book on Taxation* written in the period of Hārūn al-Rashīd (786–809) by the jurist Abū Yūsuf, and also in the works of the great theologian al-Ashʿarī. These comments are not, however, systematic in character. The first systematic treatise to discuss the conditions and characteristics of the caliphate is that written by al-Māwardī (died 1058). It is important to note how the need to formulate a coherent doctrine with regard to the caliphate becomes urgent (in the 11th century) at a time when the institution was facing a serious and irreparable decline. Earlier, when the caliphate was at the peak of its prestige and effectiveness, it had had no need of theoretical justification to defend its prerogatives against powers that were potentially arbitrary and hostile or, at least, more structured. It was not until, first with the Buyid and then with the

Seljuk dynasties, a sultanate of patrimonial strength and power (*mulk*) was imposed on the legitimate caliphate prescribed by God and unifier of the entire Islamic community, the *Ummah*, that it became clear that there was a need to define precisely the rights and duties, the characteristics and the religious sanction of the system of power that had governed Islam ever since the death of Mohammad. The rules of government as drawn up by al-Māwardī sought to establish power, and particularly that of the caliph, on the basis of a rigorous application of legal prescriptions. The caliphate is the supreme form of Islamic government: its necessity is revealed rather than rational. The caliph, who must belong to the Quraysh, Mohammad's tribe, defends religion and applies it. He knows the Law and is able to wage war. All other authorities – emirs, sultans and military leaders – are subordinate to his authority which legitimates theirs; without the sanction of the caliph there is no legitimacy in any other power. Al-Māwardī describes a utopia with a caliph who is effectively the master of the Islamic state. As the caliphate fell into decadence, historically exhausted, it was replaced by a sultanate based on force and the power of the armies. It was al-Ghazālī who now produced a reworking of al-Māwardī's 'classical' doctrine.

According to al-Ghazālī, the powers of the caliph and the sultan should be complementary: the caliph holds religious authority and the religious prestige derived from his position, whereas the sultan holds political authority and this political authority is legitimated by the use of force (with no need, therefore, of the caliph's sanction). Al-Ghazālī recognises the caliph as having the moral primacy, but this primacy would be ineffective without a robust sultanate with the power to defend him. The sultan no longer needs the caliph in order to rule whereas the caliph needs the sultan to defend his role as religious leader of the Community. It is the sultan who guarantees that the state will protect religion and, conversely, that religion will provide the ethical and moral foundations of the state:

> Worldly life and the safety of people and property are only guaranteed by a power the authority of which is respected. The experience of unrest and the assassination of sultans and caliphs [that has occurred in our time] shows this. [. . .] Religion and power are in perfect agreement; religion is that solid foundation of which the sultan must be the guardian. That which has no foundations will

> collapse and that which is not overseen will be lost. It will not escape any intelligent man that, given the differences of class and opinions, the people will perish if there is no powerful and obeyed sultan capable of asserting himself over differing and opposed tendencies. To conclude, political authority is indispensible in guaranteeing religion, and religion is necessary for the life hereafter.[34]

Al-Ghazālī's intention is to protect and guarantee religious and social peace. This leads him to preach an absolute quietism not least in response to an oppressive power. In such a way, the sage and the mystic are then able, through meditation and study, to gain space and freedom for themselves.

By the time Ibn Khaldūn produced his historical and pragmatic analysis of the sociological characteristics of power, the caliphate had given way to a sultanate and government was no longer framed according to religious law but had become a natural and social phenomenon. The evolution from a state of nature to a political system ruled over by a coercive and sovereign power is, as we have seen, a natural process. Ibn Khaldūn is explicit in his assertion that the goal of human group feeling is regal authority, or, in other words, its aim is the establishment of a state that will discipline human activities and enable that collaboration between individuals and citizens that leads to prosperity. In this sense, according to Ibn Khaldūn, regal authority itself does not have a divine basis but is a natural fact. Regal authority determines the birth of the state. Since regal authority is natural, so also does the state represent a natural mechanism subject to the rules of birth, growth and decay. In making these assertions, Ibn Khaldūn seems to depart from the orthodox Islamic view that considers that as power is derived from God, so also are the favours and advantages enjoyed by society and the civil community bestowed on them by God. He seeks to demonstrate, both historically and in the development of societies in his own time, how power and the state are phenomena originating from the dialectic of the group and its group feeling, from the cyclical resolution of the relationship between the country and the town, and so on (see Chapter 1 for a discussion of this concept). This posits the existence of a state of nature in which religion has not yet fulfilled its civilising and ethical role. Obviously, as has already been said and as we shall see again in relation to the caliphate, this does not entirely exclude the idea that religion and the Law may have a qualitative influence on political and social human forms: indeed, such forms are in some way ennobled and supported by religion, they function better and more usefully.

According to Ibn Khaldūn, there are three types of power. These have been clearly summarised by Francesco Gabrieli as follows:

> natural rule (*mulk tabīʿī*), pure tyrannical autocracy; political rule (*mulk siyāsī*), economic, secular and worldly state based on rational principles; and lastly caliphate (*khilāfah*) which is nothing other than a *mulk* where the legislation is divine and revealed in origin and where it is the duty of the head of state to guard and apply it as the successor (*khalīfa*) of the law-giving Prophet'.[35]

The text where these can be found expressed most systematically and usefully is Section XXIII of the third chapter of the *Muqaddima*:

> This makes it clear what the caliphate means. (To exercise) natural royal authority [*mulk tabīʿī*] means to cause the masses to act as required by purpose and desire. (To exercise) political (royal authority) means to cause the masses to act as required by intellectual (rational) insight [*al-nazar al-ʿaqlī*] into the means of furthering their worldly interests and avoiding anything that is harmful in that respect. (To exercise) the caliphate [*khilāfa*] means to cause the masses to act as required by religious insight into their interests in the other world as well as in this world. (Worldly interests) have bearing upon (the interests in the other world), since according to Muhammad all worldly conditions are to be considered in their relation to their value for the other world. Thus, (the caliphate) in reality is a substitute for Muhammad inasmuch as it serves, like him, to protect the religion and to exercise leadership of the world.[36] (Rosenthal 2005: 155)

This examination of the concept of power makes it possible to identify three levels: the state of nature, characterised chiefly by man's aggression toward his fellow man where power is inevitably oppressive and tyrannical; the rational state, concerned with the well-being of the community but not illuminated and inspired by the moral strength of religion; and, finally, the caliphate, provided for by religious Law.

Ibn Khaldūn holds a traditional view of the caliphate, strongly influenced by the classical doctrine of al-Māwardī. Nevertheless, from his point of view, the point of view of a witness to the collapsing unity of the Muslim empire, the caliphate is not a dead ideology but rather a hope that I have already defined as *teleological*. The caliphate is, for him, the best type of power to have appeared on Earth: because it is divine in origin (according to the classic doctrine of the jurists the necessity of the caliphate is revealed) and because with force and the moral glue of religion it has integrated the *ʿasabiyya*, or group feeling, of a chosen clan in the most productive way possible. For these reasons, Ibn Khaldūn puts forward a view of the caliphate which, if not idealised, is at least broadly positive, particularly with regard to the 'Rightly-Guided' caliphs. He gives his seal of approval to the Umayyad dynasty, or at least that of the first Umayyads including Muʿāwiya. In the evolution of Islamic history, the early caliphate, particularly of the golden age of the ʿAbbasids and the reign of Hārūn al-Rashīd, degenerated into a *mulk* dominated by personal autocracy and selfishness; in other words, theocratic power was corrupted, becoming a political realm where the rationality of its constitutive principles did not prevent the decline that strikes – fatally – at all human institutions.

Ibn Khaldūn's writings highlight the progressive process of disintegration of the power of the caliphate from its beginnings, in an almost mythical past, where the dedication of the sovereigns and subject-citizens themselves to the collective and state good had made it possible for the moral values of religion to be fully identified with and integrated with the political praxis of managing power. With the passing of time, the increasing decadence of the institutions began to coincide with a weakening of group feeling and the moral bond of prophecy. Ibn Khaldūn's theoretical reconstruction would seem to make sense from a teleological and ethical point of view. Government as described in the *Muqaddima*, however, is that which is possible from a natural point of view and also the one practised by the Islamic world of his time and historically determined by the political evolution of the Muslim world, particularly in the Maghreb. Ibn Khaldūn believes in the existence of a perfect state: it is the state of the first Umayyad and ʿAbbasid caliphs, the 'Rightly-Guided'. Consistent with the dominant viewpoint of classical Islamic political thought, he is, then, anti-utopian, in that he projects the reality of the just society into the past. Even if the *mulk* can exist without the sanction of religion, the ideal state will bring together a basis of ethics and religion with a secular and impersonal form of power in a fruitful combination that will guarantee the moral foundations on which every healthy social organisation should be constructed.

Notes

Part One

Chapter 1

1. Fakhry, *A History of Islamic Philosophy*, Longman/Columbia University Press, London and New York, 1983, p. 4.

2. Al-Shahrastānī, *Kitāb al-Milal wa al-Nihal* (*Libro delle religioni and delle sette*), ed. ʿA. M. al-'Abid, Maktaba al-Anglū al-Misriyya, Cairo, 1977, p. 48.

3. O. Leaman, *La filosofia islamica medievale*, Il Mulino, Bologna, 1991, p. 31.

4. Fakhry, *A History of Islamic Philosophy*, Longman/Columbia University Press, London and New York, 1983, p. 54.

5. A. Bausani, 'Cosmologia and religione nell'Islam', in *Scientia*, LXVIII, 1973, pp. 723–46; p. 727. The close relationship between atomism and religion has, however, been questioned by D. Gimaret, *La Doctrine d'al-Ash'arī*, Cerf, Paris, 1990.

6. A. Ivry, *Introduction to Al-Kindī's Metaphysics. A Translation of al-Kindī's Treatise 'On First Philosophy'*, SUNY Press, Albany, 1974, pp. 18–19.

7. D. Urvoy, *Les Penseurs Libres dans l'Islam Classique: l'Interrogation sur la Religion chez les Penseurs Arabes Indépendants*, Albin Michel, Paris, 1996.

8. Al-Fārābī, *L'Harmonie entre les Opinions de Platon et d'Aristote*, ed. F. Najjar and D. Mallet, Institut Français de Damas, Damascus, 1999, pp. 54 and 56.

9. Fakhry, *A History of Islamic Philosophy*, Longman/Columbia University Press, London and New York, 1983, p. 21.

10. C. D'Ancona Costa, *La casa della sapienza. La trasmissione della metafisica greca and la formazione della filosofia araba*, Guerini and Associati, Milan, 1996, pp. 80–1.

11. Fakhry, *A History of Islamic Philosophy*, Longman/Columbia University Press, London and New York, 1983, p. 31.

12. Al-Fārābī, *L'Harmonie entre les Opinions de Platon et d'Aristote*, ed. F. Najjar and D. Mallet, Institut Français de Damas, Damascus, 1999, p. 130.

13. P. Walker, Early *Philosophical Shiism. The Ismaili Neoplatonism of Abū Ya'qūb al-Sijistānī*, Cambridge University Press, Cambridge, 1993, p. 35.

14. I. R. Netton, *Muslim Neoplatonists. An Introduction to the Thought of the Brethren of Purity*, Edinburgh University Press, Edinburgh, 1991, p. 31.

15. J. Kraemer, *Humanism in the Renaissance of Islam. The Cultural Revival during the Buyid Age*, Brill, Leiden, 1992, p. 6.

16. Avicenna, *Le Livre de Science*, ed. M. Achena and H. Masse, Les Belles Lettres/ Unesco, Paris, 1986, Part I, p. 132.

17. Cf., for example, H. Corbin, *Avicenne et le Récit Visionnaire*, Berg, Paris 1979.

18. D. Gutas, *Avicenna and the Aristotelian Tradition*, Brill, Leiden 1988; but see also Gutas's more recent 'Avicenna's Eastern ("Oriental") Philosophy: Nature, Contents, Transmission', in *Arabic Sciences and Philosophy*, X, 2000, pp. 159–80.

19. R. Frank, *Creation and the Cosmic System*, Cari Winter Verlag, Heidelberg, 1992. On this subject see also J. Janssens, 'Al-Ghazālī's "Tahafut". Is it really a Rejection of Ibn Sīnā's Philosophy?', *Journal of Islamic Studies*, XII, 2001, l, pp. 1–17.

20. M. Cruz Hernández, *Historia del Pensamiento en al-Andalus*, Biblioteca de Cultura Andaluza, Seville, 1985, vol. I, pp. 44–9.

21. M. Cruz Hernández, 'Los Problemas del Pensamiento Islámico Andalusí en el Sigio XI', in *Ensayos sabre la Filósofia en el-Andalus*, ed. A. Martínez Lorca, Trotta, Madrid, 1990, pp. 178–93.

22. Avempace, *Il regime del solitario*, ed. M. Campanini and A. Illuminati, Rizzoli, Milan 2002, pp. 213 and 215.

23. Maimonides, *La guida dei perplessi*, ed. M. Zonta, UTET, Turin, 2003, p. 402.

24. Ibn Tufayl, *Epistola di Hayy Ibn Yaqzān*, ed. P. Carusi, Rusconi, Milan, 1983, p. 32.

25. Ibid., pp. 108–9.

26. M. Geoffroy, 'L 'Almohadisme Théologique de Averroes', in *Archives d'Histoire Doctrinale et Litteraire du Moyen Age*, LXXVI, 1999, p. 17.

27. Averroes, *Il Trattato decisivo*, ed. M. Campanini, Rizzoli, Milan, 1994, p. 47.

28. Averroes, *L'incoerenza dell' incoerenza dei filosofi*, ed. M. Campanini, UTET, Turin, 1997, p. 533.

29. Ibid., p. 534.

30. Averroes, *Discours Décisif*, ed. M. Geoffroy, introd. by A. De Libera, Flammarion, Paris, 1996.

31. Averroes, *Il Trattato decisivo*, ed. M. Campanini, Rizzoli, Milan, 1994, p. 115.

32. M. Parodi, 'Il tempo del confronto e dell'ascolto', in M. Bianchetti (ed.), *L'Islam e la filosofia. Tradizioni, identità, confronto*, Alboversorio, Milano 2006, pp. 15–26

33. H. Corbin, *Storia della filosofia islamica*, Adelphi, Milan, 1989, p. 209.

34. G. C. Anawati, *Introduction* to Avicenna, *La Metaphysique du Shifā'*, Vrin, Paris, 1978, vol. I, p. 47.

35. H. Ziai, 'Shihāb al-Dīn Suhrawardī', in *History of Islamic Philosophy*, ed. S. H. Nasr and O. Leaman, Routledge, London, 1996, vol. I, p. 443.

36. H. Corbin, *Storia della filosofia islamica*, Adelphi, Milan, 1989, pp. 339–40.

37. Cf. R. Arnaldez, *Grammaire et Théologie chez Ibn Hazm de Cordoue*, Vrin, Paris, 1981, p. 52.

38. R. Arnaldez, *Grammaire et Théologie chez Ibn Hazm de Cordoue*, Vrin, Paris, 1981, p. 44.

39. See M. Lombard, *Splendore and apogeo dell'Islam*, Rizzoli, Milan 1980.

40. E. Ashtor, *Storia economica and sociale del Vicino Oriente nel Medio Evo*, Einaudi, Turin, 1982.

41. Ibn Khaldùn, *Discours sur l'Histoire Universelle. Al-Muqaddima*, trans. V. Monteil, Commission Libanaise pour la Traduction des Chefs-d'Oeuvres, Beirut, 1967, p. 5 (adapted).

42. Y. Lacoste, *Ibn Khaldoun. Naissance de l'Histoire, Passé du Tiers-Monde*, Maspero, Paris, 1981, p. 172.

43. M. A. al-Yabri (al-Jābrī), *El Legado Filósofico Árabe*, Spanish trans. of *Nah-nu wa al-Turāth. Qirā 'āt Mu'āsira fi Turāthinā al-Falsafī (Our Tradition and Us. Contemporary Readings of our Philosophical Tradition)*, Trotta, Madrid, 2001, p. 356.

Chapter 2

1. A. De Libera and M. R. Hayoun, *Averroès et l'Averroisme*, PUF, Paris, 1991.

2. Averroes, *Il Trattato decisivo*, ed. M. Campanini, Rizzoli, Milan, 1994, p. 47.

3. A. Bausani, *L'Enciclopedia dei Fratelli della Purità*, Istituto Universitario Orientale, Naples, 1978, p. 175.

4. Ibid., p. 263.

5. R. Walzer, *Greek into Arabic*, Cassirer, Oxford, 1962, p. 11.

6. D. Gutas, *Pensiero greco and cultura araba*, Einaudi, Turin, 2002, pp. 59 and 61.

7. Ibid., p. 87.

8. Ibid., pp. 97 and 111.

9. Ibid., p. 100.

10. M. A. al-Jabri, *La ragione araba*, Feltrinelli, Milan, 1996, p. 72.

11. D. Gutas, *Pensiero greco and cultura araba*, Einaudi, Turin, 2002, p. 140.

12. C. D'Ancona Costa, *La casa della sapienza. La trasmissione della metafisica greca and la formazione della filosofia araba*, Guerini and Associati, Milan, 1996, pp. 116–17.

13. Ibid., p. 141,

14. C. Baffioni, *I grandi pensatori dell'Islam*, Edizioni Lavoro, Roma 1996, p. 9.

15. R. Walzer, *Alfarabi on the Perfect State*, notes and trans., Clarendon Press, Oxford, 1985.

16. In al-Fārābī, *La città virtuosa*, ed. M. Campanini, Rizzoli, Milan, 1996.

17. M. Galston, *Politics and Excellence. The Political Philosophy of Alfarabi*, Princeton University Press, Princeton, 1990.

18. J. Puig Montada, 'El Proyecto Vital de Averroes: Explicar e Interpretar a Aristoteles', in *Al-Qantara*, XXIII, 2002, pp. 11–52; p. 51.

19. M. Cruz Hernández, *Averroes. Vida, Obra, Pensamiento, Influencia*, Caja de Ahorros de Córdoba, Cordoba, 1986, pp. 63 and 66.

20. Abi Bakr Mohammadi Filii Zachariae (Rhazes), *Opera Philosophica fragmentaque quae supersunt (Rasā 'il Falsafiyya)*, ed. P. Kraus, Dār al-Āfāq al-Jadīda, Beirut, 1977, pp. 101–2.

21. Cf. L. E. Goodman, 'The Epicurean Ethic of Muhammad ben Zakariyyā' al-Rāzī', in *Studia Islamica*, XXXIV, 1971, pp. 5–26.

22. Abi Bakr Mohammadi Filii Zachariae (Rhazes), *Opera Philosophica fragmentaque quae supersunt (Rasā 'il Falsafiyya)*, ed. P. Kraus, Dār al-Āfāq al-Jadīda, Beirut, 1977, p. 105.

23. Avempace, *Il regime del solitario*, ed. M. Campanini and A. Illuminati, Rizzoli, Milan, 2002, p. 109.

24. Ibid., pp. 95 and 97.

25. Ibid., p. 199.

26. Ibid., p. 97.

27. Averroes, *L'incoerenza dell' incoerenza dei filosofi*, ed. M. Campanini, UTET, Turin, 1997, p. 533.

28. Ibid.

29. A. Bausani, *Un filosofo laico del Medioevo musulmano: Abū Bakr Muhammad Ibn Zakariyyā Rāzī*, Istituto di Studi Islamici, Rome, 1981, pp. 47–49.

30. Al-Fārābī, *La città virtuosa*, ed. M. Campanini, Rizzoli, Milan, 1996, pp. 199 and 201.

31. Ibid., p. 219.

32. In O. Leaman, *La filosofia islamica medievale*, II Mulino, Bologna, 1991, p. 213.

33. Al-Fārābī, *La città virtuosa*, ed. M. Campanini, Rizzoli, Milan, 1996, p. 251.

34. Averroes, *Il Trattato decisivo*, ed. M. Campanini, Rizzoli, Milan, 1994, p. 83.

35. O. Leaman, *Averroes and his Philosophy*, Clarendon Press, Oxford, 1988, pp. 195–6.

36. Averroes, *Il Trattato decisivo*, ed. M. Campanini, Rizzoli, Milan, 1994, p. 107.

Chapter 3

1. H. Corbin, *Storia della filosofia islamica*, Adelphi, Milan, 1989, p. 40.

2. Ibid., p. 55.

3. Ibid., p. 40.

4. S. H. Nasr takes the view that Islamic philosophy is always correlated with religion and very often linked with Illuminationism (cf. 'The Meaning and Role of Philosophy in Islam', in *Studia Islamica*, XXXVII, 1973, pp. 57–80).

5. H. Corbin, *Storia della filosofia islamica*, Adelphi, Milan, 1989, p. 246.

6. Ibid, p. 281.

7. L. Strauss, *Scrittura e persecuzione*, Marseille, Venice, 1990 and *How Fārābī read Plato's Laws*, in *Mélanges Louis Massignon*, Institut Français de Damas, Damascus 1957, vol. III, pp. 319–44.

8. Al-Fārābī, *Compendio delle 'Leggi' di Platone*, appendix to Plato, *Dialoghi Politici. Lettere*, ed. F. Adorno, vol. II, UTET, Turin, 1996, p. 742.

9. O. Leaman, *La filosofia islamica medievale*, II Mulino, Bologna, 1991, p. 289.

10. M. A. al-Jabri, *La ragione araba*, Feltrinelli, Milan, 1996, p. 75.

11. Ibid., p.78.

12. M. A. al-Jabri, *Takwīn al-'Aql al-ʿArabī (Formation of the Arab Intellect)*, Markaz Dirāsāt al-Wahda al-ʿArabiyya, Beirut, 1994, pp. 299–323.

13. See M. A. al-Jabri, *La ragione araba*, Feltrinelli, Milan, 1996, p. 90.

14. M. A. al-Jabri, *Takwīn al-'Aql al-ʿArabī (Formation of the Arab Intellect)*, Markaz Dirāsāt al-Wahda al-ʿArabiyya, Beirut, 1994, p. 313.

15. See M. A. al-Jabri, *La ragione araba*, Feltrinelli, Milan, 1996, p. 87.

16. Other scholars have argued against this type of interpretation. D. Gutas, passionate advocate of Avicenna, accuses Averroes of being a reactionary who even sought to 'pervert the course of history'(!). D. Gutas, *Filosofia greca, filosofia araba*, in *I Greci. Storia, cultura, arte, società*, ed. S. Settis, vol. III, *I Greci oltre la Grecia*, Einaudi, Turin, 2001, p. 793.

17. See M. A. al-Jabri, *La ragione araba*, Feltrinelli, Milan, 1996, p. 141.

Part Two

Chapter 4

1. Al-Ashʿarī, *Maqālāt al-Islāmiyyn (Sayings of the Muslims)*, ed. M. M. ʿAbd al-Hamīd, Maktabat al-Nahda al-Misriyya, Cairo, 1967, vol. I, p. 235.

2. Ibid., vol. I, pp. 259–60.

3. Ibid., vol. II, p. 202.

4. Al-Baghdādī, *Al-Farq bayna al-Firaq (The difference between the Sects)*, Dār al-Kutub al-ʿIlmiyya, Beirut, 1985, p. 132.

5. Al-Shahrastānī, *Kitāb al-Milal wa al-Nihal* (*Libro delle religioni and delle sette*), ed. ʿA. M. al-'Abid, Maktaba al-Anglū al-Misriyya, Cairo, 1977, p. 57.

6. Al-Ashʿarī, *Maqālāt al-Islāmiyyn (Sayings of the Muslims)*, ed. M. M. ʿAbd al-Hamīd, Maktabat al-Nahda al-Misriyya, Cairo, 1967, vol. II, p. 204.

7. P. Walker, *Early Philosophical Shiism. The Ismaili Neoplatonism of Abū Ya'qūb al-Sijistānī*, Cambridge University Press, Cambridge, 1993, p. 79.

8. Trans. of H. Corbin in *Trilogie Ismaelienne*, Verdier, Lagrasse, 1994, p. 44.

9. Ibid., p. 25, note 19.

10. *L'Epistola degli Ikhwān al-Sāfā ' 'Sulle opinioni and le religioni'*, ed. C. Baffioni, Istituto Universitario Orientale, Naples, 1989, p. 193.

11. Al-Fārābī, *La città virtuosa*, ed. M. Campanini, Rizzoli, Milan, 1996, p. 59.

12. See *Obras Filósofico-Políticas*, ed. R. Ramón Guerrero, Debate/CSIC, Madrid, 1992, p. 3 (Arabic text).

13. See al-Fārābī, *La città virtuosa*, ed. M. Campanini, Rizzoli, Milan, 1996, p. 63.

14. Ibid., p. 75.

15. Ibid., p. 65.

16. Ibid., p. 93.

17. Ibid., p. 73.

18. Ibid., p. 91.

19. Ibid., p. 97.

20. Ibid., p. 93.

21. Ibid., p. 75.

22. Averroes, *L'incoerenza dell' incoerenza dei filosofi*, ed. M. Campanini, UTET, Turin, 1997, p. 131.

23. L. E. Goodman, *Avicenna*, Routledge, London, 1992, p. 102.

24. Cf. L. Gardet and G. C. Anawati, *Introduction à la Théologie Musulmane*, Vrin, Paris, 1981.

25. J. Jolivet, *Aux Origines de l'Ontologie de Ibn Sīnā*, in J. Jolivet and R. Rashed (eds), *Etudes sur Avicenne*, Les Belles Lettres, Paris, 1984, pp. 19–28.

26. Al-Ghazālī, *La Nicchia delle luci*, TEA, Milan 1989, pp. 64–5.

27. Al-Ghazālī, *L'Unicità divina and l'abbandono fiducioso*, ed. P. Urizzi, Il Cerchio, s.l.e., 1995, pp. 26–7.

28. Cit. in I. R. Netton, *Allah Transcendent*, Curzon, Richmond 1994, p. 271.

29. Ibn ʿArabi, *La Sagesse des Prophètes (Fuçūç al-Hikam)*, ed. T. Burckhardt, Albin Michel, Paris, 1974, pp. 99–102 *passim*.

30. A. Ventura, *Introduzione* to T. Izutsu, *Unicità dell'esistenza*, Marietti, Genoa 1991, pp. XI–XV.

31. Al-Ghazalī, *Il libro della meditazione*, ed. G. Celentano, Siti, Trieste, 1988, p. 67.

32. See Al-Ghazālī, *La Nicchia delle luci*, TEA, Milan 1989, p. 71.

33. Ibid., pp. 94ff.

34. Cf. *La Profession de Foi d'Ibn Taymiyya. La Wāsitiyya*, ed. H. Laoust, Geuthner, Paris, 1986, p. 59.

Chapter 5

1 Al-Fārābī, *La città virtuosa*, ed. M. Campanini, Rizzoli, Milan, 1996, p. 97.

2. Ibid., p. 105.

3. Cit. in I. R. Netton, *Muslim Neoplatonists. An Introduction to the Thought of the Brethren of Purity*, Edinburgh University Press, Edinburgh, 1991, p. 34.

4. Cit. in S. H. Nasr, *An Introduction to Islamic Cosmological Doctrines*, Thames and Hudson, London, 1978, p. 67.
5. S. Afnan, *Avicenna. Vita e opere*, Patron, Bologna, 1969, p. 244.
6. A. Badawi, *Histoire de la Philosophie en Islam*, Vrin, Paris, 1972, vol. II, p. 656.
7. H. Davidson, *Alfarabi, Avicenna and Averroes on Intellect*, Oxford University Press, London and New York, 1992, p. 82.
8. See G. Endress, 'Averroes' De Coelo. Ibn Kushd's Cosmology in his Commentaries on Aristotle's On the Heaven', in *Arabic Science and Philosophy*, V, 1995, pp. 9–49.
9. Averroes, *L'incoerenza dell' incoerenza dei filosofi*, ed. M. Campanini, UTET, Turin, 1997, pp. 238–42.
10. Cf. H. Davidson, *Alfarabi, Avicenna and Averroes on Intellect*, Oxford University Press, London and New York, 1992, p. 256.
11. *Ibn Rushd's Metaphysics: A Translation with Introduction of Ibn Rushd's Commentary on Aristotle's Metaphysics. Book Lam*, ed. C. Genequand, Brill, Leiden, 1986, p. 149.
12 Ibid., p. 154.
13. Ibid., p. 151.

Chapter 6

1. Fakhry, *A History of Islamic Philosophy*, Longman/Columbia University Press, London and New York, 1983, p. 87.
2. H. Davidson, *Alfarabi, Avicenna and Averroes on Intellect*, Oxford University Press, London and New York, 1992, p. 28.
3. Al-Fārābī, *Epistola sull'intelletto*, ed. F. Lucchetta, Antenore, Padua, 1974, pp. 96–100.
4. Ibid., p. 102.
5. Al-Fārābī, *La città virtuosa*, ed. M. Campanini, Rizzoli, Milan, 1996, p. 177.
6. Ibid., pp. 180–1.
7. Ibid., p. 179 (modified).
8. Ibid., p. 217.
9. Ibid., p. 219.
10. H. Davidson, *Alfarabi, Avicenna and Averroes on Intellect*, Oxford University Press, London and New York, 1992, p. 85.
11. Avicenna, *Livre des Directives et des Remarques*, ed. A. M. Goichon, Vrin, Paris, 1951, pp. 324–6.
12. The numbering of the paragraphs follows that in the edition prepared by M. Asín Palacios, *Tratado de Avempace sobre la Unión del Intelecto con el Hombre*, in 'Al-Andalus' VII, 1942, pp. 1–47.
13. Averroes, *Commentarium Magnum in Aristotelis de Anima Libros*, recensuit F. Crawford, reprint Bayt al-Hikma, Tunis, 1999, p. 496.
14. Ibid., pp. 410–11.
15. Ibid., p. 495.
16. In Averroes, *L'Intelligence et la Pensée. Grand Commentaire du «De Anima». Livre III*, ed. A. De Libera, Flammarion, Paris, 1998, p. 386.
17. Averroes, *Commentarium Magnum in Aristotelis de Anima Libros*, recensuit F. Crawford, reprint Bayt al-Hikma, Tunis, 1999, p. 411.
18. H. Davidson, *Alfarabi, Avicenna and Averroes on Intellect*, Oxford University Press, London and New York, 1992, p. 297.
19. Averroes, *Commentarium Magnum in Aristotelis de Anima Libros*, recensuit F. Crawford, reprint Bayt al-Hikma, Tunis, 1999, p. 481.
20. Ibid., p. 499.

21. Ibid., p. 406.

22. See R. Taylor in 'Personal Immortality in Averroes' Mature Philosophical Psychology', in *Documenti e studi sulla tradizione filosofica medievale*, IX, 1998, pp. 87–110; Taylor discusses and rejects O. Mohammed's theory according to which Averroes' doctrine in the commentary on Aristotle can be justified in the light of Qur'anic anthropology (O. Mohammed, *Averroes' Doctrine of Immortality. A Matter of Controversy*, Wilfried Laurie University Press, Ottawa, 1984).

23. Averroes, *Commentarium Magnum in Aristotelis de Anima Libros*, recensuit F. Crawford, reprint Bayt al-Hikma, Tunis, 1999, p. 409.

24. Ibid., p. 476.

25. Ibid., pp. 407–8

26. Al-Fārābī, *La città virtuosa*, ed. M. Campanini, Rizzoli, Milan, 1996, pp. 217–19.

27. Cf. A. Illuminati, *Completa beatitudo. L'intelletto felice in tre opuscoli averroisti*, L'Orecchio di Van Gogh, Chiaravalle, 2000, pp. 50–1 and 56–7.

28. Averroes, *Commentarium Magnum in Aristotelis de Anima Libros*, recensuit F. Crawford, reprint Bayt al-Hikma, Tunis, 1999, p. 451.

29. H. Davidson, *Alfarabi, Avicenna and Averroes on Intellect*, Oxford University Press, London and New York, 1992, pp. 339–40.

Chapter 7

1. For a methodological framework, J. Puig Montada, 'Ibn Rushd vs. al-Ghazālī: Reconsideration of a Polemic', in *The Muslim World*, LXXXII, 1992, pp. 113–31, which seeks to show how the positions of the two thinkers are not necessarily always as inflexible and straightforward as is sometimes thought.

2. Al-Ghazālī, *Scritti scelti*, ed. L. Veccia Vaglieri and R. Rubinacci, UTET, Turin, 1970, p. 93.

3. M. Marmura, 'Al-Ghazālī and Demonstrative Science', in *Journal of the History of Philosopy*, III, 1965, pp. 183–204; pp. 184 and 188.

4. M. Cruz Hernández, *Historia del Pensamiento en al-Andalus*, Biblioteca de Cultura Andaluza, Seville, 1985, vol. II, pp. 74. See also *Storia del pensiero nel mondo islamico*, Paideia, Brescia, 2000, vol. II, p. 619.

5. Averroes, *L'incoerenza dell' incoerenza dei filosofi*, ed. M. Campanini, UTET, Turin, 1997, p. 153.

6. Ibid., p. 306.

7. Ibid., p. 489.

8. Al-Ghazālī , *The Ninety-Nine Beautiful Names of God*, ed. D. Burrell and N. Daher, The Islamic Texts Society, Cambridge, 1995, p. 68.

9. B. Kogan, *Averroes and the Metaphysics of Causation*, SUNY Press, Albany, 1985, p. 214.

10. Averroes, *L'incoerenza dell' incoerenza dei filosofi*, ed. M. Campanini, UTET, Turin, 1997, p. 208.

11. Ibid., p. 200.

12. Averroes, *Il Trattato decisivo*, ed. M. Campanini, Rizzoli, Milan, 1994, pp. 73ff.

13. See Averroes, *L'incoerenza dell' incoerenza dei filosofi*, ed. M. Campanini, UTET, Turin, 1997, p. 168.

14. Ibid., pp. 103–4.

15. Ibid., pp. 105–6.

16. Ibid., p. 124.

17. Ibid.

18. Ibid., pp. 153–4 (my italics).

19. Ibid., p. 156.
20. Ibid., p. 155.
21. Ibid., p. 189.
22. Averroes, *Damīma o Appendice, Il Trattato decisivo*, ed. M. Campanini, Rizzoli, Milan, 1994, pp. 125–7.
23. See Averroes, *L'incoerenza dell' incoerenza dei filosofi*, ed. M. Campanini, UTET, Turin, 1997, p. 190.
24. Ibid., p. 478.
25. Ibid., p. 488.
26. Ibid., p. 478.
27. Ibid., p. 482.

Chapter 8

1. Ibn Khaldūn, *Discours sur l'Histoire Universelle. Al-Muqaddima*, trans. V. Monteil, Commission Libanaise pour la Traduction des Chefs-d'Oeuvres, Beirut, 1967, p. 85.
2. Ibid., p. 86.
3. Ibid., p. 88.
4. Al-Fārābī, *La città virtuosa*, ed. M. Campanini, Rizzoli, Milan, 1996, p. 205.
5. Ibid., p. 183
6. Al-Fārābī, *The Attainment of Happiness*, in *Alfarabi's Philosophy of Plato and Aristotle*, ed. M. Mahdi, Free Press, Glencoe, 1962, p. 13.
7. Ibid., p. 27.
8. Avempace, *Il regime del solitario*, ed. M. Campanini and A. Illuminati, Rizzoli, Milan, 2002, p. 199.
9. *Averroes' Commentary on Plato's Republic*, ed. E. Rosenthal, Cambridge University Press, Cambridge, 1956, p. 112.
10. Ibid., pp. 112–13.
11. Ibid., p. 188.
12. Ibid., p. 183.
13. Ibid., p. 182.
14. Al-Ghazālī, *Scritti scelti*, ed. L. Veccia Vaglieri and R. Rubinacci, UTET, Turin, 1970, pp. 179-180.
15. Ibid., pp. 178–9.
16. Cit. in E. Ormsby, *Theodicy in Islamic Thought*, Princeton University Press, Princeton, 1990, p. 39.
17. Al-Ghazālī, *Kitab al-Arba'īn fī Usūl al-Dīn (Libro sui quaranta princìpi della religione)*, Maktabat al-Jindī, Cairo, 1970, p. 268.
18. Al-Ghazālī, *Counsel for Kings*, ed. F. R. C. Bagley, Oxford University Press, Oxford and New York, 1964, pp. 57–8.
19. Averroes, *Svelamento dei metodi di prova*, trans. in Averroes, *L'Islam et la Raison*, ed. M. Geoffroy and A. De Libera, Flammarion, Paris, 2000, pp. 143–4.
20. Al-Ghazālī, *Scritti scelti*, ed. L. Veccia Vaglieri and R. Rubinacci, UTET, Turin, 1970, p. 175.
21. Averroes, *L'Islam et la Raison*, ed. M. Geoffroy and A. De Libera, Flammarion, Paris, 2000, p. 136.
22. Ibid., p. 137.
23. Al-Ghazālī, *Counsel for Kings*, ed. F. R. C. Bagley, Oxford University Press, Oxford and New York, 1964, pp. 45–6.
24. Cf. also Ibn Taymiyya, *Il buon governo dell'Islàm (Siyâsa Shar'iyya)*, ed. G. M.

Piccinelli, suppl. no. 2 to 'Tatuino-Taqwim' (Journal of the Centro Interdipartimentale di Scienze dell'Islam 'Re Abdulaziz' of Bologna University), Bologna, 2001.

25. Ibn Khaldūn, *Discours sur l'Histoire Universelle. Al-Muqaddima*, trans. V. Monteil, Commission Libanaise pour la Traduction des Chefs-d'Oeuvres, Beirut, 1967, p. 746.

26. Ibid., p. 786.

27. Ibid., pp. 574–5.

28. Averroes' Commentary on Plato's Republic cit., p. 115.

29. Ibid., p. 160.

30. Ibid., p. 119.

31. Ibid., p. 209.

32. Ibid., p. 216.

33. Ibn Khaldūn, *Discours sur l'Histoire Universelle. Al-Muqaddima*, trans. V. Monteil, Commission Libanaise pour la Traduction des Chefs-d'Oeuvres, Beirut, 1967, pp. 78–9.

34. Al-Ghazālī, *Al-Iqtisād fī al-Iʿtiqād* (*Il giusto medio nella credenza*), Maktabat al-Jindī, Cairo, 1972, pp. 196–7.

35. F. Gabrieli, 'Il concetto di 'asabiyya nel pensiero storico di Ibn Khaldūn', in *L'Islam nella storia*, Dedalo, Bari, 1984, p. 240.

36. Ibn Khaldūn, *Discours sur l'Histoire Universelle. Al-Muqaddima*, trans. V. Monteil, Commission Libanaise pour la Traduction des Chefs-d'Oeuvres, Beirut, 1967, p. 370.

Bibliography

General works

E. Rosenthal, *Political Thought in Medieval Islam*, Cambridge University Press, Cambridge, 1958.
A History of Muslim Philosophy, ed. M. M. Sharif, Harassowitz, Wiesbaden, 1963 (2 vols).
A. Badawi, *Histoire de la Philosophie en Islam*, Vrin, Paris, 1972 (2 vols).
M. Fakhry, *A History of Islamic Philosophy*, Longman/Columbia University Press, London and New York, 1983.
C. Bouamrane and L. Gardet, *Panorama de la Pensée Islamique*, Sindbad, Paris, 1984.
M. Cruz Hernández, *Pensamiento islámico: investigación su tradición y actualidad*, Anthropos, Barcelona, 1988.
C. Baffioni, *Storia della filosofia islamica*, Mondadori, Milan, 1991.
H. Corbin, *History of Islamic Philosophy*, trans L. and P. Sherrard, Institute of Ismaili Studies, London, 1993.
W. M. Watt, *Islamic Philosophy and Theology*, Edinburgh University Press, Edinburgh, 1995.
C. Baffioni, *I grandi pensatori dell'Islam*, Edizioni Lavoro, Rome, 1996.
History of Islamic Philosophy, ed. S. H. Nasr and O. Leaman, Routledge, London, 1996 (2 vols).
A. Black, *The History of Islamic Political Thought*, Edinburgh University Press, Edinburgh, 2001.
O. Leaman, *An Introduction to Classical Islamic Philosophy*, Cambridge University Press, Cambridge, 2002.
M. Campanini, *Islam e politica*, II Mulino, Bologna, 2003.
C. D'Ancona (ed.), *Storia delle filosofia nell'Islam medievale*, Einaudi, Turin, 2005 (2 vols).
P. Adamson and R. Taylor (eds), *The Cambridge Companion to Arabic Philosophy*, Cambridge University Press, 2005.

Websites

www.muslimphilosophy
www.alwaraq.com

Works on the authors mentioned in the text

Muʿtazilites and Ashʿarites

Texts

Al-Shahrastānī, *Livre des Religions et des Sectes*, vol. I, ed. D. Gimaret and G. Monnot, Peeters-Unesco, Leuven, 1986; vol. II, ed. J. Jolivet and G. Monnot, Peeters-Unesco, Leuven, 1993.

Studies

H. A. Wolfson, *The Philosophy of the Kalam*, Harvard University Press, Cambridge, MA and London, 1976.
C. Baffioni, *Atomismo and antiatomismo nel pensiero islamico*, Istituto Universitario Orientale, Naples, 1982.
D. Gimaret, *La Doctrine d'Al-Ash'arī*, Cerf, Paris, 1990.
J. Van Ess, *Theologie und Gesellschaft im 2 und 3 Jahrhundert Hidschra Eine Geschichte des religiösen Denkens im frühen Islam*, De Gruyter, Berlin and New York, 1991–7 (6 vols).
J. Van Ess, *Prémices de la Théologie Musulmane*, Albin Michel, Paris, 2002.

Al-Kindī

Texts

Al-Kindī's Metaphysics. A Translation of al-Kindī's Treatise 'On First Philosophy', ed. A. Ivry, SUNY Press, Albany, 1974.
Oeuvres Philosophiques et Scientifiques d'al-Kindī, ed. R. Rashed and J. Jolivet, Brill, Leiden, 1998 (2 vols).

Studies

J. Jolivet, *L'Intellect selon Kindī*, Brill, Leiden, 1971.
E. Tornero, *Al-Kindī. La Transformación de un Pensamiento Religioso en un Pensamiento Racional*, CSIC, Madrid, 1992.

Rhazes and the 'free thinkers'

Texts

Abi Bakr Mohammadi Filii Zachariae, *Opera Philosophica fragmentaque quae supersunt (Rasā'il Falsafiyya)*, ed. P. Kraus, Dār al-Āfāq al-Jadīda, Beirut, 1977.

Studies

D. Urvoy, *Les Penseurs Libres dans l'Islam Classique: l'Interrogation sur la Religion chez les Penseurs Arabes Indépendants*, Albin Michel, Paris, 1996.
S. Stroumsa, *Freethinkers of Medieval Islam: Ibn al-Rawāndī, Abū Bakr al-Rāzī and their Impact on Islamic Thought*, Brill, Leiden, 1999.

Al-Fārābī

Texts

Alfarabi's Philosophy of Plato and Aristotle, ed. M. Mahdi, Free Press, Glencoe, 1962.
Epistola sul'intelletto, ed. F. Lucchetta, Antenore, Padua, 1974.
Alfarabi on the Perfect State, ed. R. Walzer, Clarendon Press, Oxford, 1985.
Obras Filosófico-Politicas, ed. R. Ramón Guerrero, Debate/CSIC, Madrid, 1992.
La città virtuosa, ed. M. Campanini, Rizzoli, Milan, 1996.
L'Harmonie entre les Opinions de Platon et d'Aristote, ed. F. Najjar and D. Mallet, Institut Français de Damas, Damasco, 1999.
Alfarabi. The Political Writings, 'Selected Aphorisms' and Other Texts, ed. C. Butterworth, Cornell University Press, Ithaca, 2001.
Epâtre sur l'Intellect, ed. D. Hamzah, L'Harmattan, Paris, 2001.
Scritti politici, ed. M. Campanini, UTET, Turin, 2007.

Studies

M. Galston, *Politics and Excellence. The Political Philosophy of Alfarabi*, Princeton University Press, Princeton, 1990.
M. Mahdi, *La Cité Vertueuse d'Alfarabi*, Albin Michel, Paris, 2000.
M. Mahdi, *Alfarabi and the Foundation of Islamic Political Philosophy*, Chicago University Press, Chicago, 2001.
M. Fakhry, *Al-Fārābī, Founder of Islamic Neoplatonism*, Oneworld, Oxford, 2002.

Renaissance in the Buyid Era

Texts

Al-Miskawayh, *Traité d'Ethique*, ed. M. Arkoun, Institut Français de Damas, Damasco, 1969.

Studies

M. Arkoun, *Contribution à l'Etude de l'Humanisme Arabe au IV/X Siècle. Miskawayh, Philosophe et Historien*, Vrin, Paris, 1970.
J. Kraemer, *Humanism in the Renaissance of Islam. The Cultural Revival during the Buyid Age*, Brill, Leiden, 1992.
I. R. Netton, *Al-Fārābī and his School*, Routledge, London, 1992.

Ismaelite thinkers and the Brothers of Purity

Texts

Abu Ya'qub Sejestani, *Le Dévoilement des Choses Cachées*, ed. H. Corbin, Verdier, Lagrasse, 1988.

L'Epistola degli Ikhān al-Safā ' sulle Opinioni and le Religioni, ed. C. Baffioni, Istituto Universitario Orientale, Naples, 1989.

Trilogie Ismaélienne. Abū Ya'qūb Sejestānī, 'Le Livre des Sources'. Al-Hosayn Ibn 'Alī, 'Cosmogonie et Escatologie'. Mahmūd Shabestarī 'La Roseraire du Mystère', ed. H. Corbin, Verdier, Lagrasse, 1994.

Studies

Y. Marquet, *La Philosophie des Ikhwān al-Safā '*, Algers, 1975.

A. Bausani, *L'Enciclopedia dei Fratelli della Purità*, Istituto Universitario Orientale, Naples, 1978.

I. R. Netton, *Muslim Neoplatonists. An Introduction to the Thought of the Brethren of Purity*, Edinburgh University Press, Edinburgh, 1991.

P. Walker, *The Wellsprings of Wisdom: A Study of Abū Ya'qūb al-Sijistānī's 'Kitāb al-Yanābi''*, Salt Lake City, Utah, 1994.

D. De Smet, *La Quiétude de l'Intellect: Néoplatonisme et Gnose Ismaélienne dans l'Oeuvre de Hamīd al-Dīn al-Kirmānī*, Louvain, 1995.

P. Walker, *Hamīd al-Dīn al-Kirmānī. Ismaili Thought in the Age of al-Hākim*, I. B. Tauris, London and New York, 1999.

Avicenna

Texts

Livre des Directives et des Remarques, ed. A. M. Goichon, Vrin, Paris, 1951.

Epistola sulla vita futura, ed. F. Lucchetta, Antenore, Padua, 1969.

La Métaphysique du Shifā ', ed. G. Anawati, Vrin, Paris, 1978–85 (2 vols).

Le Livre de Science, ed. M. Achena and H. Masse, Les Belles Lettres/UNESCO, Paris, 1986.

Metafisica, ed. O. Lizzini and P. Porro, Bompiani, Milan, 2002.

Studies

L. Gardet, *La Pensée Religieuse d'Avicenne*, Vrin, Paris, 1951.

A. Afnan, *Avicenna. Vita and opere*, Patron, Bologna, 1969.

H. Corbin, *Avicenne et le Récit Visionnaire*, Berg, Paris, 1979.

J. Jolivet and R. Rashed (eds), *Etudes sur Avicenne,* Les Belles Lettres, Paris, 1984.

D. Gutas, *Avicenna and the Aristotelian Tradition*, Leiden, Brill, 1988.

L. Goodman, *Avicenna*, Routledge, London, 1992.

M. Sebti, *Avicenne. L'Ame humaine*, Presses Universitaires de France, Paris, 2000.

Avicenna and his Heritage, ed. J. Janssens and D. De Smet, Leuven University Press, Leuven, 2002.

Al-Ghazālī

Texts

Scritti scelti, ed. L. Veccia Vaglieri and R. Rubinacci, UTET, Turin, 1970.
Freedom and Fulfillment, ed. J. McCarthy, Twayne, Boston, 1980.
The Faith and Practice of al-Ghazali, ed. W. M. Watt, Oneworld, Oxford, 1994.
The Incoherence of the Philosophers, ed. M. Marmura, Brigham Young University, Provo, 1997.
Le perle del Corano, ed. M. Campanini, Rizzoli, Milan, 2000.

Studies

A. Wensinck, *La Pensée de Ghazālī*, Maisonneuve, Paris, 1940.
F. Jabre, *La Notion de Certitude selon Ghazālī*, Vrin, Paris, 1958.
H. Laoust, *La Politique de Ghazālī*, Geuthner, Paris, 1970.
R. M. Frank, *Creation and the Cosmic System. Al- Ghazālī and Avicenna*, Carl Winter, Heidelberg, 1992.
D. Burrell, *Al-Ghazālī: Faith in Divine Unity and Trust in Divine Providence*, Four Courts Press, Dublin, 2001.

Website

www.ghazali.org

Avempace

Texts

El Regimen del Solitario, ed. J. Lomba, Trotta, Madrid, 1997.
'Avempace. Tratado de la Unión del Intelecto con el Hombre', ed. J. Lomba, in *Anaquel de Estudios Arabes*, XI, 2000, pp. 369–91.
Il regime del solitario, ed. M. Campanini and A. Illuminati, Rizzoli, Milan, 2002.

Studies

G. Zainaty, *La Morale d'Avempace*, Vrin, Paris, 1979.
J. Lomba, *Avempace, Deputación de Aragon*, Zaragoza, 1989.
S. Harvey, 'The Place of the Philosophers in the City according to Ibn Bājjah', in *Political Aspects of Islamic Philosophy*, ed. C. Butterworth, Harvard University Press, Cambridge, MA, 1992, pp. 199–233.
J. Lomba, 'Lectura de la Etica Griega por el Pensamiento de Ibn Bāyya', in *Al-Qantara*, XIV, 1993, 1, pp. 1–43.

Ibn Tufayl

Texts

Ibn Tufayl's Hayy Ibn Yaqzān, ed. L. Goodman, Twayne, New York, 1972.
L'Epistola di Hayy Ibn Yaqzān, ed. P. Carusi, Rusconi, Milan, 1983.
El Filósofo Autodidacto, ed. A. González Palencia and E. Tornero, Trotta, Madrid, 1995.

Studies

S. Hawi, *Islamic Naturalism and Mysticism: a Philosophic Study of Ibn Tufayl's Hayy Ibn Yaqzān*, Brill, Leiden, 1974.
L. I. Conrad (ed.), *The World of Ibn Tufayl: Interdisciplinary Perspectives on Hayy Ibn Yaqzān*, Brill, Leiden, 1996.

Averroes

Texts

The Incoherence of the Incoherence, ed. S. Van den Bergh, Luzac, London, 1962.
Averroes on Plato's 'Republic', ed. R. Lerner, Ithaca, 1974.
Grand Commentaire de la 'Metaphysique' d'Aristote. Livre Lam-Lambda, ed. A. Martin, Vrin, Paris, 1984.
Discours Décisif, ed. M. Geoffroy and A. De Libera, Flammarion, Paris, 1996.
L'Incoerenza dell'incoerenza, ed. M. Campanini, UTET, Torino, 1997.
L'Intelligence et la Pensée. Grand Commentaire du 'De Anima'. Livre III, ed. A. De Libera, Flammarion, Paris, 1998.
L'Islam et la Raison, ed. M. Geoffroy, Flammarion, Paris, 2000.
Trattato decisivo sull'accordo della religione con la filosofia, ed. M. Campanini, Rizzoli, Milan, 2001.
Averroes' Middle Commentary on De Anima, ed. A. Ivry, Brigham Young University Press, Provo, 2002.

Studies

Multiple Averroès, ed. J. Jolivet, Les Belles Lettres, Paris, 1978.
C. Butterworth, *Philosophy, Ethics and Virtuous Rule. A Study of Averroes' Commentary on Plato's 'Republic'*, American University in Cairo Press, Cairo, 1986.
D. Urvoy, *Ibn Rushd (Averroes)*, Routledge, London and New York, 1991.
A. Martinez Lorca (ed.), *Al Encuentro de Averroes*, Trotta, Madrid, 1993.
A. Illuminati, *Averroè and l'intelletto pubblico*, Manifestolibri, Rome, 1996.
M. Cruz Hernández, *Abū 'l-Walīd Ibn Rushd (Averroes). Vida, Obra, Pensamiento, Influencia*, Cajasur, Córdoba, 1997.
D. Urvoy, *Averroès. Les Ambitions d'un Intellectuel Musulman*, Flammarion, Paris, 1998.
O. Leaman, *Averroes and his Philosophy*, Curzon Press, Richmond, 1998.
G. Endress and J. Aertsen (ed.), *Averroes and the Aristotelian Tradition*, Brill, Leiden, 1999.
M. Fakhry, *Averroes (Ibn Rushd). His Works and Influence*, Oneworld, Oxford, 2001.
J. B. Brenet (ed.), *Averroès et les Averroismes juif et latin*, Vrin, Paris, 2007

Website

www.thomasinst.uni-koeln.de/averroes

The Avicennian 'School'

Texts

Sohravardi, *Le Livre de la Sagesse Orientale*, ed. H. Corbin and C. Jambet, Verdier, Lagrasse, 1986.

Molla Sadra Shirazi, *Le Livre des Pénétrations Métaphysiques*, ed. H. Corbin, Verdier, Lagrasse, 1993.

Suhrawardī, *Philosophy of Illumination*, ed. J. Walbridge and H. Ziai, Brigham Young University Press, Provo, 1999.

Studies

J. Walbridge, *The Science of Mystic Lights: Qutb al-Dīn Shirāzī and the Illuminationist Tradition in Islamic Philosophy*, Harvard University Press, Cambridge, MA, 1992.

M. Aminrazavi, *Suhrawardī and the School of Illumination*, Curzon Press, Richmond, 1997.

J. Walbridge, *The Wisdom of Mystic East: Suhrawardī and Platonic Orientalism*, State University of New York Press, Albany, 2001.

Ibn Khaldūn

Texts

The Muqaddimah. An Introduction to History, ed. F. Rosenthal, Princeton University Press, Princeton, 1967 (3 vols).

Discours sur l'Histoire Universelle. La Muqaddimah, ed. V. Monteil, Sindbad, Paris, 1978 (3 vols).

Ibn Khaldūn e la Muqaddimah, ed. G. Pizzi, All'Insegna del Pesce d'Oro Scheiwiller, Milan, 1985.

Studies

M. Mahdi, *Ibn Khaldūn's Philosophy of History*, University of Chicago Press, Chicago, 1964.

N. Nassar, *La Pensée Realiste d'Ibn Khaldūn*, PUF, Paris, 1967.

M. Talbi, 'Ibn Khaldūn et le sense de l'Histoire', in *Studia Islamica*, XXVI, 1967, pp. 73–148.

Y. Lacoste, *Ibn Khaldūn, Naissance de l'Histore, Passe du Tiers Monde*, Maspero, Paris, 1981.

A. Al-Azmeh, *Ibn Khaldūn*, Routledge, London, 1990.

J. Sayyah, *Politique de l'Islam. L'Idée de l'Etat de Ibn Khaldūn à Aujourd'hui*, L'Atelier de l'Archer, PUF, Vendôme, 2000.

G. Turroni, *Il mondo della storia secondo Ibn Khaldūn*, Jouvence, Rome, 2002.

Bibliography of English-language Versions

S. Van Den Bergh (trans. and ed.), Averroes's *Incoherence of the Incoherence*, The Trustees of the E. J. W. Gibb Memorial, London, 1954.

Lenn Evan Goodman (trans. and ed.), Ibn Tufayl's *'Hayy Ibn Yaqzān': A Philosophical Tale*, Twayne, New York, 1972.

P. Morewedge (trans. and ed.), *The Metaphysics of Avicenna*, Routledge and Kegan Paul, London, 1973.

A. K. Kazi and J. G. Flynn (trans and eds), Al-Shahrastānī's *Muslim Sects and Divisions*, Kegan Paul International, London, 1984.

Oliver Leaman, *An Introduction to Medieval Islamic Philosophy*, Cambridge University Press, Cambridge, 1985.

R. Walzer (trans. and ed.), al-Fārābī's *On the Perfect State*, Oxford University Press, Oxford, 1985.

L. and P. Sherrard (trans), H. Corbin's *History of Islamic Philosophy*, Institute of Ismaili Studies, London, 1993.

D. Buchman (trans. and ed.), al-Ghazālī's *The Niche of Lights*, Brigham Young University Press, Provo, 1998.

D. Gutas, *Greek Thought, Arabic Culture*, Routledge, London, 1998.

C. E. Butterworth (trans. and ed.), Averroes's *Decisive Treatise*, Brigham Young University Press, Provo, 2001.

F. Rosenthal (trans. and ed.), Ibn Khaldūn's *The Muqaddimah*, abridged edition, Routledge and Kegan Paul, London, 2005.

Index

Note: names beginning with **al-** are filed under the second element (e.g. **al-Fārābī** is filed under **F**)